Rebirth of the Blue: 35-3

One Great Ride!

Copyright© 2010 • ISBN: 1-59725-230-0

Published by Pediment Publishing, a division of The Pediment Group, Inc. www.pediment.com Printed in Canada

Acknowledgments

Rebirth of the Blue: 35-3, One Great Ride! | Kentucky 2009–2010 Season

Publisher: Timothy M. Kelly and *The Lexington Herald-Leader*

Sports Editor: Gene Abell

Writers: Jerry Tipton, Ryan Alessi, Valarie Honeycutt Spears, Mark Story, Beverly Fortune, John Clay, Amy Wilson, Seth Emerson

Photographers: Mark Cornelison, David Perry, Charles Bertram, Pablo Alcalá, Ron Garrison, Jonathan Palmer, Matt Goins, Erik Campos

Graphics and Sports Page Design: Brian Simms, Chris Ware, Camille Weber, Jeff Bowen, Brian Malasics, Dennis Varney, Elizabeth Price, Monica Flint, Dean Holt

Book Design: Lillie Reich, Winding Road Communications

Assistance in Editing: Mat Graf, Gene Abell

Assistance in Design and Photos: Julie Achauer, Ron Garrison, Sharon Ruble, Steve Medley, Ashlee Garrett

Executive Editor: Peter Baniak

Foreword

When John Calipari arrived as Kentucky's new coach in April 2009, he downplayed the notion of an immediate revival.

He did not walk on water, he said. He only promised to work diligently and, in a few seasons, Kentucky would be Kentucky again.

Then Calipari tried mightily to contradict himself. He began the resurrection of Kentucky basketball by persuading the stars of his recruiting class at Memphis to follow him to UK.

No one knew then that the freshmen, led by point guard John Wall and DeMarcus Cousins, would evoke comparisons to Michigan's iconic Fab Five.

Wall made an immediate impression. In his debut, he hit the game-winning shot in the final seconds to beat Miami (Ohio). It was a preview of things to come by one of Kentucky's best clutch players in a long time.

Cousins supplanted All-American candidate Patrick Patterson as the team's low-post anchor. The Cats won their first 19 games, giving Calipari the best start by any first-year Kentucky coach.

Perhaps most gratifying, UK personified a quality Coach Cal prized enough to use as a book title: Refuse to lose.

That quality came in handy as the freshmen showed their age. Stretches of brilliance often bled into periods of distraction. Almost always the Cats rode a palpable refuse-to-lose attitude to victory.

A final record of 35-3 served as a clever disguise for a team not nearly so dominant. Half the games were decided by 12 or fewer points. UK's 16-3 record in those games reflected the players' resourcefulness, desire and sheer talent.

Aside from the winning (which at Kentucky is like saying aside from the oxygen), the season returned a sense of spectacle.

It started with Big Blue Madness and Calipari's state-of-the-program address. Then there was the blizzard of confetti in Rupp Arena that signaled UK beating North Carolina to the milestone 2,000th victory. The Southeastern Conference regular-season and tournament championships restored Kentucky's status as the flagship program. So did a No. 1 national ranking.

Ashley Judd got company in the celebrity-fan category. LeBron James, Magic Johnson, Drake, Mike Tomlin and Ben Roethlisberger attended games in Rupp Arena.

Calipari's fan-friendly embrace of Kentucky basketball made his reclusive predecessor, Billy Gillispie, and an appearance in the 2009 NIT fade from memory. Along the way, from the beginning to the NCAA Tournament East Region, Kentucky won.

In UK's long, storied basketball history, only the Fabulous Five season of 1947–48 saw more victories: 36-3. Even by Kentucky's standards, that was noteworthy.

"We did a lot of successful things," said Cousins, a double-double machine with 20. "But we didn't get our main goal, which was winning the national championship."

Throughout the season, Calipari candidly preached the reality of college basketball: all is prelude to the NCAA Tournament. Wall picked up on that reality when he said going into March Madness, "Kentucky fans, they don't hang banners for conference championships or SEC championships. They want banners for national championships."

Through the first three NCAA Tournament games, Kentucky seemed on schedule with its self-envisioned destiny. The Cats beat East Tennessee State, Wake Forest and Cornell by a combined 76 points. Only in 1993 and 1996 had UK won its first three NCAA Tournament games by more points (99 and 93, respectively).

Then came West Virginia, a veteran team from the rugged Big East Conference, to snatch a happy ending from this season of renewal and hope. "It was a look we weren't used to and we just couldn't adjust," Cousins said of the West Virginia 1-3-1 zone that stymied the Cats in the East Region championship game. "I wish we'd had more time."

Time, Kentucky did not have.

With its core of presumed one-and-done freshmen, UK embodied the one-shining-moment anthem of the NCAA Tournament. And for all the glitter this season, they knew their all-too-brief time together would be no more.

"It was an amazing year," Wall said. "But I came up short of my goal I had for myself and my teammates. And I'll always think of that."

Patterson, the rare selfless star, looked beyond the immediate sting of defeat.

"I think eventually we'll look back on this and say, 'Hey, we were a stepping stone to getting Kentucky back to national (prominence),' " he said. "Back to the kind of team Kentucky basketball is."

Jerry Tipton
Lexington Herald-Leader

Table of Contents

Calipari Comes to UK

April 1, 2009

Cal's a Cat

Calipari lured from Memphis with 8-year, $31.65 million deal
Background checks leave UK satisfied

John Calipari has accepted the University of Kentucky's offer to become its men's basketball coach, UK confirmed Tuesday night. With the hire, college basketball's leader in overall victories gained the coaching star power its fan base has craved for more than a decade.

Calipari, whose leadership at Memphis caused that school to mount a determined effort to keep him, gives UK a high-profile coach whose national prominence rivals that of Rick Pitino, who left Lexington 12 years ago.

Calipari also becomes the highest-paid coach in college basketball.

UK called a news conference for 9:30 a.m. Wednesday to formally introduce Calipari, a big winner on the court and in recruiting during earlier coaching stops at Massachusetts and Memphis. UK also called an Athletic Association Board of Directors meeting for 9 a.m. to approve Calipari's hiring and contract.

In checking Calipari's background, UK President Lee T. Todd Jr. said the school found nothing to kill the widely anticipated deal.

LEFT: New UK Coach John Calipari at the Joe Craft Center, April 1, 2009. LEXINGTON HERALD-LEADER/MARK CORNELISON

While at UMass, one of Calipari's players, Marcus Camby, admitted to accepting $28,000 from agents. That caused the NCAA to vacate the Minutemen's advancement to the 1996 Final Four. Calipari was not linked to the infraction.

Questions have also been raised about Calipari's association with William "Worldwide Wes" Wesley, a behind-the-scenes figure linked to Memphis recruiting efforts.

"We've looked into all those things," Todd said. "That guy works for a whole lot of people. I never had heard of him until we started this process. He doesn't work for just any one coach."

As for the contract, UK confirmed on its Web site that the deal is for eight years and $31.65 million.

Todd said he was unaware of any effort to raise private funds to supplement Calipari's pay.

In terms of players as well as coach, Calipari's move may prove Kentucky's gain and Memphis' setback.

Several players or recruits spoke of leaving Memphis and joining him at Kentucky.

In Miami for Wednesday's McDonald's All-American Game, heralded prospect DeMarcus Cousins (who had committed to Memphis) told *The Miami Herald* on Tuesday afternoon that he spoke with Calipari before the decision was made.

LEXINGTON HERALD-LEADER

WWW.KENTUCKY.COM

APRIL 1, 2009 | WEDNESDAY | METRO FINAL EDITION ★ | 75¢

HIGHEST-PAID COLLEGE COACH

CALIPARI LURED FROM MEMPHIS WITH 8-YEAR, $31.65 MILLION DEAL

CAL'S A CAT

John Calipari won 252 games at Memphis and lost 69. He took the Tigers to the NCAA championship game in 2008 only to lose to Kansas in overtime. He also guided Massachusetts to the Final Four in 1996. His overall record over 17 college seasons is 445-140. UK will introduce its new coach at a 9:30 a.m. news conference on Wednesday.

PHOTOS BY MARK WEBER | THE (MEMPHIS) COMMERCIAL APPEAL

Background checks leave UK satisfied

By Jerry Tipton and Ryan Alessi
jtipton@herald-leader.com
ralessi@herald-leader.com

John Calipari has accepted the University of Kentucky's offer to become its men's basketball coach, UK confirmed Tuesday night. With the hire, college basketball's leader in overall victories gained the coaching star power its fan base has craved for more than a decade.

Calipari, whose leadership at Memphis caused that school to mount a determined effort to keep him, gives UK a high-profile coach whose national prominence rivals that of Rick Pitino, who left Lexington 12 years ago.

Calipari also becomes the highest-paid coach in college basketball.

UK called a news conference for 9:30 a.m. Wednesday to formally introduce Calipari, a big winner on the court and in recruiting during earlier coaching stops at Massachusetts and Memphis. UK also called an Athletic Association Board of Directors meeting for 9 a.m. to approve Calipari's hiring and contract.

In checking Calipari's background, UK President Lee T. Todd Jr. said the school found nothing to kill the widely anticipated deal.

While at UMass, one of Calipari's players, Marcus Camby, admitted to accepting $28,000 from agents. That caused the NCAA to vacate the Minutemen's advancement to the 1996 Final Four.

See UK COACH, A7

Memphis fans Nathan Bradshaw, left and Brett Wynne, were among those gathered outside coach John Calipari's house in East Memphis Tuesday afternoon in a last ditch effort to keep the coach from leaving for Kentucky. Calipari bought pizza for fans and media who maintained the vigil.

Fans love idea of recruiting a top recruiter

JOHN CLAY
HERALD-LEADER SPORTS COLUMNIST

John Calipari is a give-the-people-what-they-want hire.

Sure, he brings risk.

He also promises reward.

There is a reason most of the Big Blue Nation is dancing in the streets at the thought of the Memphis coach leaving Beale Street for the Bluegrass.

Calipari gets players. He gets big players. He gets quick players. He gets talented players. He gets monstrously talented players.

You can question the methods he uses to get those players.

You can't question his results.

Look at this year. Daniel Orton is the top signee of the 2009 Kentucky basketball recruiting class brought in by former UK head coach Billy Gillispie. Rivals rates Orton as the 22nd best player in the current recruiting crop. That's excellent. But ...

If John Wall, the nation's No. 1 prep player — who continues to say that Memphis tops his list — were to commit to the Tigers, Calipari would have the No. 1 (Wall), No. 2 (DeMarcus Cousins) and No. 3 (Xavier Henry) players on Rivals' list.

Consider this: Let's say, for the sake of speculation,

See CLAY, A7

Will recruits follow him? Two of John Calipari's highly-ranked recruits could also consider becoming Wildcats. **Page A6**

Playing by the rules Questions have dogged Calipari throughout his years as a head basketball coach. **Page A6**

The deal-maker Calipari's coaching reputation and personality make him a sought-after commodity. **Page A7**

Online: Kentuckysports.com Get the latest on today's 9:30 a.m. announcement of Calipari as coach.

HOW TO HELP KIDS PICK PETS
A PRIMER • COMMUNITIES

INSIDE TODAY

Pistachios scare: FDA reacting more swiftly than during peanut crisis. **Nation | World, A3**

Cobb ready: UK sophomore back after knee surgery. **Sports, C1**

ONLINE TODAY | KENTUCKY.COM

Search public records, including university salaries, property records and more.

COMING UP | THURSDAY

Traditional Greek sweets again are available at annual pastry sale. **A la Carte**

7 01540 10891 0

SUNNY
Chance of precipitation less than 20%. **Weather, D12**
59 HIGH | 45 LOW

INDEX
Vol. 25, No. 88
© 2008

Business D6-D7
City | Region ...... D
Classified D9-D11
Comics B8-B9
Crosswords .. B9, D11
Dear Abby B9
Horoscope B8
Movies B6
Obituaries D4-D5
Opinions A12-A13
Sports C
Your Health D12

HOW TO REACH US
Delivery: 1-800-999-8881
Classified: 233-7878 or 1-800-933-7355

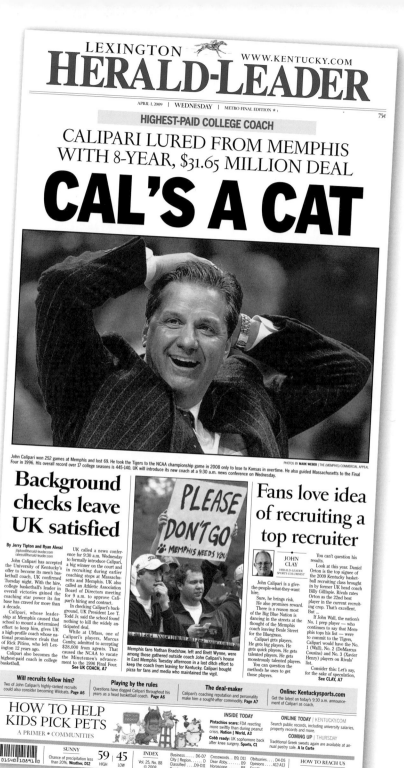

"I'm trying to stay focused right now and have fun," Cousins said. "When I get back home, it's time to get back down to business. I did get a chance to talk to Coach Cal, and he said he was considering the job. Now I'm basically waiting like everybody else to see what he does."

Another McDonald's All-American committed to Memphis, Xavier Henry, said he would reopen the process.

"I could get out of my letter of intent if he wasn't there for any reason," Henry told reporters in Miami. "It reopens my whole recruitment to everybody and anybody."

Meanwhile, point guard Tyreke Evans, who won several national Freshman of the Year honors this past season, told FoxSports.com that he was leaving Memphis for a shot at the NBA.

"If he's leaving, I'm not staying," Evans told FoxSports.com. "Coach leaving did it for me.

"I'm shocked he left, especially with the class he had coming in. I know it was tough for him, but it was his dream job. You can't get mad at him for that."

Calipari fits the criteria Kentucky desired after firing Billy Gillispie on Friday: a well-rounded coach who can perform the UK job's varied duties on and off the court.

In terms of coaching, Calipari is one of only 13 coaches to take two schools to a Final Four. He guided Massachusetts in 1996 and Memphis in 2008 to college basketball's grandest stage.

Only Rick Pitino has taken three schools to a Final Four: Providence (1987), Kentucky (1993, 1996 and 1997) and Louisville (2005).

Calipari has compiled a record of 445-140 in 17 seasons as a college head coach. That includes a nine-season record of 252-69 at Memphis.

As for the job's public component, Calipari has been a highly visible presence in Memphis. The Commercial Appeal newspaper of Memphis once called Calipari not only "this city's most beloved sports celebrity but as Citizen Cal, a Memphian as integral as shipping envelopes and barbecue."

When many sports figures avoid taking sides on public issues, Calipari

FOLLOWING TOP: New Kentucky coach John Calipari sat in between Athletics Director Mitch Barnhart, left, and school president Lee Todd during his introductory news conference held in the Joe Craft Center on April 1, 2009.
LEXINGTON HERALD-LEADER/CHARLES BERTRAM

FOLLOWING BOTTOM: Elijah Stamper, 2, pointed toward a plane as he sat atop the shoulders of Dan Eads. The two came from Harrodsburg in hopes of seeing John Calipari arrive at Blue Grass Airport. LEXINGTON HERALD-LEADER/MARK CORNELISON

freely addressed non-basketball issues.

"I used to think I had a lot of ideas," Memphis banker Harold Byrd once told the Commercial Appeal. "His mind races a million miles an hour."

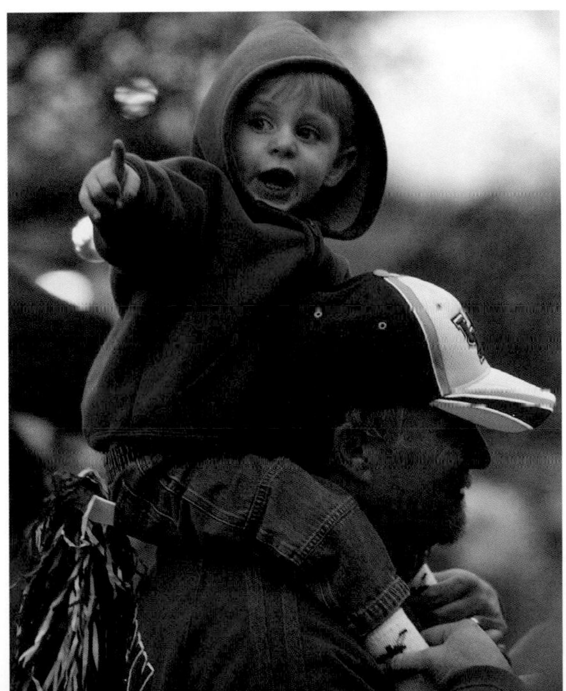

Calipari opened his home to fund raisers for local politicians. He also offered opinions on civic problems like crime and poverty. He solicited advice from business leaders and reached out to state legislators.

"If this program or me or my family can bring light to something good in this community, I get involved in it," Calipari told the Commercial Appeal. "Whoever is sitting in that (head coach's) seat, if you're not getting involved in the community, you're cheating this place. … (If) people recognize you, then use it to bring light to good stuff. It's almost an obligation."

Before making the decision, Calipari spoke with former UK coaches Joe B. Hall and Eddie Sutton on Tuesday.

Hall noted the difficult decision Calipari faced: lead Kentucky or cement Memphis' standing as a national power.

"I know he hates to leave the players there and the friends he's made," Hall said. "That's a big step."

Sutton said he gave Calipari a balanced appraisal of UK basketball.

"I told him all the good things about Kentucky," Sutton said. "Kentucky has the best things (a coach) would ever want.

"Maybe there are a couple drawbacks.

"I told him it was a great place to coach."

"Most of the people there are just great basketball fans. There are a few who probably take it a little serious. It's almost a religion to them."

When asked about drawbacks to the Kentucky job, Sutton said, "You lose some of your privacy. It's hard to go out and take the family to dinner without a lot of people wanting autographs. It's something you live with.

"But it also has some real pluses. I didn't say anything negative."

For many UK fans, Calipari's hiring added a new plus. ■

— Jerry Tipton and Ryan Alessi

April 1, 2009

Calipari pushes envelope, but not 'off the table'

Since leaving the University of Massachusetts 13 years ago with the program under NCAA investigation, John Calipari has been dogged at every stop by questions of how clean a program he runs.

Those who have worked with Calipari say he is aggressive in all aspects of coaching — particularly recruiting — but does not cross the line.

"John knows the rules and regulations of the NCAA. He knows the rules of recruiting. And if he pushes the envelope, he knows when to stop pushing it," said Howard Davis, a former UMass sports information director. "In my opinion, he will not make the next step and push the envelope off the table."

UK President Lee T. Todd Jr. confirmed that university officials dug into Calipari's recruiting record and association with a man who serves as a sort of majordomo to current and aspiring basketball stars.

UK was satisfied that Calipari, who is leaving Memphis to take the UK job, is on the up-and-up, Todd said.

"We've looked into all those things," he said.

The most trouble a Calipari program has been in came at the end of his tenure at UMass in 1996. The NCAA sanctioned the school, and it forfeited its 35 wins after a probe revealed Marcus Camby, then a junior, took money and gifts from an agent, which is against the rules. David K. Scott, the former chancellor at the UMass Amherst campus for most of Calipari's tenure, said officials thoroughly vetted whether Calipari knew of any wrongdoing.

"I don't believe he did," Scott said.

By all accounts from Memphis athletic boosters and former UMass officials, Calipari is the type of hyper-focused coach who likes to be involved in all facets of the program.

"You knew right away that John was going to be in total control of his program," as Davis put it.

In the Camby case, Scott said, UMass officials were "convinced" after lengthy interviews with the staff that Calipari didn't know of the player's dealings with the agent.

"I guess things like that can happen, yes, even to a coach who's pretty on top of everything," Scott said. "I don't know how much he was dealing with the students' personal lives."

Calipari left UMass for a brief stint as an NBA coach just as the NCAA probe was heating up. Since taking the helm at Memphis in the 2000–01 season, Calipari has been haunted by similar issues.

In 2006, a Norfolk, Va.— based sports lawyer claimed he gave former Memphis player Shawne Williams nearly $50,000 in exchange for getting to represent him. The aspiring agent filed a suit against Williams — then dropped it — when the player chose someone else.

And William "Worldwide Wes" Wesley, who has ties to scores of NBA, college and prep athletes, also has been associated with Memphis.

Calipari was quoted in a GQ story about Wesley saying the man is an "ambassador" to the Memphis program.

What exactly that entails is unclear. Wesley, according to reports, is skilled at connecting players with whatever they want, whether it's meeting celebrities or a stylist.

Wesley has been linked to helping Memphis land two recent star players, Derrick Rose and Tyreke Evans.

Todd, however, dismissed any notion that Calipari's association with Wesley is improper and said Wesley "doesn't work for just any one coach."

Harold Byrd, a Memphis banker who served as president of Memphis' Rebounders booster club, said recruiting is watched carefully and he has seen "no evidence" Calipari ever broke rules.

Byrd said he has seen Wesley at some Tigers games, including at last month's NCAA Tournament games.

"Does he have a friendship with Coach Calipari, I think, yes," Byrd said.

"It's sort of like the world of politics where, unfortunately, there are a lot of people who are involved in your campaign and many people are people you'd not like to have there," Byrd said. "But they're going to be there, and you have to deal with them." ■

— Ryan Alessi

PRECEDING: John Calipari gave a big hug to Karen Keightley, daughter of former UK equipment manager Bill Keightley, who passed away a year ago, after he was introduced as the new head basketball coach at the University of Kentucky. LEXINGTON HERALD-LEADER/MARK CORNELISON

BELOW: John Calipari was interviewed at a news conference held in the Joe Craft Center. LEXINGTON HERALD-LEADER/CHARLES BERTRAM

April 2, 2009

Can-Do Cal

New coach manages to lead communities and players

As a young assistant coach in 1988, John Calipari burst into his interview for the University of Massachusetts head coaching job hauling notebooks that outlined his plan to remake a beleaguered basketball program on and off the court.

He even laid the groundwork for the interview in Amherst by making the unusual move of calling UMass athletics department staff to introduce himself and ask for their support.

That preparation and commitment wowed officials who had brought in some other big names who have become coaching luminaries, such as Texas' Rick Barnes and eventual NBA Coach Stu Jackson.

"He came into that interview and absolutely blew the search committee away," said Glenn Wong, a professor of sports management at UMass who served on the panel.

Calipari's sales pitch didn't stop with the hiring, Wong said. A year later, Calipari called the search committee back and handed them a report on how the program fared compared with what he laid out in his job interview.

Measuring success goes beyond a win-loss record, those who have been around Calipari in Amherst and Memphis say.

That includes mingling with fans, courting boosters, suggesting marketing strategies, trying to bolster the players' academic performances and investing in the community.

"It indicates his passion for the program and goal to make the whole program succeed," said Wong, who served as interim athletics director at one point during Calipari's eight seasons at UMass.

In that time, Calipari took the program from a 10-win team to a national championship contender.

Calipari said when he was introduced Wednesday as the University of Kentucky's new men's basketball coach that he understands how high the on-court expectations are at Kentucky. But he said he still believes running a basketball program comes with broader responsibilities.

Churchill wants to try night racing
HORSE RACING — B5

SPORTS

Cards top Cats 5-1 in softball
UK SPORTS — B6

THURSDAY, APRIL 2, 2009 | KENTUCKY.COM/SPORTS | LEXINGTON HERALD-LEADER SECTION B

Can-Do Cal

Losing changed UK's mind

2 YEARS AGO, CATS DIDN'T PURSUE CAL

MARK STORY
HERALD-LEADER SPORTS COLUMNIST

John Calipari waited for the phone call. And waited. And waited.

Two years ago, after Tubby Smith bolted for the Great White North, Calipari figured he was a logical candidate to become the new head man at Kentucky.

"I called my wife (Ellen) every day for six days. 'Did they call? Did they call?' " Calipari said of UK. "Then I kind of figured out; they're not calling."

Two years and one ill-fated Kentucky coaching hire later, the call that ultimately made Coach Cal into the Cats' coach finally arrived.

John Calipari's initial foray as head men's basketball coach of the Kentucky Wildcats played to boffo reviews Wednesday.

In a morning news conference from the plush Joe Craft Center carried live on ESPN and TV stations around Kentucky, the now ex-Memphis coach was charming, funny, even poignant.

When he opened his remarks, Calipari noted that he had officially agreed to take the UK job on March 31 — the one-year anniversary of the death of Bill Keightley.

At the mention by the new coach of the beloved Mr. Wildcat, you could almost feel eyes misting from Paducah to Pikeville.

This guy is *good*.

So why was the man greeted as UK's basketball savior in 2009 a coaching-search outcast when Lee Todd and Mitch Barnhart went looking in 2007?

See STORY, B3

KENTUCKY SPORTS.COM

The Calipari Era begins: Go online to get all the latest news and connect with other Cats fans.

MORE COVERAGE

All the Cal you can handle: Read more about Wednesday's press conference. **Page A1**

New coach manages to lead communities and players

By Ryan Alessi
ralessi@herald-leader.com

As a young assistant coach in 1988, John Calipari burst into his interview for the University of Massachusetts head coaching job hauling notebooks that outlined his plan to remake a beleaguered basketball program on and off the court.

He even laid the groundwork for the interview in Amherst by making the unusual move of calling UMass athletics department staff to introduce himself and ask for their support.

That preparation and commitment wowed officials who had brought in some other big names who have become coaching luminaries, such as Texas' Rick Barnes and eventual NBA coach Stu Jackson.

"He came into that interview and absolutely blew the search committee away," said Glenn Wong, a professor of sports management at UMass who served on the panel.

Calipari's sales pitch didn't stop with the hiring, Wong said. A year later, Calipari called the search committee back and handed them a report on how the program fared compared with what he laid out in his job interview.

Measuring success goes beyond

See CALIPARI, B4

Meeks, Patterson optimistic about hire

By Jennifer Smith
jsmith3@herald-leader.com

Neither Patrick Patterson nor Jodie Meeks has decided what his future holds, but each sounded optimistic about the future of Kentucky basketball under John Calipari.

The two Kentucky stars were in class when the news conference about their new coach was held, but they met with Calipari on Wednesday morning, and both seemed pleased with the hire.

"We know the possibilities that could be next year. Jodie and I always talk about the future," Patterson said through UK media relations. "We always talk about what could be, what could possibly be in the future with Kentucky and with this great coach we have in Calipari right now. We're just looking forward to it, and I'm sure we'll come to a

See PLAYERS, B4

A beautiful day for Brooks

"I also make a commitment to create an environment that fosters discipline," he said. "And most importantly, my job is to hold players accountable on and off the court."

A people person Calipari has attracted much attention over the years for his colorful quotes and big personality.

"Although he's flashy and can be brash, he's also got this other side I've seen these last couple years," said Randy Fishman, a Memphis lawyer and a university athletic advisory board member.

Fishman said he once mentioned to Calipari that a good friend was very ill.

"He called him to cheer him up," Fishman said. "He does a lot of things that don't show up in the newspaper."

Calipari keeps up with his former players and colleagues even after they part ways.

He made a surprise visit to Amherst in February 2006 when UMass dedicated its court to former coach and broadcaster Jim Lehman.

And UK President Lee T. Todd Jr. said he was impressed with Calipari when, at the end of his job interview over the weekend, he was able to list the whereabouts of the players from one of his early UMass teams.

That personal connection is often what endears him to the die-hard fans and donors.

"The boosters love him because he knows them. He takes time to talk to them. He knows their grandchildren's names, and he asks about their children," Wong said.

Calipari showed glimpses of that Wednesday. He acknowledged the one-year anniversary of the death of beloved UK equipment manager Bill Keightley, pointed out Herky Rupp in the room and recognized former UK player Richie Farmer as the state's agriculture commissioner.

Engaging the community Calipari is not the type of coach to remain confined in the gym.

When he found the UMass program almost demoralized in the late 1980s, Calipari embarked on a one-man campaign to fire up students.

"He went into dormitories, and went into the fraternity houses. He wanted kids to have cut-off basketballs on their heads and painted faces," said Howard Davis, who served as Calipari's first sports information director. "Nobody ever heard of that at UMass. He really generated a lot of enthusiasm."

To engage families, he created a group at UMass, the Mini Minutemen, for dozens of 5- to 12-year-olds to practice ball handling skills with the college coaches and perform during halftimes, Wong said.

Supporters also praised Calipari's community and university involvement in Amherst and Memphis.

Former UMass-Amherst chancellor David K. Scott recalled that Calipari made a "six-figure donation" to the university's library.

Each year, he has raised money at his Memphis home for scholarships and held political fund-raisers for both Republican and Democratic candidates who were big supporters of the university, said Harold Byrd, a Memphis-area banker and booster.

The coach formed the Calipari Family Foundation for Children.

And in 2007, Calipari expanded his reach to the basketball community in China by establishing a series of coaching clinics.

All the while, he's managed to keep tabs on nearly every

RIGHT: John Calipari laughed with former UK player and current Kentucky Agriculture Commissioner Richie Farmer after being introduced as UK's new head basketball coach. LEXINGTON HERALD-LEADER/MARK CORNELISON

facet of his program.

"He's fantastic on the details," said Jim Hillhouse, a board member of Memphis' booster club.

For instance, seven hours before last month's student-athlete award ceremony at Memphis' Peabody Hotel, Calipari stopped in to check on arrangements. He ended up suggesting to move the pre-ceremony reception to the hotel's roof, Hillhouse said.

The academic side.

Both the NCAA and UK administrators have increased their focus on their athletes' grades in recent years.

The NCAA measures student academic performance through a complex formula that takes into account eligibility, retention and graduation rates. A score of 925 in that formula is considered the NCAA's minimum bar and is roughly the equivalent of a 60 percent graduation rate.

The Memphis men's basketball team scored just above that threshold at 927 during the 2003–2007 time frame, according to the NCAA. That put the team slightly below the middle of the pack among men's basketball programs.

The UK team's score was slightly better at 941.

"We're not where I want to be yet," said Todd, who said he specifically charged Calipari with raising that bar.

Calipari's contract, for instance, calls for a $50,000 bonus if 75 percent of a class graduates.

His supporters said that as long as he brings the same level of energy and commitment to UK as he has shown in the past, Calipari can accomplish perhaps the trickiest task of all: satisfying the hungry Big Blue Nation.

"Overall, with what he has done with the attendance and with the fans, as well as the wins, people will remember him as being one of the great coaches here," said Don Mc Kinnon, a former Memphis football player and athletics supporter. "Fans love him." ■

— Ryan Alessi

BELOW: John Calipari was surrounded by Kentucky fans and signed autographs on his way to the airport after the news conference announcing his hire. LEXINGTON HERALD-LEADER/DAVID PERRY

April 2, 2009

Losing changed UK's mind
2 years ago, Cats didn't pursue Cal

MARK STORY
HERALD-LEADER SPORTS COLUMNIST

John Calipari waited for the phone call. And waited. And waited.

Two years ago, after Tubby Smith bolted for the Great White North, Calipari figured he was a logical candidate to become the new head man at Kentucky.

"I called my wife (Ellen) every day for six days. 'Did they call? Did they call?' " Calipari said of UK. "Then I kind of figured out; they're not calling."

Two years and one ill-fated Kentucky coaching hire later, the call that ultimately made Coach Cal into the Cats' coach finally arrived.

John Calipari's initial foray as head men's basketball coach of the Kentucky Wildcats played to boffo reviews Wednesday.

In a morning news conference from the plush Joe Craft Center carried live on ESPN and TV stations around Kentucky, the now ex-Memphis coach was charming, funny, even poignant.

When he opened his remarks, Calipari noted that he had officially agreed to take the UK job on March 31 — the one-year anniversary of the death of Bill Keightley.

At the mention by the new coach of the beloved Mr. Wildcat, you could almost feel eyes misting from Paducah to Pikeville.

This guy is good.

So why was the man greeted as UK's basketball savior in 2009 a coaching-search outcast when Lee Todd and Mitch Barnhart went looking in 2007?

Todd, the UK president, said Wednesday he didn't know why.

"I don't know everyone that Mitch talked to," Todd said of UK's 2007 search. "I don't remember much talk about" Calipari.

Barnhart, the Kentucky athletics director, said he entered the 2007 search with a plan and a pecking order set in his mind.

He gave Billy Donovan first crack at the job, which meant waiting until Joakim Noah and Co. finished their successful defense of the NCAA title.

Once Billy D. said no, "I talked to another coach," Barnhart said, in what I think was a reference to Rick Barnes of Texas.

"Then I got to the third name on my list," Barnhart said. "And it was Billy (Gillispie)."

Why wasn't Calipari in that top three in 2007?

"There was no real reason. It was sort of like when a coach goes out recruiting and you have a list of prospects, one, two, three, four, five, six," Barnhart said. "I entered that search with a firm plan in mind. And stuck to it."

OK.

Since they won't say it, I will.

I think the reason Todd and Barnhart didn't call Calipari in 2007 was that they were scared by the coach's reputation for working in the college basketball gray areas.

The reason they did call him in 2009 was that Kentucky's athletics honchos were feeling a whiff of desperation to get UK basketball back to winning at a " Kentucky level."

At the University of Kentucky, when you are coming off four straight double-digit-loss seasons; when you've just played in the NIT; and when you've been forced to acknowledge you've completely bungled the prior coaching search after two years by firing the coach; well, then an athletics director's hold on his job can start feeling a little shaky.

At Kentucky, it could even be that a university president's hold on his job could start feeling a little less than secure.

You really need a hire of the magnitude that changes the conversation.

Under those circumstances, the positives of a charismatic coach who can energize a fan base, recruit and flat-out coach begin to come rather starkly into focus.

Meanwhile, all those gray areas — Worldwide Wes; players on the police blotter; Massachusetts and its vacated Final Four trip — become a lot easier to look past.

So, two years after Calipari expected the call from Kentucky, Todd and Barnhart finally got Memphis on the line.

Now, they have their reputations staked on Coach Cal.

"I'm totally comfortable with John," Barnhart said after Wednesday's news conference. "Just getting to know him, he's not the person that you often see portrayed. I told him, I know what that feels like."

Five years from now, if the Calipari legacy at UK is about basketball — not the gray areas — we'll know that Kentucky's tardy call was a good call. ■

April 2, 2009

Fans welcome UK's latest coach
They like what they hear from Calipari

In his first news conference, the University of Kentucky's new men's basketball coach, John Calipari, won over skeptical Wildcats fan Tom Rougeux.

When Calipari said he would be here to serve the community and the players, "that was the watershed moment for me," Rougeux said as he waited outside the Joe Craft Center, the basketball practice facility behind Memorial Coliseum, on Wednesday morning.

"That sounded to me like the leader we're looking for," said Rougeux, who listened to the news conference on his BlackBerry. Several people crowded around, also listening. "That's the thing about a winning program: It's how you think about others, no matter if you're a coach or a boss."

Dozens of students, families with children, and people from the community — some had traveled from as far as Ashland — waited in glorious sunshine to catch a glimpse of the newly appointed men's basketball coach.

The coach received a positive reception from assembled fans. Several viewed Calipari's hiring as the shot in the arm the program needed.

"He had an immediate impact on UK's basketball program before he even stepped foot on campus," said Randy Van Hoose, who left Ashland at 4 a.m. with his business partner, Rick Brizendine. The two run the Web site www.wildcatnation.net.

Calipari not only knows how to win basketball games, "He has the perfect personality to project the program," Van Hoose said. "He loves the public. He loves the camera. He loves the history of this program."

Van Hoose said he couldn't see any negatives, which Brizendine said is a good

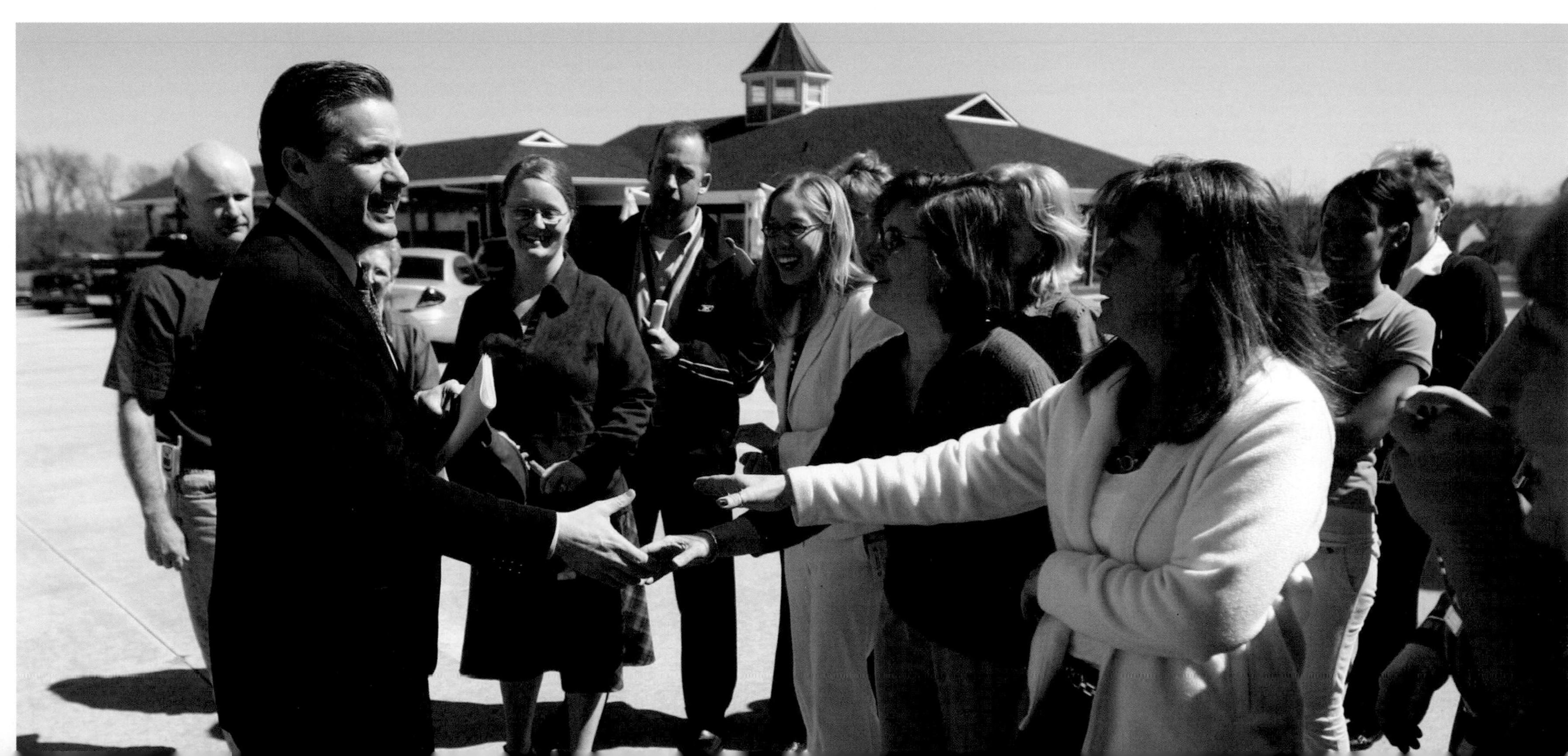

thing.

"If he didn't work out, it would have been a long drop to the next candidate," he said.

A pep rally was not scheduled Wednesday, university officials said, because Calipari was on a tight schedule. He was due back in Memphis about noon.

During the news conference, fans nodded as Calipari described his coaching style and spoke of his commitment to community involvement and how he wanted his players to have fun as they played. Van Hoose said the remarks were in sharp contrast to those of his immediate predecessor, Billy Gillispie, who was fired Friday.

"Before hearing him, I thought, 'Am I the only one who appreciated Tubby's clean program?'" said Rougeux, who delayed getting to his job at Krauth Electric Co. on Wednesday morning in order to swing by the Craft Center.

After the news conference, Rougeux admitted that he was a Calipari convert. Reports that the coach had gone to early Mass also impressed Rougeux.

Calipari reminded UK student Todd Weatherholt of Rick Pitino, the former UK basketball coach who now leads the University of Louisville.

"He has that charisma about him like Pitino," said Weatherholt, who hoped to see Calipari before going to Spanish class. "I'm excited."

"We have a coach committed to making his players great, and that makes a great program," said Jeremy Sheffel, a senior engineering major from Jackson.

When asked his reaction to Calipari's $31.65 million deal, UK senior Bryan Hicks said, "Pricey."

"But worth it," chimed in his roommate Bruce Arlinghaus, a sophomore from Northern Kentucky.

Hicks agreed: "You win one national championship, and you get all that money back in national exposure."

Faculty member Don Lowe liked what he heard when Calipari said the college graduation rates for his former players at UMass and the University of Memphis jumped while he was coach.

"I really like what he said about holding students accountable, because I have most of the basketball players" in a communications class, Lower said.

Fans took delight in Calipari's humor and quick wit, both during the news conference and afterward. As he left the Craft Center, he signed autographs all the way to the black SUV awaiting him. Gina Lysell, a UK staff member, yelled, "We love you, coach!"

Calipari quipped, "Oh, darlin', what are you gonna say when I lose my first game?" ■

— Beverly Fortune

PRECEDING: After being introduced as the new coach, John Calipari greeted employees at the RJ Corman Railroad Group in Nicholasville. Calipari was about to board an RJ Corman jet for a return trip to Memphis.
LEXINGTON HERALD-LEADER/ CHARLES BERTRAM

BELOW: Del Weatherford helped keep shirts with a Calipari theme on display at Hands on Originals on South Broadway in Lexington. A second run was planned for the fast-selling shirts.
LEXINGTON HERALD-LEADER/PABLO ALCALÁ

April 2, 2009

UK gets a coach who really gets UK

JOHN CLAY

HERALD-LEADER SPORTS COLUMNIST

What Billy Gillispie couldn't do in two years, John Calipari did in two minutes.

First thing at Wednesday's press conference, the new Kentucky basketball coach asked for Hazel Keightley. He mentioned Rex Chapman and Joe B. Hall and Richie Farmer — "He's going to be governor; it's crazy" — and Herky Rupp and told an anecdote about working a Five-Star camp with Kyle Macy.

He gets it is one of the overused phrases I've come to loathe. Yet I can't think of another one that fits. Billy Gillispie never got it at Kentucky. John Calipari arrived with it. And then some.

As a personality, he's the perfect fit. John Calipari, a Catholic of Italian descent, via Pennsylvania and West Virginia ("dandelion soup") and UMass and the Nets — "They don't bring up how I got fired," he said — and Memphis is an over-the-top personality for an over-the-top job.

He talks, and he croons, and he schmoozes, and he flatters, and he cajoles, and all of those are good things. How do you think the man recruits? That annual Rotary Club commitment that Billy G. blew off? Cal will be there. And the Rotarians might want to reschedule their afternoon appointments.

We can claim we want a nice, mild-mannered guy, but that's our insurance man. For a basketball coach at a program like Kentucky, we want inspiration and motivation and someone who can look us in the eye and make us feel like we're going to get where we want to go.

"Charisma," said Farmer afterward. "He's got that charisma."

Oh, his critics say he also has a temper and a vindictive streak. The Memphis people will tell you Coach Cal can be all over the

LEFT: Connie Barnhart, left, wife of UK Athletics Director Mitch Barnhart; Brad Calipari, 12; Megan Calipari, 19; and Ellen Calipari laughed during a news conference in UK's Joe Craft Center, where John Calipari was introduced as the university's new basketball coach.

LEXINGTON HERALD-LEADER/CHARLES BERTRAM

place, all the time, from touchingly nice to shockingly mean, as part of a complex package that sometimes rubs people raw.

Here's another thing the Memphis people will tell you: Cal might give the vibes of a slickster, but he's really a committed family man who was heavily invested in the community.

That insecure city thought it was getting an East Coast short-timer who would use it as a quick pit stop on the way to a better job. Turned out, it took nine years. As badly as Calipari wanted the Kentucky job, he almost couldn't make himself leave.

They will also tell you he'll stick up for his players, sometimes past the line of political correctness.

But the part I liked best Wednesday was his talk about how he wants the players to have fun. After the past two years, we could use a lot more of that around here, and a little less of someone who throws kids under the bus.

"You want that coach who's going to walk 100 steps with you," Bobby Perry, the ex-Cat, said after the press conference. "If you mess up too many times, he's going to let go. But we all mess up, you're going to mess up, but what he said about the players says a lot."

Yeah, yeah, Calipari can sometimes be too much the salesman, and he can lay it on Bruce Pearl thick. But all coaches have their own shtick. North Carolina's Roy Williams is down-home Roy. Kansas' Bill Self is that good-looking Middle American. Rick Pitino is the driven New Yorker who is going to outwork everyone, or make you think he has. They all have their parts to play.

But here's the thing: Calipari won't shrink from the role. That's why he's here. He buys into the "Kentucky is Kentucky" part. You could tell that early, from the "We want to double (the banners)" line to "This is the right place if you want to win championships and recruit the best of the best."

It was just about then, you could feel the state swell with love.

To say John Calipari won the opening press conference is to say they could have hung another banner in the Craft Center right then and there.

Might be time to invest in a really good ladder. ■

April 2, 2009

A busy day for Coach Calipari, 'A hard job' ahead

Charismatic Calipari promises no quick fix

At an introductory news conference as bright and sunny as the weather, only one discordant note was heard. And it came from the man of the hour: new University of Kentucky basketball coach John Calipari.

"I do not walk on water," he told the audience in the Craft Center. "I do not have a magic wand. I'm day to day."

Then referencing UK President Lee T. Todd Jr. and Athletics Director Mitch Barnhart (who were reduced to silent partners on the podium), Calipari added, "I told Dr. Todd and Mitch, if you want something to happen in a year, do not hire me. That's not how I do things."

Todd and Barnhart seemed like the reporters, deep-pocketed boosters, former players and current Cats in attendance: enthralled.

Yet throughout his bravura performance, the likes of which had not been seen around UK basketball since Rick Pitino commanded the Cats and media attention, Calipari repeatedly reduced himself to human dimensions.

His grandparents on his father's side came through Ellis Island. His grandfather worked in the coal mines of West Virginia, contracted black lung and died at age 58.

His mother's family was from Webster Springs, W.Va. Their diet included dandelion soup.

"I'm not the grand pooh-bah," he said. "I'm not the emperor. That's not what I want to be. We're regular people."

Calipari will have an irregular salary: $31.65 million over eight years, which makes him college basketball's highest-paid coach. That includes a buyout of $3 million per year remaining on the deal should UK decide to fire him without cause.

That didn't seem likely as Calipari

touched just about every iconic note in Kentucky basketball's storied history.

He mentioned Hazel Keightley and Karen Marlowe, widow and daughter of the late Bill Keightley.

He noted talking to all but one of his living predecessors: Joe B. Hall, Eddie Sutton, Tubby Smith and Pitino. Conspicuous by his absence was Billy Gillispie, who was fired on Friday after two seasons. "I don't have his number," Calipari said of Gillispie. "There was no intent."

Other names dropped included Kyle Macy, Rex Chapman, Nazr Mohammed, Tayshaun Prince, Adolph Rupp and Herky Rupp.

In leading what he referred to as "the commonwealth's team," Calipari acknowledged that he has an unusually difficult job.

"This is a hard job and a hard life," he said. "It's a challenge I am so excited about taking on. I know it's going to be hard. There's no givens here. We're not just walking and waltzing. It's not going to happen that way."

Calipari all but called for help in a collective effort to lift Kentucky basketball back to the heights of college basketball.

"I'm a gatherer," he said. "Folks, if this happens here, my vision of this program, it's going to happen because of all of us working together ... it takes a village ...

"If I'm doing my job, 10,000 people will say, 'Without me, they couldn't have done it.' "

Barnhart described a simple and direct hiring process. "We quickly zeroed in on (a) coach," the UK athletics director said. "And, frankly, he zeroed in on us as well."

That raised an obvious question: Why didn't this news conference happen two years ago? Why didn't Kentucky zero in on Calipari two years ago when Gillispie was the ill-fated — and ill-suited — choice?

When a reporter noted that Calipari was not on the radar, he quipped, "Well, I was on the radar."

Then he added, "But I called my wife every day for six days. 'Did they call? Did they call?' Then I kind of figured out, they're not calling."

With perfect hindsight, Barnhart called that decision, "My mistake."

Barnhart said of Gillispie's hiring, "I had a guy that was the hot coach. I watched him play. I watched his team. I liked the way they did it. He had built a couple programs. I felt we had the right guy, and I missed. My fault."

Barnhart did not say specifically why he bypassed Calipari. When asked if the perception of potential NCAA rules issues played a part, Barnhart said, "No, no. Don't start that."

A check with the NCAA not only showed no problems, Barnhart said, but NCAA compliance staffers spoke of how they "enjoyed" working with Calipari.

"Our commitment at the University of Kentucky to compliance and discipline has always been strong, and that will not change," Barnhart said. "John's commitment to compliance and discipline has always been strong, and that will not change."

Calipari noted the difficult choice he faced: a Kentucky job he'd dreamed of or continuing a blessed existence as University of Memphis coach.

After completing the UK news conference, Calipari returned to Memphis, where he spoke to reporters outside his home.

"I know people are going to be angry," he said of Memphis fans. "... But I hope over a period of time that people will understand that we absolutely loved it here.

"You have to know I had a lot of opportunities to leave here for more money than I was making, and I never did. If I stayed, I would have made more money (at Memphis) next year than at Kentucky. They asked me a hundred times, 'Can we pay you more? Can we do more?' It had nothing to do with that."

With that, Calipari paused and then walked into his front door to presumably regain his composure.

A few minutes later, the Memphis team chaplain, Ken Bennett, came out with a message for the media.

"This is very hard for him," Bennett said. "Give him a minute."

A few hours earlier, Calipari had gotten sentimental as he recalled his first experience with Kentucky basketball. His Massachusetts team played at UK on Dec. 4, 1991. Kentucky beat the tired Minutemen, who stopped in Lexington for a game while returning from the Great Alaska Shootout.

"I could not believe the environment," he said. "At that point, I said, 'I'd love to coach there someday.' ■

— Jerry Tipton

RIGHT: With University of Kentucky President Lee T. Todd Jr. at his left and UK Athletics Director Mitch Barnhart at his right, John Calipari was introduced as UK's new head basketball coach, April 1, 2009. LEXINGTON HERALD-LEADER/CHARLES BERTRAM

NATIONAL CHAMPIONS
1998
NATIONAL CHAMPIONS
1978
NATIONAL CHAMPIONS
1951

April 9, 2009

Calipari shows a softer side
At UK practice

The $32 million coach walked into Kentucky's $30 million practice facility looking like "Joe Bag of Donuts," the real John Calipari he suggested he was at his introductory news conference.

A long white sleeved T-shirt. Blue sweat pants. The beginning of a paunch (apparently he wasn't kidding about liking Dunkin' Donuts). Definitely not the persona of a grand pooh-bah of basketball.

Nor did Calipari rule Wednesday's 45-minute workout with an imperial air. Calipari made it clear what he wanted, then watched the 17 players try to execute. (Matt Pilgrim, tweaked hamstring, and walk-on Matt Scherbenske, knee injury, watched from the sideline.) UK invited the media to observe the practice in the Craft Center.

UK spent the time working on driving to the basket with purpose. "Fifty layups a game," the new coach told the players. "If you don't go hard for layups, I can't play you."

Perhaps mindful of talk that his predecessor, Billy Gillispie, beat the players down verbally, Calipari sprinkled his instruction with encouragement.

"Good job."

"It's different. You're doing fine."

"You're doing great."

Early on, Calipari blew a whistle to comment on a drill. The whistle, which he tooted softly, failed to halt several dribbles and side conversations. A coaching eruption seemed impending.

"Please stop," he said. "When the whistle blows, please stop talking, managers and everyone."

Everyone stopped.

Later, when he apparently didn't believe the players were paying enough attention, Calipari said, "Please listen."

When Calipari saw players frown because a manager failed to make a good pass, he said, "Don't be mad at a manager because I got things I can be mad at you about."

The coaches' attire added to the informal atmosphere. Three staff members he's bringing from Memphis — John Robic, Orlando Antigua and Rod Strickland — were not uniformly dressed.

(UK spokesman DeWayne Peevy said Robic and Antigua were hired as assistant coaches. Strickland could be an assistant or hold the job he had at Memphis, Director of Basketball Operations. That leaves Calipari needing to fill one spot.)

Early on, the players worked on scoring while being hit with pads wielded by managers or assistant coaches. The players had to absorb two blows while either on the drive or at the basket.

"You have to play through bumps," Calipari said. "If you can't play through bumps, it will be hard for me to play you.

"When you miss, you'll look over at me and say, 'I got fouled.'

"I don't care about you getting fouled. Make the layup."

NCAA rules allow teams to practice for two hours a week until April 15.

When this workout ended, Calipari gathered the players near mid-court and could be heard to say, "That was a great job. Hey, that was great."

A few moments later, the new coach said something that elicited chuckles from the players. ■

— Jerry Tipton

LEFT: Former UK great Kenny Walker talked with John Calipari before he ran his players through practice at Joe Craft Center.
LEXINGTON HERALD-LEADER/MARK CORNELISON

FOLLOWING: John Calipari, who led his Cats through practice, also evaluated who would fit best in his dribble-drive system.
LEXINGTON HERALD-LEADER/MARK CORNELISON

1948
NATIONAL CHAMPIONS
1951
NATIONAL CHAMPIONS
1958
NATIONAL CHAMPIONS
1978
NATIONAL CHAMPIONS
1996

Building The Team

Cal Meets Big Blue Nation

April 9, 2009

Cousins commits to Cats

Highly touted big man 'comfortable' with Cal

Highly regarded prospect DeMarcus Cousins became the first recruiting notch in John Calipari's belt as Kentucky coach late Tuesday night.

That's when Cousins made it official. After first committing to Memphis, he will follow Calipari to Kentucky.

"He wanted to do it at the highest level and with a coach he's grown to feel comfortable with," said Otis Hughley, Cousins' high school coach, in explaining the decision.

Calipari's success with NBA-bound players like Derrick Rose and Marcus Camby probably played a role in Cousins' decision, Hughley said.

So did style of play.

"I think he likes the opportunity to play pro sets," Hughley said. "Pick and roll. Pick and pop. That will highlight the arsenal and variety he has in his game. ... He wanted to find a place to do more than sit on the block or just play outside. He wants to play the whole game."

Cousins, a 6-foot-10 player for John LeFlore High in Mobile, Ala., is rated as the nation's No. 2 prospect in the class of 2009, according to the recruiting service Rivals.com.

Cousins averaged "close to 27 (points) and 11 (rebounds)" for LeFlore last season, Hughley said. He'll come to Kentucky with the expectation of being a so-called "one-and-done," a player who only plays one season at the college level, as Rose and Tyreke Evans did for Calipari at Memphis.

When asked if Cousins would be a one-and-done player, Hughley said, "He can be. All that stuff is contingent on too many variables."

Hard work and a good attitude can make Cousins a one-and-done player, the LeFlore coach said.

"A lot of guys can practice all day every day, that doesn't mean it's going to happen," Hughley said. "He certainly has everything he would need."

Recruiting analysts see Cousins as a top-shelf prospect.

Jerry Meyer of Rivals.com said Cousins was one of the most skilled big men he'd seen in more than six years appraising prospects. He rated Cousins over Al Jefferson, who jumped from high school to the Boston Celtics, because Cousins has greater shooting range and is a better passer.

"He'll be a good NBA player," said analyst Brick Oettinger of the Prep Stars recruiting service.

LEFT: DeMarcus Cousins addressed the media.
LEXINGTON HERALD-LEADER/MARK CORNELISON

Cousins has not taken a college entrance exam, so his academic eligibility remains unfulfilled.

One other question hangs over Cousins. He's had fits of temper while playing in the summer AAU circuit.

"There are flare-ups," Meyer said before adding, "That's better than being soft and won't compete. … He plays with a chip on his shoulder. He doesn't mind getting physical. It's just a matter of controlling and channelling (the anger)."

Hughley all but guaranteed that Cousins will not have any flare-ups for however long he plays for Kentucky.

"He won't do that under Coach Cal," the LeFlore coach said. "He didn't do that under me. All that is really directly correlated to how he's led. A lot of it is just being young."

Orton wavering?

Internet buzz suggested signee Daniel Orton was wavering on his commitment to UK. He's scheduled to play in the Derby Festival high school all-star game on Saturday.

But the player's father said there was no change in his son's commitment to UK. Daniel still intended to play for Kentucky, but he also might consider the option of seeking a release.

Derby Festival organizer Dan Owens called the player's father on Wednesday to make sure Orton still intended to play in the all-star game.

"We'll be there, looking forward to it," Larry Orton told Owens. ■

Jerry Tipton

May 7, 2009

Bledsoe provides Cats with missing piece

Signing fills void at point guard

Kentucky met its top remaining recruiting need on Wednesday when Eric Bledsoe signed with UK.

Bledsoe, whom the recruiting service Rivals.com ranks as the third-best point guard in the high school class of 2009, picked Kentucky over Memphis.

Bledsoe's commitment is not expected to adversely affect Kentucky's pursuit of another point guard, the celebrated John Wall.

Bledsoe, a native of Birmingham, Ala., cited new UK coach John Calipari and Kentucky's love for basketball as factors.

"When Alabama recruited him at the end, he said, 'Coach, it's pretty much football, football, football all the time,' " said Maurice Ford, Bledsoe's coach at Birmingham's Parker High School.

"'I'm a basketball player. Every time I pick up the paper, they're writing about football. Coach, I want to go where basketball is important, where everyone knows and loves the game.'"

Calipari, who earlier recruited Bledsoe for Memphis, played a "big role" in the decision, Bledsoe said.

"I hung out with him a lot when I was up there," he said of an official visit last weekend. "He told me I'd be his starting point guard."

Calipari, whom Bledsoe called a "really funny dude," spoke of playing more than one point guard should Wall also sign with Kentucky.

"He's very competitive, very tough," Rivals analyst Jerry Meyer said of Bledsoe. "He understands how to win basketball games. He can do pretty much everything you need a point guard to do except shoot. He's not a great shooter. But he's good enough to keep the defense honest."

Another analyst, Brick Oettinger of Prep Stars, cited shooting as a reason his recruiting service only rated Bledsoe at No. 80 among the prospects in the class of 2009.

"I don't think he's a very good shooter," Oettinger said. "That was the major thing. What he's best at is pushing the ball on the break and dishing. When having to set up in the half-court, he's not as effective. But he's quick."

The 6-foot-1 Bledsoe did well in the Derby Festival Basketball Classic in Louisville in April. He scored nine points, grabbed a team-high eight rebounds and had four assists in 24 minutes.

"What makes him special is, he's a competitor," Meyer said. "He's a down-and-dirty, gritty player."

Rivals ranks Bledsoe at No. 23 among the nation's prospects in the class of 2009.

Bledsoe averaged 20.3 points and 11.5 assists as a senior in leading Parker High to the Alabama 5A state championship. The Birmingham News named him No. 1 in its annual Super Senior listing.

Bledsoe has not yet gained his academic

eligibility as a college freshman. Ford, his high school coach, voiced confidence that Bledsoe will be eligible.

Ford told the Birmingham News that Bledsoe had scored a 17 on the ACT and passed the Alabama High School Graduation Exam. Ford told the newspaper that Bledsoe has to make at least a B in a core-curriculum math course he's taking now to reach the grade-point average he needs to be eligible as a college freshman.

"He's on track," Ford told the Birmingham News. "This is the first time he's been challenged academically. He knows what he has to do."

Bledsoe's commitment does not end Kentucky's search for help at point guard. UK has been prominent in its pursuit of Wall, from Raleigh, N.C., who is a consensus choice as the nation's best player.

Wall is expected to narrow his list of eight schools any day.

Meyer dismissed the thought that Bledsoe's commitment might cause Wall to drop Kentucky.

"I don't think John Wall is really worried about any player in terms of competition for playing time," Meyer said with a chuckle.

Calipari has reportedly been trying to sell Bledsoe and Wall on the idea of playing together on the court.

The analysts disagreed on how plausible that scenario might be.

"Kentucky could definitely play the two together," Meyer said. "The dribble drive is the ultimate offense to play two point guards because it's dribble based. … Guys are expected to put it on the floor and create plays."

Oettinger was dubious. He suggested a more powerful selling point for Bledsoe.

"You'll get to practice against Wall every day," he said. "See how good you'll become. "I can see that argument rather than playing them both together."

Bledsoe joined a Kentucky recruiting class that includes big men Daniel Orton of Oklahoma City; and DeMarcus Cousins of Mobile, Ala.; plus wings Darnell Dodson of Greenbelt, Md.; and Kentucky Mr. Basketball Jon Hood of Madisonville.

As with Cousins, Dodson and perhaps Wall, Bledsoe's arrival at Kentucky can be linked directly to Calipari becoming UK coach.

"If Cal had stayed in Memphis, I would have signed with Florida," Bledsoe said. "I wanted to play in the SEC." ■

— Jerry Tipton

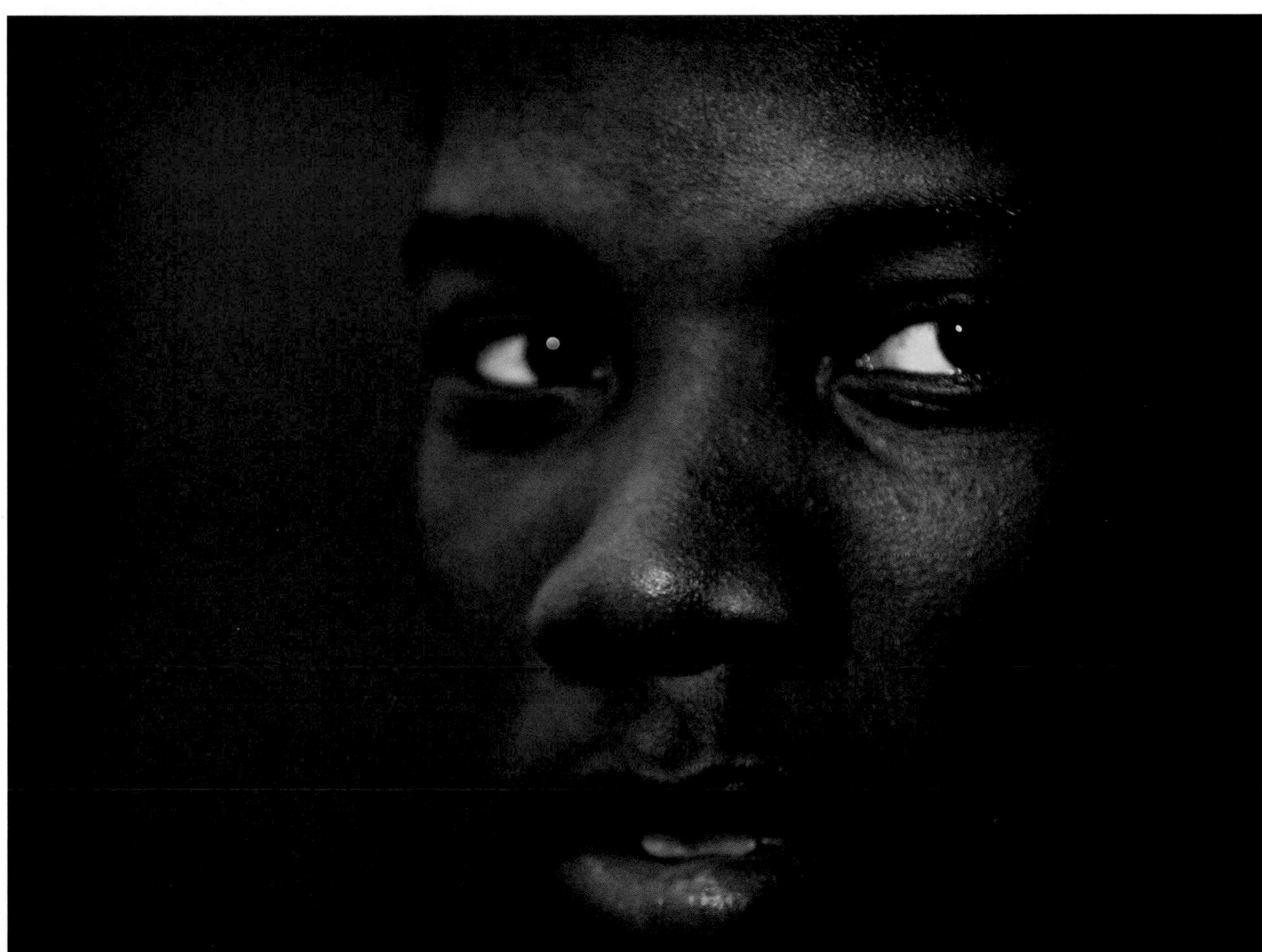

RIGHT: Eric Bledsoe addressed the media.
LEXINGTON HERALD-LEADER/MARK CORNELISON

May 9, 2009

Patterson stays true to Blue

Big man withdraws from NBA Draft to pursue NCAA

Citing the chance to play for a national championship-caliber team next season and graduate next spring, big man Patrick Patterson has decided to withdraw his name from the 2009 NBA Draft.

The University of Kentucky made Patterson's intentions known Friday afternoon, leaving teammate Jodie Meeks as the only Wildcats player in the NBA Draft.

Meeks' father acknowledged his surprise that Patterson withdrew from the draft.

"If it's the right thing for him and his family, I'm happy for him," Orestes Meeks said. "My deal is more surprise than anything else. He couldn't have done any workouts (for NBA teams) because the workouts haven't started yet."

His son won't begin workouts for NBA teams for more than a week, the elder Meeks said. Meeks' decision to stay in the draft or return to Kentucky would come after the workouts.

"He's just starting the process," Orestes Meeks said. "There's no update because nothing has happened yet."

Meeks, who led UK and the Southeastern Conference in scoring last season, is one of about 50 players to be invited to the NBA's Pre-Draft Camp in Chicago later this month.

When asked to put that invitation in perspective, NBA consultant Chris Ekstrand said, "The draft has 60 picks. Draw your own conclusions."

The elder Meeks noted that Patterson's return enhances UK's attraction for Jodie Meeks.

"I think it'll be a very big tug," Orestes Meeks said. "He knows how good they'll be. They'll be extremely good."

Patterson, a 6-foot-9 forward, led the SEC and ranked 11th in the country in field goal percentage (60.3 percent) last season. He was one of the league's most productive players.

"I have the chance to graduate in three years, which is important to me and my family," Patterson said in a statement released by UK. "I want to help Kentucky compete for a national title, and even more than that win its eighth national championship. I'm also really excited about playing for Coach Cal and developing my game in the dribble-drive offense."

UK's first-year coach, John Calipari, expressed happiness with getting to coach Patterson next season.

"In the month that I've been at Kentucky, I've been blown away by Patrick Patterson," Calipari said in a UK news release. "He is one of the nicest individuals I've met and one of the fiercest competitors that I've been around. I'm thrilled I get to coach him next year."

As for the curious timing of Patterson's withdrawal before working out for teams, Ekstrand speculated that Patterson could have learned already where he projected in the draft. The NBA's

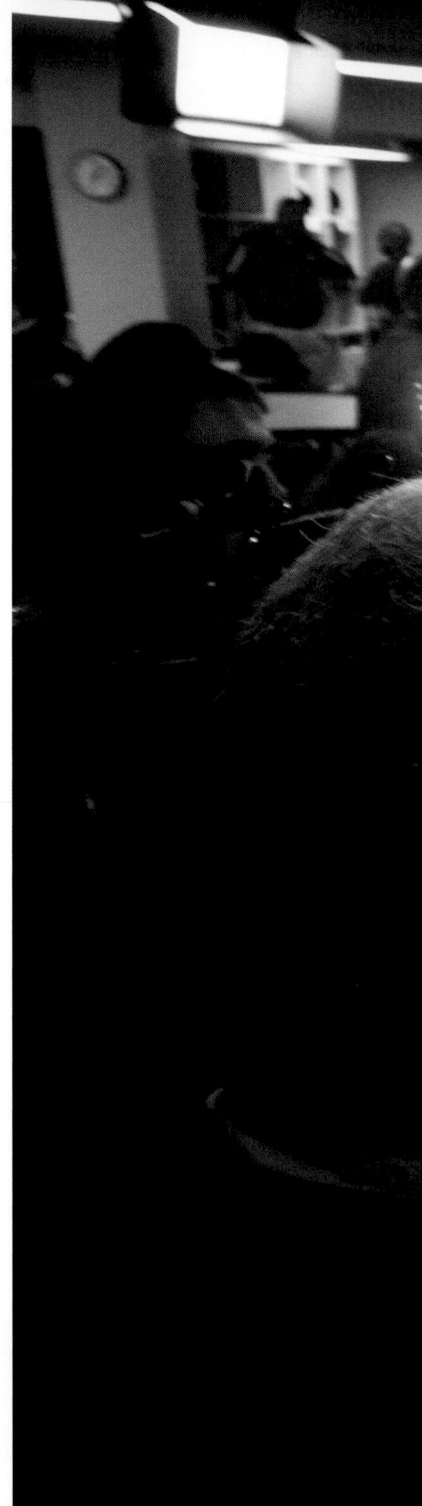

RIGHT: UK's Patrick Patterson held a news conference in Memorial Coliseum to give his reasons for returning to the Wildcats after exploring the possibility of entering his name in the NBA Draft. LEXINGTON HERALD-LEADER/DAVID PERRY

UK

Undergraduate Advisory Committee could have given Patterson an estimate by now on where he might be drafted, Ekstrand said.

Earlier this spring, Calipari spoke of Patterson being able to make himself a lottery pick in the 2010 NBA Draft if he returned to Kentucky next season. That supported the general view of Patterson being taken in the second half of the first round at the earliest.

UK plans to make Patterson and Calipari available to answer media questions on Monday.

Patterson was the only player in the SEC to rank in the top five in scoring (17.9 ppg) and rebounding (9.3 rpg). Patterson also led the league in double-doubles with 15, the eighth most in a single season in UK history.

Dick Vitale, ESPN's Hall of Fame commentator on college basketball, saw Patterson's return as making Kentucky a "legit top-10, top-15 team" next season.

Vitale noted that UK remains in contention for point guard John Wall, generally considered the nation's top high school prospect. Plus, Meeks could return.

"If they get John Wall and Jodie Meeks comes back, they'll be ready to take on the Atlanta Hawks," Vitale said. "Never mind the NCAA title. They'll be going for the NBA title." ■

—Jerry Tipton

BELOW: UK's Patrick Patterson, center, flanked by parents Tywanna, left, and Buster, held a news conference in Memorial Coliseum to give his reasons for returning to the Wildcats after exploring the possibility of entering his name in the NBA Draft. LEXINGTON HERALD-LEADER/DAVID PERRY

May 20, 2009

Wall in the family

UK's class of 2009 No. 1 in nation 'by far'

Adding mega point guard prospect John Wall to Kentucky's recruiting haul inspired attempts to put the class in historic terms. Guesstimates quickly zoomed past best this year and best in 10 years.

Analyst Dave Telep of the Scout.com recruiting service put Kentucky's class in biblical terms.

"It's like Noah's Ark," he said. "They got two of everything. Two point guards. Two centers. Two wings."

Wall, a 6-foot-4 player from Raleigh, N.C., is one of the point guards. More precisely, he's the No. 1 high school point guard in the country, according to all the major recruiting services.

Analyst Jerry Meyer of the Rivals.com recruiting service likened Wall to a mix of Derrick Rose and Rajon Rondo.

To describe Wall's speed and athleticism, analyst Brick Oettinger of Prep Stars cited one of the greatest Olympic champions.

"Picture Carl Lewis," Oettinger said before adding, "with a basketball in his hands."

When the person on the other end of the telephone laughed, Oettinger said, "I'm serious. He's faster than anybody on the court."

Wall joins a UK recruiting class that includes big man DeMarcus Cousins of Mobile, Ala. Rivals.com ranks them as the top two players in the high school class of 2009. Another big man, Daniel Orton, is generally considered a top-25 national prospect. Rivals also rates point guard Eric Bledsoe in its top 25.

Other players in UK's class are junior-college wing Darnell Dodson (Rivals considers him a four-star prospect) and Kentucky Mr. Basketball Jon Hood.

"By far, the No. 1 recruiting class in the country," said Bob Gibbons, an analyst for the All-Star Sports service. "Everybody had North Carolina No. 1. This class by far surpasses that."

Wall, who must still gain academic eligibility, faces one other minor hurdle. He is due in court May 29 to answer to a misdemeanor breaking and entering citation. He is eligible for a first-offender program in which punishment is usually community service. As a first offender, he can also petition the court to remove the citation from his record.

Wall is scheduled to talk about his choice of Kentucky at a 2 p.m. news conference on Wednesday. He had also been considering Duke, Miami (Fla.), North Carolina State, Florida, Kansas and Baylor.

Once again in this spring's astounding recruiting haul, new UK coach John Calipari was cited as the key factor.

"I had a group of great schools and I admire them all," Wall told the Raleigh News and Observer. "But the relationship I had with Coach Cal was the biggest factor."

In a separate interview with the recruiting service Rivals.com, Wall said, "In the end, I just felt I wanted to play for Coach Cal. Coaches give different visions of what they can do for you when they talk to you. And all of those are impressive. But my long relationship with Coach Cal and what he can do for me in his program was the main thing."

Although Wall spoke of an "easy decision," his travel-team coach and adviser, Brian Clifton, suggested a more deliberate process.

"We had an at-length conversation last night," Clifton told Rivals. "He felt that the risks that were at Kentucky were acceptable risks for him."

The risks were the presence of two other point guards at UK: sophomore-to-be DeAndre Liggins and Bledsoe. Bledsoe is considered one of the most talented point guards in the high school class of 2009, as was Liggins in the class of 2008.

"It's not like John is a guy who wants to take two or three years to figure it out and get things together," Clifton told Rivals. "He needs to hit the ground running in short order. But John said to me, 'When I came to your program, I wasn't the guy. I had to listen to you and turned it around. It doesn't matter to me who is there.'

"I believe in John Wall as a person, forget basketball. If he believes in the situation, then I trust him and respect him. If he believes he can do it, that's all I need to hear."

Wall, whom the analysts say must improve his perimeter shot and overall decision making, welcomed the competition.

"Being able to play against Eric (Bledsoe) is a big plus," Wall told Rivals. "I told Brian and my mom that I've always had to fight for my position. That's what I had to do when I first played for Brian. I'm used to fighting. It's another challenge for me to come to Kentucky and fight for my position."

Wall is considered the final piece of the puzzle to complete Kentucky's revamped lineup. He would be the point guard to lead a potential lineup that would include holdover stars Patrick Patterson and Jodie Meeks, plus sophomore Darius Miller.

Gibbons likened Wall to the player's hero, Derrick Rose, a one-and-done point guard who led Memphis to the 2008 Final Four.

"John Wall, I predict, can do for Kentucky what Derrick Rose did for Memphis," the analyst said. ■

— Jerry Tipton

BELOW: John Wall addressed the media.
LEXINGTON HERALD-LEADER/MARK CORNELISON

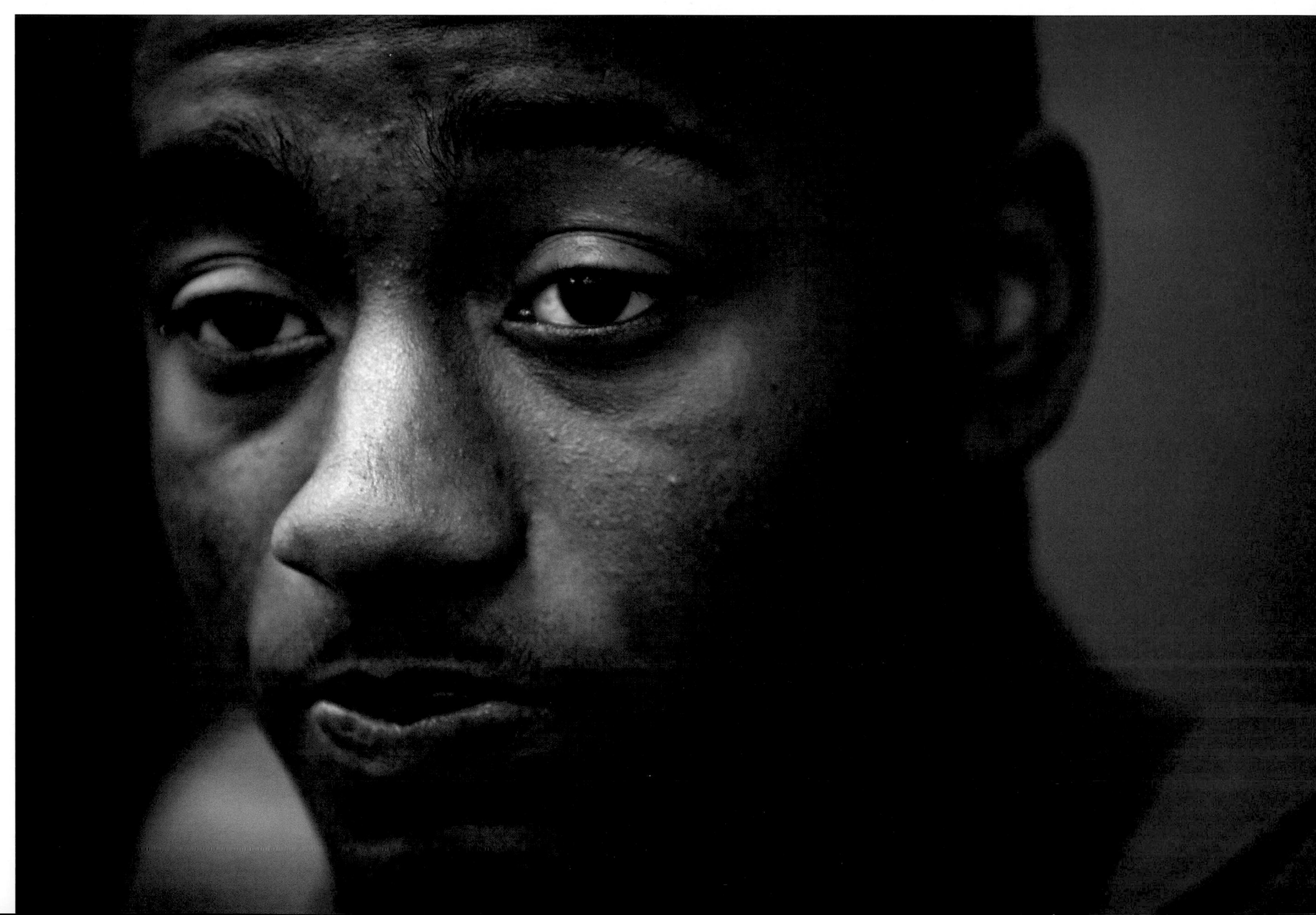

May 24, 2009

ALL THE RIGHT MOVES

He eats. He tweets. He lives among the mere mortals ...

He took a star turn in the Governor's Mansion. He rode a special train to the Kentucky Derby. He recruited the nation's No. 1 class of prospects.

He was named an honorary member of the Lexington Rotary Club. He coaxed a shy employee of Wheeler Pharmacy to pose with him for a picture. He created a deafening buzz around Kentucky basketball.

He goes to church each morning. He calls a newfound friend from Kentucky daily to check on his ongoing battle with bone cancer. His Twitter audience is 80,000-plus.

He bought a house, hired a basketball staff, returned to Memphis to visit his wife, watched his son play youth basketball, dropped in unexpectedly at an on-campus charity event and sat with UK softball players in a Lexington restaurant as they watched ESPNU's unveiling of the NCAA Tournament bracket.

Asked how John Calipari is doing as the new basketball coach for the University of Kentucky, school president Lee Todd said, "Oh, I think he's doing great. I think there's about six of him."

The seemingly omnipresent Calipari seems to be the total package: coach, father, husband, friend, ambassador, promoter, comforter of the afflicted, confident of the comfortable.

He made a big splash when he accepted Kentucky Gov. Steve Beshear's invitation to attend a reception. Todd, who also attended the event, came away doubly pleased.

Before making a few remarks, Calipari got Todd aside to ask whether there were any university projects the president wanted mentioned.

"So I found him to be someone who's wanting to embrace the whole university," Todd said.

The UK president also soaked in the scene of Calipari shaking hands, posing for pictures and charming the governor's guests.

LEXINGTON WWW.KENTUCKY.COM

HERALD-LEADER

MAY 24, 2009 | SUNDAY | METRO FINAL EDITION $2.00

He eats. He tweets. He lives among the mere mortals ...

He took a star turn in the Governor's Mansion. He rode a special train to the Kentucky Derby. He recruited the nation's No. 1 class of prospects.

He was named an honorary member of the Lexington Rotary Club. He coaxed a shy employee of Wheeler Pharmacy to pose with him for a picture. He created a deafening buzz around Kentucky basketball.

He goes to church each morning. He calls a newfound friend from Kentucky daily to check on his ongoing battle with bone cancer. His Twitter audience is 80,000-plus.

He bought a house, hired a basketball staff, returned to Memphis to visit his wife, watched his son play youth basketball, dropped in unexpectedly at an on-campus charity event and sat with UK softball players in a Lexington restaurant as they watched ESPNU's unveiling of the NCAA Tournament bracket.

Asked how John Calipari is doing as the new basketball coach for the University of Kentucky, school president Lee Todd said, "Oh, I think he's doing great. I think there's about six of him."

See CALIPARI, A15

Article by **Jerry Tipton** jtipton@herald-leader.com Illustration by **Camille Weber** cweber1@herald-leader.com

Kathleen Imhoff, the Lexington Public Library executive director, said she is now reviewing all credit card bills.

What else library charged

19 employees spent $350,000

MOST CARDS NOW CANCELED

By John Cheves
jcheves@herald-leader.com

Nineteen Lexington Public Library employees who had active library credit cards, other than chief executive Kathleen Imhoff, spent about $350,000 with them over the past three years, according to a Herald-Leader review of library documents.

Checking out the books

Earlier this month, the library board voted to cancel most of those credit cards after a Herald-Leader story detailing $134,000 that Imhoff spent in five years on travel, meals, gifts and other items. Imhoff and four others were allowed to keep their cards.

The majority of the 19 employees charged for work-related travel and materials, as the credit cards are intended under library policy. Several employees seldom used their cards.

But thousands of dollars also were spent on beer, wine and liquor; parties and gifts for

See LIBRARY, A8

Who might fly Somerset to D.C. and back?

TAXPAYERS SUBSIDIZE SERVICE THAT COINCIDES WITH WEEKEND

By Halimah Abdullah
habdullah@mcclatchydc.com

WASHINGTON — The lone commercial airline serving Republican Rep. Hal Rogers' hometown of Somerset offers discounted fares starting at $39 on half-empty nine-seat planes thanks to a $1 million taxpayer-subsidized grant.

Customers zip through security at Lake Cumberland Regional Airport's $3 million, federally funded commercial terminal, which sat virtually empty for three years as local

INSIDE TODAY | HERALD-LEADER

Harrodsburg children's author inspired by mom who read to her

Heather Henson

ARTS + LIFE — PAGE E1

Track finals: Louisville Male wins; Henry Clay, Dunbar, Bryan Station in top 10. **Sports, B1**

State tennis finals: Lexington high school players all finish as runners-up. **Sports, B1**

UK's Jarmon accepts blame for taking banned substance

By Chip Cosby
ccosby@herald-leader.com

The career of University of Kentucky football star Jeremy Jarmon has come to an abrupt end after he tested positive for a substance banned by the NCAA and was ruled ineligible for his senior season.

Jarmon's result was positive in a random NCAA test conducted Feb.

"Someone asked me a question," Todd said. "I told him, I'm actually just standing here enjoying seeing everybody happy."

No one seemed happy two short months ago. Athletics Director Mitch Barnhart spoke of former coach Billy Gillispie, a solitary figure in every sense, needing to make "adjustments." Gillispie recoiled at the suggestion of being a celebrity/public figure. Maybe most importantly, the team failed to receive an NCAA Tournament bid for the first time since 1991.

Now it all seems like a bad dream. Billy Wilcoxson, a former Board of Trustees member for 21 years, likened Calipari's arrival as "a fresh drink of water from the head of a stream."

Perpetually parched Kentuckians have chug-a-lugged Calipari.

Luther Deaton, the long-time chairman, president and CEO of Central Bank, rode the train to the Kentucky Derby with Calipari. He recalled a stop at Valhalla Golf Club, where the new UK coach suggested they get off the train and mingle.

"He was like a magnet," Deaton said. "Ninety percent of the people were saying, 'John, thank you for coming and saving us.' "

The messianic fervor surrounds a man who talks about himself as Joe Bag-o-Dunkin' Donuts. At his introductory news conference, he told UK fans about his love for Dunkin' Donuts and his desire to reduce his caffeine intake.

Rick Corman, whose Nicholasville-based company builds railroad tracks and cleans up accident sites, was asked to send one of his private planes to Memphis when Calipari agreed to become UK coach.

To avoid media detection, Corman set a flight plan for a trip from Nicholasville to Houston. As the plane began a descent into Memphis, an FAA controller radioed the pilot: "Please don't take our coach."

Corman did not know Calipari. He noticed the new UK coach insisted on carrying his own bag onto the plane. He heard "Cal" make sure his son, Bradley, said "please" and "thank you" when offered a soft drink.

Corman and Calipari became friends. Calipari spoke of how he goes to Catholic mass each morning, and goes to a Methodist church on Sunday. His wife, Ellen, was raised a Methodist.

Corman spoke of his bone cancer and how he's undergone two bone marrow transplants.

Now Corman and Calipari talk or text-message every day.

"He prays for me every day," Corman said. "He'll call and say, 'Did you feel it?'

"How can I not like the guy? If I don't go to games, I should be horse-whipped."

Calipari the recruiter made the biggest public impression this spring. If presidents are judged, albeit artificially, by the first 100 days in office, UK's new coach could be posing for basketball's Mount Rushmore after a mere 54 days on the job.

"What he's done (in recruiting) is probably the equivalent of solving Obama's auto industry problem," recruiting analyst Dave Telep of Scout.com said. "I don't think anybody in the last decade made a spring statement the way Kentucky has. What happened to Kentucky this spring — in theory — shouldn't happen."

By late spring, all the best prospects are gone. But Calipari took a good class and made it better by adding two top-25 point guards (John Wall and Eric Bledsoe), a top-five big man (DeMarcus Cousins) and a junior college wing (Darnell Dodson). Like a pied piper, he got all four to follow him from Memphis to Kentucky.

"No one out there could have handled things like he has," said Joe B. Hall, who ought to know.

Hall coached UK for 13 seasons, beginning in 1972.

"He's handled everything deftly and with aplomb," Hall said. "He's prepared. He solves things. He comes up with solutions."

Calipari inherited problems. Two months ago, it seemed possible that Kentucky could lose its two best players (Patrick Patterson and Jodie Meeks) to the NBA Draft. The point guard position remained a question mark. To quote Telep, UK's team now looks like Noah's ark: two of everything.

C. M. Newton, once a UK player, later athletics director and now a basketball consultant to the Southeastern Conference, laughed when asked about Calipari's first 54 days as Kentucky coach.

"It exceeds anything I've ever seen or dreamed of, really," Newton said.

Newton noted how Calipari fit the criteria for coaching at Kentucky: He had demonstrated an ability to produce a high-level program, he understood the job and, maybe most importantly, he wanted the job.

Newton called Calipari a "power coach," someone who thrives in the spotlight and bends it to his will.

An example was Twitter, Newton said. The 80,000-plus who receive Calipari's Twitter messages dwarf the 5,700 signed up for the Twitter account produced by his friend, Indiana Coach Tom Crean. Such coaching heavyweights as Roy Williams, Bill Self and Ben Howland do not yet use the Twitter technology.

In his early press conferences, Calipari exuded confidence and thorough preparation. His soliloquy on scheduling suggested someone who had researched the art and science of finding opponents.

"I sense he's pushing all the right buttons as he tries to move the program to where we want it to be," Barnhart said. "He seems to have a clear road map, and he's running at a fast pace."

Of course, the destination is college basketball's ultimate stage, the Final Four, and a national championship.

Two months ago, that customary Kentucky goal seemed a few seasons away. No more.

When it was suggested that Kentucky will be Kentucky again, Hall said, "I bet you money that North Carolina, Duke, Kansas, UCLA, Connecticut feel that way. That Kentucky is back in the picture."

Newton offered a word of caution.

"I'm a true believer he'll take the program to great heights," he said of Calipari. "But anybody who thinks you'll have one dominant program Ã la UCLA back in the day or when Kentucky ruled the roost, you can forget that. There's too many national programs now.

"But he'll be one of them. I have no doubt of that. But he hasn't done it yet."

Newton has spoken to Calipari more than once. The new coach told him of the first impression UK basketball had made on him.

"This is crazy," Calipari told Newton.

To which, Newton replied, "Just enjoy the honeymoon. It will end, I will promise you."

Maybe so. But for now, Calipari is the Prince Charming who has swept a blue-clad damsel in distress off her feet.

He has done little wrong. He can do little wrong.

Deaton, who has helped every UK coach going back to Hall, paid Calipari the ultimate compliment.

"I think he's one of us," the banker said. "To be honest, I think he's a Kentuckian." ■

— Jerry Tipton

RIGHT: Coach John Calipari saluted the fans during a timeout of the Alabama vs. Kentucky football game, Oct. 3, 2009. LEXINGTON HERALD-LEADER/MARK CORNELISON

KENTUCKY
BASKETBALL

October 3, 2009

Calipari goes camping
Coach and his son join in the Madness

Kentucky Coach John Calipari and his son, Bradley, decided to go on a camping trip Friday night with hundreds, if not thousands, of their new-found friends.

Calipari went to the Memorial Coliseum/Joe Craft Center complex to camp out with UK fans, many of whom have been at the site since Wednesday waiting for Saturday morning's distribution of Big Blue Madness tickets.

When asked why he decided to camp out, Calipari said, "Because my wife is out of town." The UK coach wasn't sure where he and his son would pitch their tent.

"We brought a tent and two sleeping bags," he said. "They'll set it up somewhere."

Before pitching the tent, Calipari and his staff sat at tables outside the entrance to the Joe Craft Center. A long line of UK fans got autographs and posed for pictures with the coach.

Among the items Calipari signed were basketballs, caps, t-shirts, a pizza box, a construction helmet, yearbooks and the back of a wheelchair. ■

— Jerry Tipton

LEFT: Patrick Patterson signed autographs as UK players served pizza and signed autographs for fans who were camping out for Big Blue Madness.
LEXINGTON HERALD-LEADER/MARK CORNELISON

RIGHT: Coach John Calipari posed for a photo with Dalton Neff, of Harlan, outside the Joe Craft Center. The coach joined fans camping out for Big Blue Madness tickets. LEXINGTON HERALD-LEADER/MARK CORNELISON

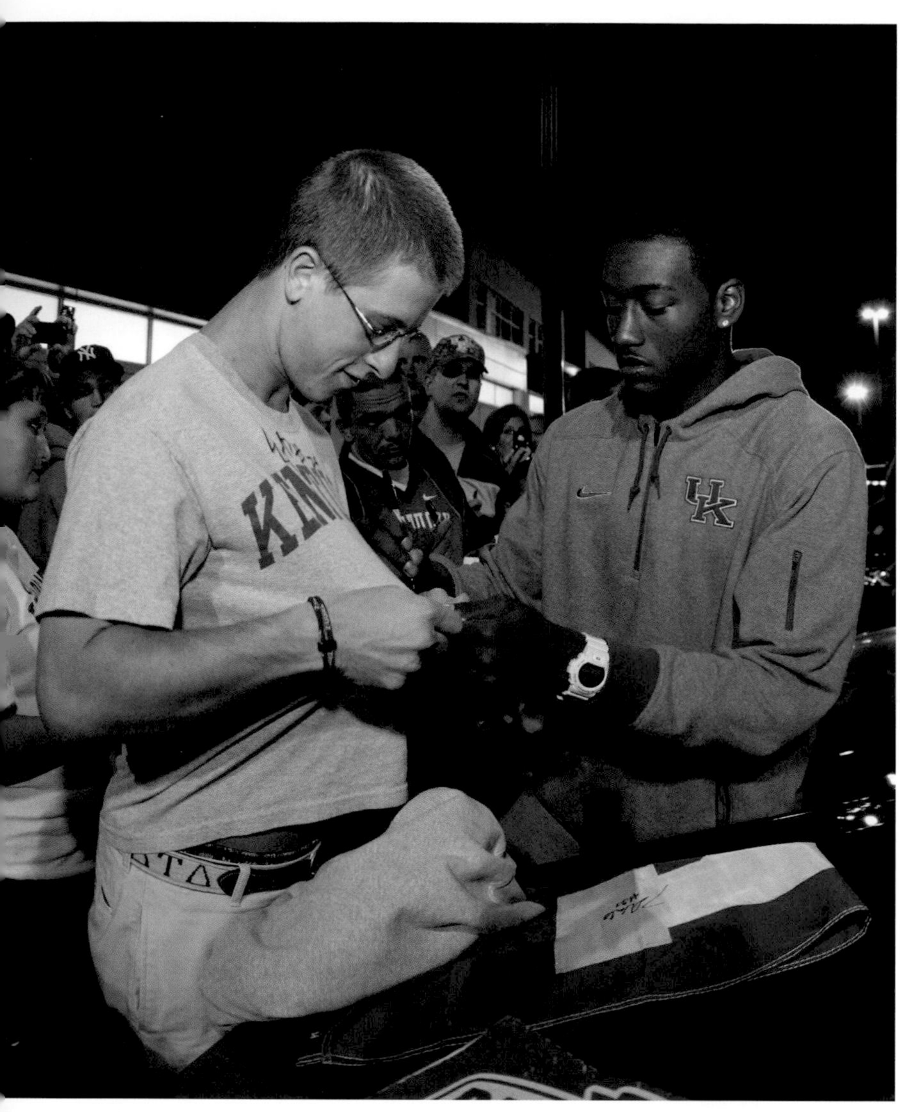

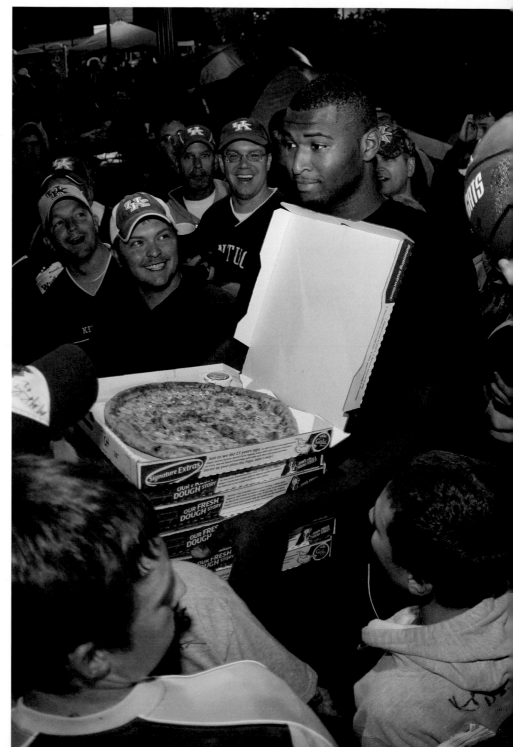

ABOVE: John Wall signed the shirt of Blake Breathitt.
LEXINGTON HERALD-LEADER/MARK CORNELISON

RIGHT: DeMarcus Cousins delivered pizza to fans who were camping out for Big Blue Madness. LEXINGTON HERALD-LEADER/MARK CORNELISON

October 16, 2009

Calipari mixes the old and new
Six newcomers and seven veterans

Tuesday night means bowling. Video games, especially NBA 2K10, unite players of varied backgrounds. Meals at the Blazer Hall cafeteria are communal gatherings.

Kentucky players have done everything but sit around a campfire and sing Kumbaya, it seems. As first-year coach John Calipari noted at UK's Media Day on Thursday, the objective of all this togetherness carries the utmost importance for the 2009–10 season.

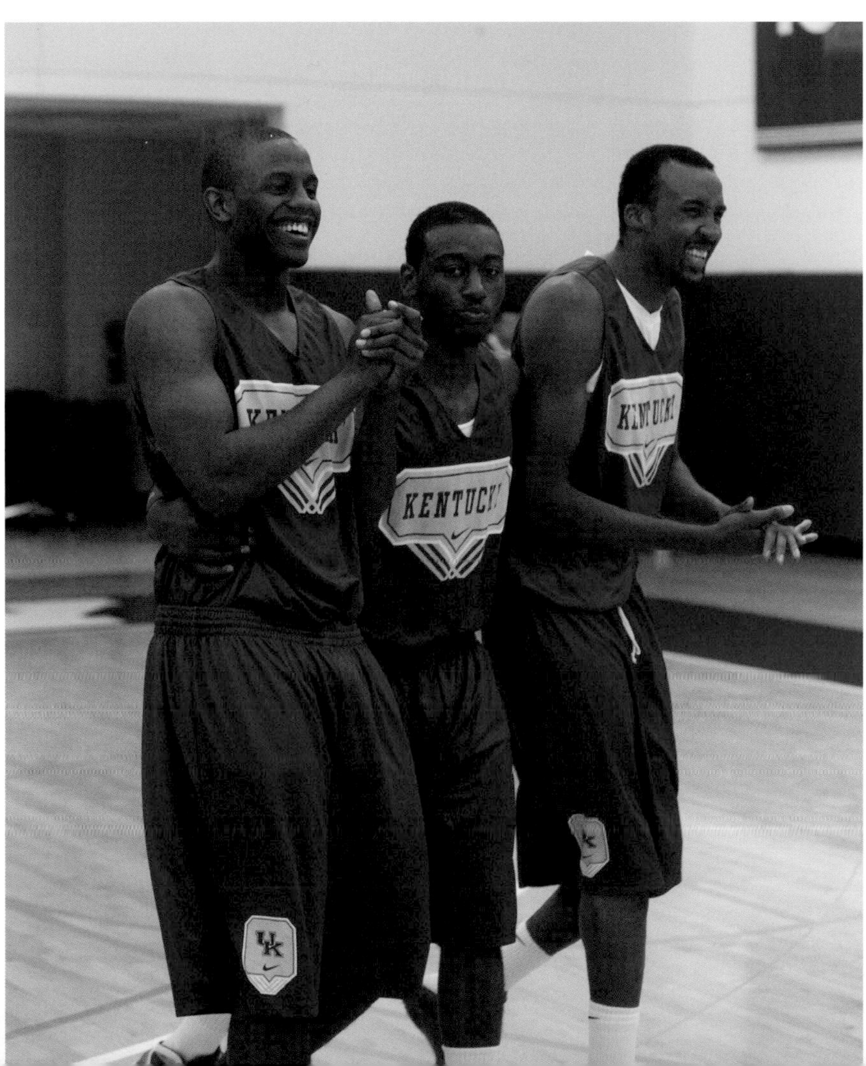

Talent alone won't get done what Kentucky wants to get done.

So one of Calipari's first moves was to have the players congregate to watch the movie Remember the Titans. The movie depicted football players from two different schools learning to consolidate. Not so coincidentally, this UK team can be almost perfectly halved: six heralded newcomers and seven veteran holdovers.

In the movie, mutual respect leads to affection. Affection evolves into a kind of love that frees grown men to cry shamelessly.

"When you get to that kind of love, you care about the other person more than yourself," Calipari said. "If we can get to that point with this team, we won't lose many games."

That's as close as Calipari got to embracing the outsized expectations for this Kentucky team.

"We don't have much time to get there," Calipari said in reference to opening night against Morehead State in less than a month (Nov. 13). "We have to go through wars to see who's really with us."

Calipari likened the process to soldiers in a foxhole. "Who do you send for ammo?" he said. "Who's coming back?"

Typically on Media Day, long before the metaphorical bullets fill the air, the players say all the right things. UK's Media Day was no exception.

Senior forward Perry Stevenson said the freshmen were "not arrogant, not egotistical."

Stevenson acknowledged his concern about incoming players hyped as instant stars. "I had a lot of thoughts," he said. "Then I figured that being recruited by a place like Kentucky, you're not only a good player, you're a good person."

John Wall, the most heralded of the UK freshmen, noted his concern with blending in.

"One of my biggest concerns was to try to be a team player and team leader," he said. "Most of the freshmen have high expectations. Would some of the upperclassmen feel bad? 'Oh, he thinks he's all that.'

LEFT: John Wall, center, walked with his arms around Darius Miller, left, and Perry Stevenson as the University of Kentucky basketball players addressed the media. LEXINGTON HERALD-LEADER/MARK CORNELISON

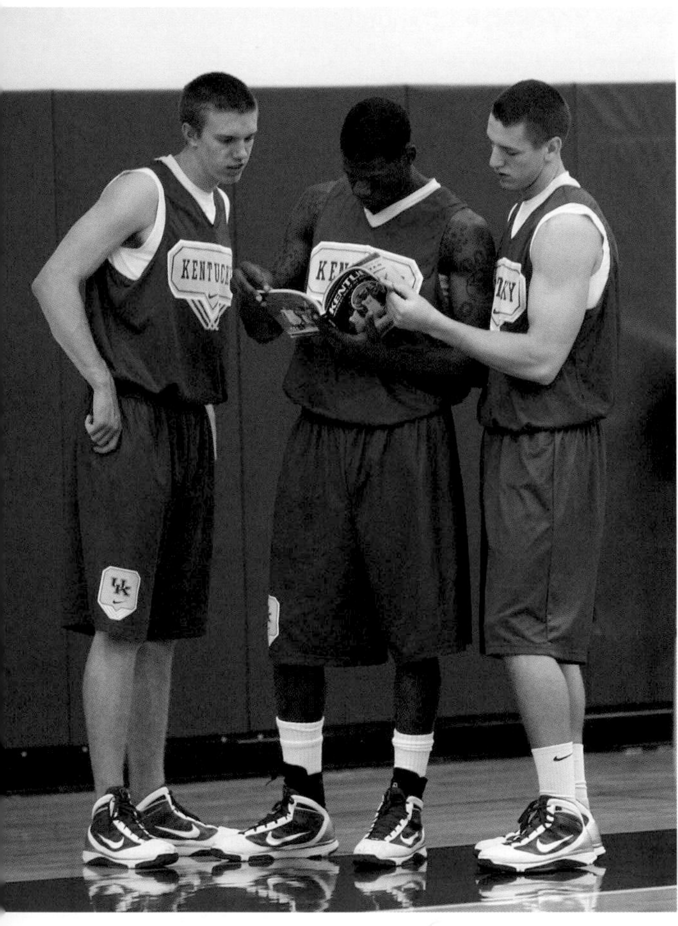

"But they didn't try to push us to the side. They helped us out."

Wall said he tried to blend in to the point of making sure he turned his practice jersey to the same side — blue or gray — as his teammates so as not to stand out. He acknowledged the complicating factor of being widely projected as the No. 1 pick in the 2010 NBA Draft.

"It's pretty tough," he said. "Some people might look at me differently."

Freshman DeMarcus Cousins, whose unabashed exuberance led Calipari to compare him affectionately to a 12-year-old, said a gap between veterans and newcomers does not exist.

"You might as well say everybody here is a freshman," he said. "No one has played for (Calipari) before. So we're all learning. We're all coming from the bottom up."

While labeling junior Patrick Patterson as the main man, Cousins dismissed the appeal of taking on the team's fastest gun.

"It's not about who is the man," Cousins said. "Nothing like that. We came here to win."

Another freshman big man, Daniel Orton, spoke of divine intervention aligning this group of UK stars.

"Everybody here has a good heart," he said. "We're a bunch of good guys. It's kind of funny how things worked out. God has mysterious ways of working everything out. I really think that's what happened. God put this team together."

Of course, Calipari is no stranger to meshing individual talents. His teams at Massachusetts and Memphis epitomized collective effort. He noted the importance of living together. He cited the help of the best player having a one-for-all approach. Like Marcus Camby at UMass, Patterson fits that description, the coach said.

But Calipari noted that those UMass and Memphis teams did not carry the national expectations of this Kentucky team. He said he spoke for an hour with one of his coaching mentors, Larry Brown, earlier Thursday.

"This is a little virgin territory for me as a coach," Calipari said. "I'm going to be learning ... I don't have all the answers. Some of it will be guessing. And if I'm wrong, I'll change." ■

— Jerry Tipton

ABOVE: UK's Jon Hood, left, DeAndre Liggins, center, and Mark Krebs flipped through a team media guide after media day.
LEXINGTON HERALD-LEADER/CHARLES BERTRAM

RIGHT: Josh Harrellson, left, Darius Miller, center, and Ramon Harris left the practice court at Joe Craft Center. LEXINGTON HERALD-LEADER/CHARLES BERTRAM

FOLLOWING: Patrick Patterson high-fived fans from the stage during UK's Big Blue Madness festivities in Rupp Arena.
LEXINGTON HERALD-LEADER/MARK CORNELISON

October 17, 2009

Manic, Mystical
Calipari shares his vision of returning UK to 'rightful place'

Envy our past. Fear our future.

That immodest message — delivered on a video accompanied by a thumping, teeth-rattling bass line — began the business portion of Kentucky's Big Blue Madness in Rupp Arena on Friday night.

Then first-year coach John Calipari added a bask-in-our-present addendum in a keynote address/acceptance speech.

Throwing plenty of red meat — or in this case, blue meat — to the capacity crowd, Calipari spoke of returning Kentucky basketball "back to its rightful place atop the mountain."

Earlier in the 15-minute address from a podium sitting on an H-shaped stage, Calipari set an even higher objective.

"That we are the gold standard not just for college basketball," he said, "but for all of college athletics."

He talked about a program "rooted in integrity" and always "run with class."

One hopes the possible secondary NCAA rules violations committed by the crowd when it chanted prospects' names were a misstep to be written off to runaway zeal. That happened four times, each an apparent violation of NCAA rule 13.11.4 which forbids the chanting of prospects' names at an event open to the public.

Madness as recruiting tool always hangs in the air. In this, Calipari set an equally lofty goal.

"My vision is for every high school player in the country to dream of putting on this uniform," he said. The energy and buzz of Madness "will attract the best student-athletes to our program."

Calipari noted UK basketball's history and tradition. A "mystical" experience, he described it.

"Our history is rooted in our coaches: Rupp, Hall, Smith," he said.

Intentionally or not, Calipari did not mention Rick Pitino, who weaved similar enthusiasm into championships in the 1990s, and Eddie Sutton.

Calipari called his dribble-drive "college basketball's most exciting offense." As he's noted throughout the fall, he stressed again the importance of team play for a roster nearly split between veterans and newcomers.

If the Cats achieve a singular purpose, he said, "We will become unbreakable and unbeatable."

But, Calipari added, "It doesn't happen in a day or weeks."

The ensuing scrimmage showed the need for patience. And it immediately revealed that some UK fans will struggle to exercise that quality.

When the first possession in the 20-minute scrimmage began with a series of passes, a fan could be heard saying, "Looks like Tubby ball."

As expected, the Cats struggled with perimeter shooting. During the first eight minutes, there were only two baskets other than dunks or layups: a pull-up 10-footer by heralded freshman John Wall and a 15-footer by freshman Daniel Orton.

Josh Harrellson stood out. He made four three-point shots.

But there also were three-point airballs by Patrick Patterson, DeMarcus Cousins and DeAndre Liggins. Plus, Eric Bledsoe and Patterson missed badly on other three-point attempts.

There were crowd-pleasing plays, too. Twice Wall drove to thunderous dunks, on the first freeing himself with a nifty behind-the-back dribble.

But overall, the scrimmage seemed to leak a bit of enthusiasm out of the crowd.

During a break in the action, Calipari took a microphone and said, "Folks, are you enjoying it?"

Then he added, "But do you see how far we have to go? Just so everybody understands it."

The coach's candid comment drew applause.

Madness began on time at 7:30. The celebration got off to a rousing start when a fan made a three-pointer to win a home entertainment complex.

After the obligatory appearance by the cheerleaders, the UK women's team was introduced at 7:55. Ten minutes later, Coach Matthew Mitchell introduced his special "assistant coach" for Madness: country music star Eddie Montgomery. ■

— Jerry Tipton

FOLLOWING: Before the men's scrimmage, Coach John Calipari spoke to the packed house in Rupp Arena.
LEXINGTON HERALD-LEADER/MARK CORNELISON

LEXINGTON HERALD-LEADER » KENTUCKY.COM/SPORTS » SECTION B

SPORTS

BUSINESS, B9 DOW: 9,995.91 ▼67.03

CARDS, HUSKIES LOOKING FOR FIRST BIG EAST WIN - B3

BENGALS SELL OUT BEHIND OCHOCINCO, MOTOROLA - B2

Insight plans adding more HD, faster Internet

SATURDAY, OCTOBER 17, 2009 ★

KATHY WILLENS | ASSOCIATED PRESS

Yanks take opener

The Yankees' Alex Rodriguez ran into Angels catcher Jeff Mathis and was called out at home plate Friday in the fifth inning of Game 1 of the ALCS. The Yankees won 4-1. **Page B5.**

Cats have corner on confidence

BURDEN, NELOMS SAY THEY CAN PLAY WITH SEC RECEIVERS

By Chip Cosby
ccosby@herald-leader.com

On paper, the revamped Kentucky cornerback tandem of Randall Burden and Martavious Neloms gave up three touchdowns to South Carolina receiver Alshon Jeffery last Saturday.

But if you look beyond the numbers, there is more to see.

For one, Burden and Neloms weren't physically overmatched against the Gamecocks wideouts, running stride for stride with them most of the afternoon. Where the two corners ran into problems was trying to make plays on the ball.

But they don't seem to have lost any confidence.

"We can run with any team we play against, whether it's Florida, Alabama or South Carolina," Burden said. "It's just a matter of getting the ball out when it's time."

Two of Jeffery's TDs came on Burden. On the first, Jeffery fought through tight coverage and brought in a 10-yard slant.

"I thought I played that pretty well," Burden said. "I was all up on him before he even caught the ball. He just brought it in and secured it."

Jeffery also made an acrobatic one-handed catch in the end zone over Burden for a 28-yarder.

"That was just a great catch on his part," Burden said.

Burden and Neloms might have to hold down the fort for another week or two. Star corner Trevard Lindley is out with a high ankle sprain, and fellow starter Paul Warford will try to play through an

See UK FOOTBALL, B4

Kentucky at Auburn

WHEN: 7:30 p.m. Saturday
TV: ESPNU
RADIO: WBUL-FM 98.1; WLAP-AM 630
RECORDS: Kentucky (2-3, 0-3 SEC); Auburn (5-1; 2-1)
SERIES: Auburn leads 24-5-1
LAST MEETING: Auburn won 49-27 in Lexington in 2005

Miss World has something to prove

HARD-LUCK GOZZIP GIRL BACK AS THE FAVORITE

By Alicia Wincze
awincze@herald-leader.com

The connections of Miss World say they are confident their filly will prove her first Grade I victory was the result of her talent and not a rival's misfortune when she faces another Grade I field on Saturday at Keeneland.

After pulling an upset in the Grade I Garden City Stakes at Belmont on Sept. 12, Miss World goes for her fourth straight win and second graded stakes victory in the Grade I, $500,000 Queen Elizabeth II Challenge Cup over 1⅛ miles on the Keeneland turf.

Though Miss World ran away for a 1¾-length win in the 1⅛-mile Garden City, heavy favorite Gozzip Girl ran into trouble on the first turn when she clipped heels and almost went down before gathering herself to finish fourth.

While there is no denying Gozzip Girl didn't get the ideal trip, Miss World didn't exactly have things her way either.

"It was actually a tough trip for her, too. The favorite got really badly squeezed inside, but mine also got squeezed between two horses on the outside," trainer Christophe Clement said after the Garden City. "I don't think she had a great trip, it's just she was the best horse."

Winless in her first five starts — all of which were run at a mile or less — Miss World didn't break her maiden until she was stretched out to 1$\frac{1}{16}$ miles on the turf at Belmont in July.

See KEENELAND, B8

SATURDAY

Grade I Queen Elizabeth II Stakes
When: 5:05 p.m.
Where: Keeneland
TV/radio: TVG/WLXO-FM 96.1

BIG BLUE MADNESS

MANIC, MYSTICAL

MARK CORNELISON | mcornelison@herald-leader.com

Kentucky's John Wall tried a reverse dunk during Big Blue Madness on Friday night at Rupp Arena. Wall drew cheers from the crowd with a pair of big slams, but the Cats struggled with perimeter shooting during a 20-minute scrimmage.

CALIPARI SHARES HIS VISION OF RETURNING UK TO 'RIGHTFUL PLACE'

By Jerry Tipton
jtipton@herald-leader.com

Envy our past. Fear our future.

That immodest message — delivered on a video accompanied by a thumping, teeth-rattling bass line — began the business portion of Kentucky's Big Blue Madness in Rupp Arena on Friday night.

Then first-year coach John Calipari added a bask-in-our-present addendum in a keynote address/acceptance speech.

Throwing plenty of red meat — or in this case, blue meat — to the capacity crowd, Calipari spoke of returning Kentucky basketball "back to its rightful place atop the mountain."

Earlier in the 15-minute address from a podium sitting on an H-shaped stage, Calipari set an even higher objective.

"That we are the gold standard not just for college basketball," he said, "but for all of college athletics."

He talked about a program "rooted in integrity" and always "run with class."

One hopes the possible secondary NCAA rules violations committed by the crowd when it chanted prospects' names were a misstep to be written off to runaway zeal. That happened four times, each an apparent violation of NCAA rule 13.11.4 which forbids the chanting of prospects' names at an event open to the public.

Madness as recruiting tool always hangs in the air. In this, Calipari set an equally lofty goal.

"My vision is for every high school player in the country to dream of putting on this uniform," he said. The energy and buzz of Madness

See MADNESS, B5

JASON SANKOVITCH

Bryan Station's Darrian Miller sacked Lafayette quarterback Brett Durbin in the first half of Friday night's game. Both teams' offenses struggled through a scoreless first half.

BRYAN STATION 14, LAFAYETTE 7

Station earns stripes with 4th-quarter rally

DEFENDERS SCORE TWO LATE TDS AFTER OFFICIAL MISHAP

By Mike Fields
mfields@herald-leader.com

Better late than never.

That was how Bryan Station felt Friday night after it rallied to beat Lafayette 14-7, ending an eight-year losing streak to the Generals.

Bryan Station tailback Tevin McCaden, the state's leading rusher, was kept in check most of the game, but he shook free for two touchdowns in the fourth quarter.

McCaden finished with 100 yards on 27 carries.

Kickoff was two hours late on the wet, cold night, apparently because no officials were assigned to call the game at Tates Creek.

A crew was put together from

See BRYAN STATION, B6

FRIDAY'S TOP SCORES

Lexington Christian	**40**
Raceland	0
Henry Clay	**21**
Madison Central	7
Scott County	**42**
Paul Dunbar	7
Lexington Catholic	**62**
East Jessamine	0
Boyle County	**47**
West Jessamine	0
Belfry	**34**
Chalden Clark	13

HS KENTUCKY HIGH SCHOOL SPORTS

Go to **Kentucky.com/highschools** for up-to-date scores, line scores and recaps.

Hayden sets state record

Lexington Christian's Domonique Hayden scored four touchdowns to give him 117 for his career, breaking a state record. **Page B6**

UK
8

October 29, 2009

What a display of athleticism
On this Kentucky team, you see it in everyone

JOHN CLAY
HERALD-LEADER SPORTS COLUMNIST

It's always dangerous to make sweeping declarations based on something as benign as an intrasquad basketball scrimmage, even if it is played before a crowd of 14,060.

And then, all of a sudden Patrick Patterson, Kentucky's 6-foot-9 center, the junior who never strayed far from the basket his first two seasons, stepped back and popped in a three-pointer.

Rupp Arena went nuts.

In fact, it was the first of Patterson's two three-pointers.

So while who knows what exactly is going on with John Wall's eligibility, after viewing UK's Blue-White scrimmage Wednesday night, there is one thing I do know.

This is one athletic basketball team.

That's a master-of-the-obvious statement, of course, until you stop and think of it's simple importance.

And how long it has been since we could make that statement.

The past two seasons, the Cats lacked the scheme, the depth, the overall talent and athleticism to let their best, heck, their only, low-post presence slide out on the floor and prove his perimeter game.

"Patrick is skilled, man," said freshman DeMarcus Cousins. "He is skilled."

Yes, he is. And, on his team, he's no longer in the minority. There is the greased lightning that is Eric Bledsoe. There is the strength, with a bit more finesse than you might think, that is Daniel Orton. There is the smoothness that is Darius Miller. There is the point-making productivity of Darnell Dodson.

There is the attitude that is "Big Cuz," i.e. Cousins, with his headband, and his sneer one minute and grin the next.

And, of course, there is the man of mystery, Wall, who is as advertised, in case you had any sliver of a doubt. He is ridiculous.

BOTTOM LEFT: UK Coach John Calipari talked with former UK Coach Joe B. Hall before the Blue-White scrimmage. LEXINGTON HERALD-LEADER/MARK CORNELISON

BOTTOM RIGHT: UK assistant coach Tony Delk joked with Darnell Dodson on the bench during the Blue-White scrimmage.
LEXINGTON HERALD-LEADER/MARK CORNELISON

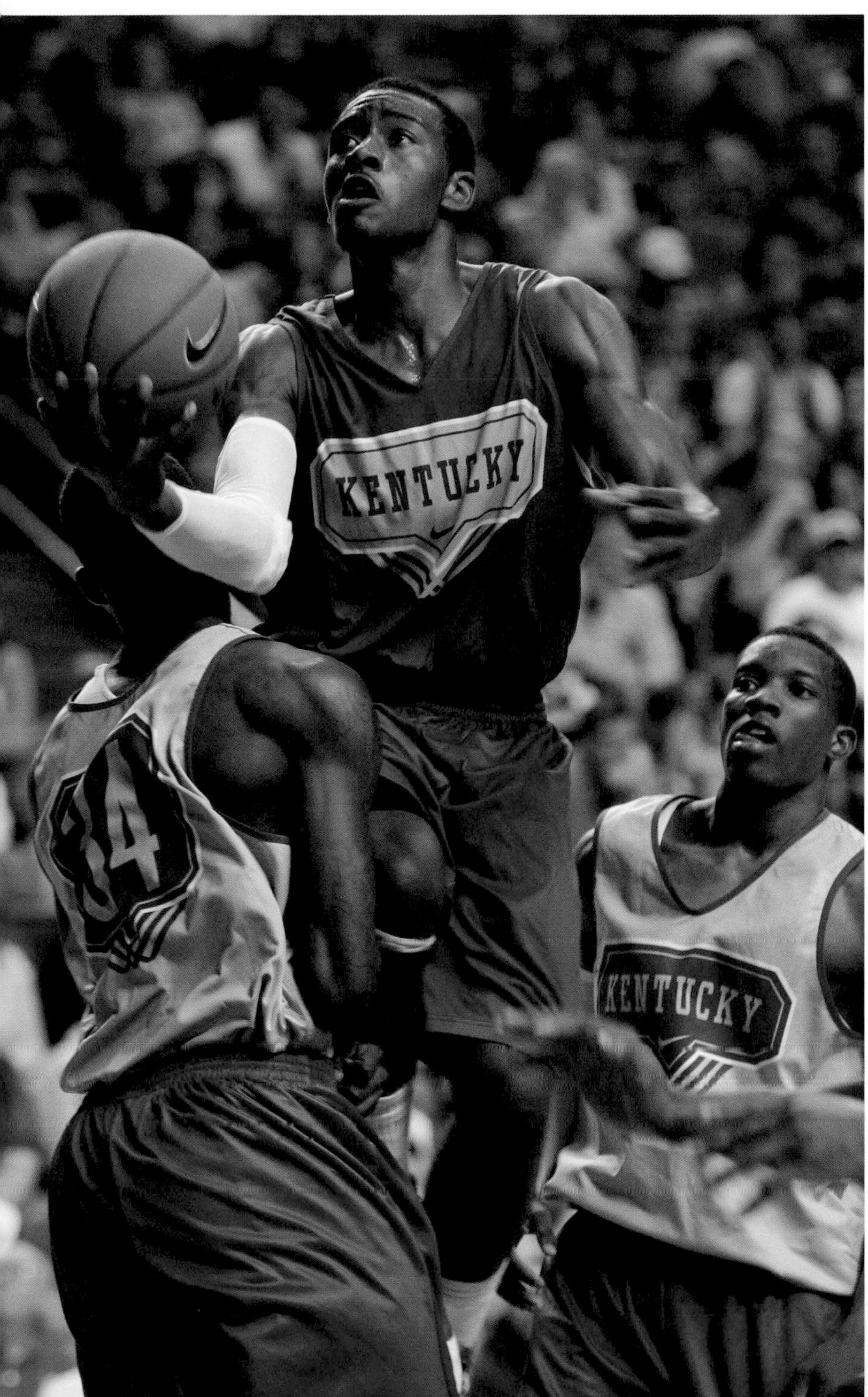

The freshman is so quick he almost glides to the basket. He can lull a defender to sleep, then blow past him.

Kentucky has boasted very good basketball players this past decade or so, even a few great players. (Take a bow, Tayshaun Prince.) But the Cats have not been overrun with a preponderance of athletes, guys who can jump out of the gym, stop on a dime or blow your doors off.

These guys can. For all the sloppiness displayed in the early stages of the dribble-drive motion offense, and the fact that the team has officially been working for only nine days — "We've had 13 practices," Coach John Calipari said — the athleticism was a joy to watch.

"We have great athleticism, length, speed, quickness," Patterson said. "I think that's going to help us out on the defensive end. We've got to learn great defense, stop the opponent."

That will come. Calipari said he coaches offense first, then defense. It's the way he operates, especially when putting in an offense that none of the team — not the six newcomers, not the seven holdovers — knows.

"But with the athleticism we have, it should make it easier to run up and down the court," Patterson said. "And bring in people off the bench and continue the top-level play that we need."

That sound you just heard was the Big Blue Nation shouting hallelujah!

Nor should we forget the team athleticism necessary to let the old low-post guy show what he can do away from the low post.

"What I liked was that he was able to play this offense yet he was still so alive under the basket," Calipari said of Patterson. "Some people worry that you play this way, but you never get to the post; you will learn how to get to the post. And we have to figure out ways to get him to the post."

But … (and this is a good but …)

"Didn't you like seeing him shooting threes?" Calipari asked. "Aren't you amazed at his skills out on the floor where he can catch it at 20 feet and then drive it and shoot a layup and go by people?"

Indeed, this has a chance to be one amazing team. ■

LEFT: John Wall scored over DeAndre Liggins in the second-half of the Blue-White scrimmage. LEXINGTON HERALD-LEADER/MARK CORNELISON

WHITAKER BANK
KENTUCK
SEC
SEC

THE SEASON BEGINS

November 8, 2009

In search of swagger

Calipari wants to renew fans' confidence, restore program's aura of invincibility

At one stop on John Calipari's travels throughout Kentucky this year, a fan asked the new University of Kentucky basketball coach a question: Did he remember the Wildcats' comeback victory against LSU?

"The one down at LSU?" Calipari said in reference to UK's 1994 rally from a 31-point deficit at LSU, thereafter dubbed the Mardi Gras Miracle. "Everybody knows that one. You'd have to be on the moon not to know that one."

That wasn't the one. The fan was talking about some home-game comeback against LSU lost in the mists of time.

"You think I was watching Kentucky games?" asked Calipari, no doubt with a smile.

Yes, the fan could have said. Doesn't everyone? Shouldn't everyone?

Kentucky games are not just games. "Not for 'fun-zees,'" as Calipari likes to say.

Every game is memorable, historic, meaningful and carved into the soul of any right-thinking basketball fan. Ditto for any coach, like Calipari until now, practicing his trade at some other (read: lesser) program.

If Calipari hadn't already gotten the message (and he had), this fan's question let him know the standard for UK basketball. All college basketball crossroads are supposed to run through Lexington. But Kentucky's program had gotten stranded at the corner of Irrelevant and Ordinary.

In the past five seasons, UK had a win-loss record of 112-58. Many programs would envy a winning percentage of .659. For Kentucky, it represented a slide toward humdrum. Tennessee became the first Southeastern Conference team to finish ahead of Kentucky in the standings four straight years. Florida became the first SEC team to beat the Cats seven straight times.

Parity could be grudgingly accepted. But this was parody.

Last season punctuated the unhappy state of affairs. The Cats dropped out of The Associated Press' pre-season Top 25 for the first time since 1990. Then Kentucky failed to receive a bid to the 2009 NCAA Tournament, snapping a streak of appearances dating to 1992.

"I really want to erase that," sophomore Darius Miller said of last season. "I didn't have fun being on

LEFT: UK took the floor as Kentucky played North Carolina, Dec. 5, 2009, in Rupp Arena.
LEXINGTON HERALD-LEADER/MARK CORNELISON

the Kentucky team that went to the NIT. I want to start over and win games."

Enter Calipari.

In less than eight months, he secured the nation's No. 1 recruiting class and used his irresistible can-do spirit to restore the belief that Kentucky will be Kentucky again.

"Back to the rightful place atop the mountain," Calipari said in his inspiring Big Blue Madness address.

Making it fun again.

In that same 15-minute oration, the new coach pledged himself to getting "the greatest fans in all sports once again pumping your chests."

That part of the restoration came before the first layup at the first practice. Such is the power of Calipari's personality and startling recruiting sweep.

"We're going to have a hoppin' team the next few years," fan Charles Wofford, 66, said while waiting in line for Big Blue Madness tickets. "It's going to be like Christmas."

Another fan in the Madness line, Jerry Roberts, likened the state of UK basketball to the glory years of the mid-1990s.

"I don't think there's anybody else they could have hired to get us back immediately," he said of Calipari. "That's the consensus (of UK fans)."

For Kentucky to be Kentucky is to set a high standard that touches college basketball's ozone.

"Those type of teams that made it to the Elite Eights, Final Fours and national championships," Patrick Patterson said after the Blue-White Game. "We want to be the type of team that people remember."

Though a native of Alabama, freshman DeMarcus Cousins is wise in the ways of Kentucky.

"I've learned quick," he said. "They're serious about this basketball. They want it as bad as we do. They're throwing wood on the fire. It's going to be roaring."

Calipari, who coincidentally wrote a self-help book aptly titled Bounce Back, knows the task he bears. During an appearance at the Kiwanis Club of the Bluegrass, he playfully asked his audience what they thought of a scenario that included a 15-point loss to Louisville en route to a national championship. Grumbles ensued.

"You don't come to Kentucky unless your plan is to win championships," Calipari told the Kiwanians. "You don't come to just win games. But I understood that when I came."

At a speech in Louisville, Calipari repeated the thought. "First, you've got to win some games," he said. "Then, that's not good enough. You have to accept it."

Jimmy Dykes, the former UK assistant (Eddie Sutton era) who now works as an SEC basketball analyst for ESPN, vouched for Calipari's

LEFT: John Calipari's coach at Clarion, Joe DeGregorio, next to Calipari, and Calipari's high school coach, Bill Sacco, far left, along with present Clarion Coach Ron Righter, second from left, presented Calipari with a jersey before Kentucky played Clarion, Nov. 6, 2009. LEXINGTON HERALD-LEADER/MARK CORNELISON

FOLLOWING: John Calipari spoke to reporters at Joe Craft Center. LEXINGTON HERALD-LEADER/PABLO ALCALÁ

HE GREATEST TRADITION IN THE HISTORY
OTB

awareness of the Kentucky job.

"He knows his main job is in Year Two, Year Three, Year Four, Five and 10," Dykes said. "It's for Kentucky fans to be having fun. And fun for Kentucky fans is making travel plans for the Final Four, not travel plans for the SEC Tournament."

To get there, Calipari has promoted Kentucky basketball tirelessly. He's sent a jersey to President Barack Obama. He's volunteered to pose for pictures with restaurant workers.

"We all see the history, the tradition, the nearly mystical (experience) of Kentucky basketball," he said at Madness.

Beware, Calipari has alliteration at his disposal, and he's not afraid to use it.

"It doesn't matter if you're from a hollow in Hazard," he said at Madness, "a farm in Frankfort or a humble home in Hodgenville."

In returning Kentucky to Kentucky status, Calipari did not take the fan interest for granted. He's worked to light an emotional fire in a fan base already known as highly flammable.

Indiana Coach Tom Crean, a good friend of Calipari's, endorsed this approach. Speaking to a convention of Kentucky high school coaches, Crean noted that IU's student attendance dropped by about 50 percent last season.

"You've got to fight for that enthusiasm," Crean said. "The moment you think the fans are locked in, you're going to make a mistake."

Calipari's Twitter and Web sites draw thousands of followers, many simply wanting to be acknowledged and feel a part of the program, he said.

"Everything he's doing is to build that enthusiasm," Crean said. "Take nothing for granted."

Getting back the swagger.

Of course, Calipari's primary concern is not the fans, but the players. He's spoken repeatedly of lifting their spirits and instilling a swagger. This echoed a theme of Rick Pitino's when he transformed a Kentucky program mired in NCAA rules violations and made it a perennial Final Four contender.

"Not arrogance," Calipari said in defining terms. "Swagger is we deserve to win because we worked. Swagger goes to officials and fans. Then you're winning. It all starts with getting kids to enjoy to work."

This swagger is an expectation of good things to come and a confidence in having made the necessary preparation to make it happen.

Calipari acknowledges that to bring swagger to Kentucky basketball is to go back to the future.

"This Kentucky program has always had a swagger," he said, "and people saw it. Players knew it. Officials knew it. Everybody knew it. You walked in and there it was. We just have to get that swagger back."

For all of Kentucky's dominance, the SEC missed Kentucky's swagger the past few years. Fairly or unfairly, the weight of its flagship program sinking brought down the league.

"It's good for the league for Kentucky to be good because the perception is when Kentucky's not good, our league is not good," said Mississippi State Coach Rick Stansbury, a native of Battletown, Ky. "We need Kentucky to be good. If Kentucky is beat by the rest of the league, well, the league is down."

At SEC Media Day, Calipari said he'd come to Kentucky at the right time of his career. At age 35 or 40, he might have failed. But at 50, he brings valuable experience to the job. His previous stops, Massachusetts and Memphis, conditioned him to be the league's heavyweight. Opponents always gave his teams their best shot.

"Here it's no different," he said. "It doesn't matter if you're hurt or who's in the uniform. We're everybody's big game. I think mentally I'm ready for it. Now I have to get my team mentally ready for it."

The experience of UMass and Memphis taught him to appreciate every practice and every possession. Each has value against an aroused opponent. That's the lesson he wants to convey to the Kentucky players.

If UK learns that lesson and brings a swagger to its game, opponents will feel the effect late in games, Calipari said.

"For other teams, if they're up, they panic," the UK coach said. "If they're down, they don't think they can beat you."

Calipari has promised no quick fixes. He's scoffed at pre-season rankings. UK was No. 4 in The Associated Press pre-season poll, its best pre-season position since being No. 4 going into the 2001–02 season.

Calipari said bringing back a swagger usually takes years. "But why waste this year?" he asked.

Whenever Kentucky is Kentucky again, Crean advised the state's high school coaches — and by extension UK fans — to credit Calipari.

"You guys are literally blessed to see that program develop again," the Indiana coach said. ■

— Jerry Tipton

November 8, 2009

UK's star cluster plans to sparkle as a team

JOHN CLAY

HERALD-LEADER SPORTS COLUMNIST

OK, OK, so the rest of college basketball is hoping, dare we say praying, that somewhere along the way Kentucky basketball will crash and burn in a 13-ego pileup in the selfish pursuit of singular stardom.

All that talent.

And only one ball.

The Cats' reply: We're one for all.

Or maybe three for all.

"Me, Eric and DeMarcus are always around," said the highly recruited freshman guard John Wall. "They call us the 'The Three Amigos.'"

"We all pretty cool," said the highly recruited freshman center DeMarcus Cousins. "We've been knowing each other since we were babies, basically, especially me, Eric and John. Me and Eric, we're from the same dirt."

"We get along real well," said the highly recruited freshman guard Eric Bledsoe. "We're like brothers."

Same goes for fellow freshmen Daniel Orton and Jon Hood, the junior-college transfer Darnell Dodson and the lucky seven veterans back from last season.

"With this team this year I see a lot more joking around," said Patrick Patterson, the junior power forward and team leader. "People getting along more, just hanging out. We're pretty much just enjoying each other's company."

You would think maybe that wouldn't be the case, the six newcomers being highly recruited and all, and the holdovers seeing their turf invaded by such a collection of sparklers.

"They had a lot of hype coming in behind them," said sophomore Darius Miller, "and I think they deserved every bit of it."

But such star clusters can often throw a team out of its orbit. Everyone wants points. Everyone wants fame. Everyone wants the ball.

But to a Cat — new and old alike - the claim is that's not the case, that this team is made up not only of hoop celebrities, but jokers.

Take Cousins, the tall drink of water who speaks in a slow, southern drawl, and admits to having a mean side on the hardwood to go with an affable side off the floor.

"I like to chill, have fun, make people laugh," Cousins said. "But on the court, when the lights come on, it's business. There's nothing to joke about."

Cousins calls himself "Big Cuz," though Orton reports that his rookie teammate has been pinned with another moniker.

"Dancing Bear," Orton said. "Because he's always dancing in the weight room."

Is Cousins a good dancer?

"He is," Orton said, "I have to give it to him."

Orton is well-spoken, a thoughtful Oklahoma native who committed early to previous coach Billy Gillispie, then was successfully re-recruited when John Calipari grabbed (with a vengeance) the UK program's reins in the spring.

"I think God put this team together," Orton said.

(Didn't Wall play for Word of God Christian Academy?)

"We came in and most of the upperclassmen were gone (during the summer)," Cousins said. "So we didn't really have a choice but to bond with each other."

That's easy to say now, of course, before the real competition for minutes begins, before the pressure of extraordinarily high expectations commences.

"I feel it's going to get us through everything this year, the humor we have between us," Orton said.

So is this initial burst of chemistry a surprise?

"We played together and against one another," said Orton, "so you kind of knew the personalities of the people coming in. So, not at all really."

"A little bit (surprised), but not really," said Miller. "I kind of figured that would happen. Every guy here that's on the team is a real good guy. We all get along and have fun together."

That could be bad news for the rest of college basketball.

"Everybody gets along great," said Cousins. "Just time, and it's gonna happen." ■

November 8, 2009

This year's Cats have the buzz meter humming

MARK STORY
HERALD-LEADER SPORTS COLUMNIST

The buzz is back.

That may as well be the slogan for Kentucky Wildcats basketball 2009–10.

After what have been, by UK's regal historical standards, four straight mediocre seasons, the arrival of a charismatic new coach and a lavishly hyped influx of new players has the Kingdom of the Blue on fire with anticipation.

What I call "Buzz Teams" — squads around which a fevered level of pre-season excitement form — are hardly unique in UK basketball history.

Let's use our "Buzz Evaluator" to examine how this year's Cats compare to other hyped teams from UK's modern history.

Season: 1983–84

Buzz Generator: The return of Sam Bowie after two missed seasons due to leg injury; the addition of highly touted freshmen Winston Bennett and James Blackmon. They joined a deep roster that included Melvin Turpin and Kenny Walker up front with Jim Master and Dicky Beal in the backcourt.

Outcome: The Cats went 29-5, swept the SEC regular season and tourney championships and made the Final Four. There, a puzzling 3-for-33 shooting performance in the second half caused a loss to Patrick Ewing and Georgetown.

Buzz Evaluator: Final Four meltdown left a bad taste.

Season: 1987–88

Buzz Generator: Return of star forward Winston Bennett from a knee injury and addition of a No. 1 recruiting class that included Eric Manuel and LeRon Ellis. They boosted returning guard standouts Rex Chapman and Ed Davender.

Outcome: Kentucky won both the SEC regular season and tournament titles, but Eddie Sutton's third UK team was upset in the NCAA round of 16 by Villanova (subsequently, UK's NCAA participation and its SEC titles were vacated due to rules violations).

Buzz Evaluator: Team that was ranked No. 1 in the country early in the season did not live up to its hype when it mattered.

Season: 1995–96

Buzz Generator: The addition of McDonald's All-Americans Ron Mercer and Wayne Turner plus Ohio State transfer Derek Anderson to a loaded roster that already had Tony Delk, Walter McCarty and Antoine Walker.

Outcome: Rick Pitino's team was dominating, going 34-2 and winning Kentucky's first NCAA title in 18 years.

Buzz Evaluator: A case when the reality exceeded the pre-season praise.

Season: 2001–02

Buzz Generator: UK stars Tayshaun Prince and Keith Bogans took their names out of the NBA Draft. Kentucky added highly touted outside shooter Rashaad Carruth and power forward Chuck Hayes to a roster — Prince, Bogans, Jason Parker, Marvin Stone, Erik Daniels, Gerald Fitch — that was the most talented of the Tubby Smith era.

Outcome: Parker hurt a knee and didn't play. Stone transferred to Louisville. After being beset by toxic team chemistry and off-the-court disciplinary issues, the remaining players became known as Team Turmoil. Cats finished 22-10 and lost in the NCAA round of 16.

Buzz Evaluator: A train wreck. One of the most disappointing teams in UK history.

Season: 2004–05

Buzz Generator: Arrival of Tubby Smith's most-touted recruiting class — Rajon Rondo, Joe Crawford, Ramel Bradley and Randolph Morris — plus the addition of Western Kentucky transfer Patrick Sparks. The newcomers joined returning forward standouts Chuck Hayes and Kelenna Azubuike.

Outcome: Went 28-6 and won the SEC regular season title, but lost to Michigan State in double overtime in the NCAA Elite Eight.

Buzz Evaluator: A good team that let the Final Four trip Tubby really needed slip through its fingers in the first OT against Michigan State.

Season: 2009–10

Buzz Generator: The arrivals of new coach John Calipari with uber-recruits John

Wall, DeMarcus Cousins and Eric Bledsoe. The decision of star forward Patrick Patterson to stay in school for his junior season.

Keys to a positive outcome: Can new (six newcomers) and old (seven returnees) mesh? Can anyone consistently make outside shots? With as many as three players (Patterson, Wall and Cousins) likely to turn pro after this season, will there be enough basketballs to go around?

Buzz Evaluator: By March, Calipari needs to have a Final Four-caliber team. But my guess is that the fans will give him a one-year honeymoon period even if UK doesn't make the final weekend in 2010. ■

November 13, 2009 | Kentucky vs. Morehead State » W 75-59

Cats too good from the start

Patterson and Bledsoe shine in Calipari's UK debut

Sip the champagne. Puff on the cigars. Check for a hotel room at the Final Four.

Well, scratch that third one … for now.

The John Calipari era began in grand style Friday night as Kentucky's talented youngsters thoroughly whipped a veteran Morehead State team 75-59. But it wasn't that grand.

The victory made Calipari happy. He saw inspired play from All-American candidate Patrick Patterson and backup — or is that 1-A? — point guard Eric Bledsoe.

Patterson answered the call for more dominant play with 20 points and 12 rebounds. Starting in place of John Wall, who sat as part of an NCAA-ordered punishment, Bledsoe set a UK record for scoring by a freshman in his collegiate debut with 24 points.

While Bledsoe's seven turnovers might have been another such record (understandable given his 37-minute workload), what caused Calipari to scoff at the notion of anyone taking bows cut to the heart of how he thinks basketball should be played.

"When I coached the last four years, I didn't have to beg my team to compete," Calipari said. "I'm so used to it, when I don't see it, I'm losing my mind."

LEFT: The E-Rupp-tion Zone roared after a block by Patrick Patterson against Kenneth Faried during the first half of the Morehead State game in Rupp Arena. LEXINGTON HERALD-LEADER/PABLO ALCALÁ

Calipari cited inattention to defensive detail such as failing to stay in a stance or allowing the ball to get to the basket area too easily.

But Morehead State, which got UK's attention because it returned four starters from an NCAA Tournament team, still had troubles. Star big man Kenneth Faried, who had 25 double-doubles last season, struggled to 17 points and seven rebounds.

Morehead Coach Donnie Tyndall noted UK's size. "We have one guy who fits that description," he said of Faried. "They have four."

Maze Stallworth, who set a school record with 87 three-point baskets last season, made only two of 15 shots (one of 12 from three-point range). Tyndall noted that Stallworth had missed almost a week of practice because of a concussion.

Led by Patterson, Kentucky threatened to KO Morehead State in the first half. UK twice led by as much as 14 points before the Eagles rallied late to reduce the lead to 33-25 at

halftime.

To explain his production, Patterson noted the encouragement he got from Calipari and assistant John Robic.

"He and I sat down and had a little heart-to-heart," Calipari said. "... It was great to see him bust out. He should be a 20-and-12 guy. I'd say 25 and 15 is what he needs to be."

Robic added a pointed observation. "I'm still waiting to see how you play," the assistant told him, Patterson said.

Patterson, who had been prodded by Calipari after taking only seven shots against Campbellsville, took eight in the first half. He seemed animated from the tip, scoring nine of the Cats' first 14 points. His second putback inside the first eight minutes extended the early lead to 14-5. That prompted a Morehead State timeout with 12:22 left.

Patterson also made the first three-point basket of his career en route to 14 first-half points.

Led by Patterson, UK dominated inside. The Cats outrebounded Morehead State 43-24 and enjoyed a 26-8 advantage in points in the paint before a lackluster final few minutes.

"For us to get outrebounded by 19, when that's a huge emphasis for

PRECEDING LEFT: Kentucky's Eric Bledsoe tangled with Kenneth Faried, left and Ty Proffitt, right as he scored a basket during the second-half of the Morehead State game. LEXINGTON HERALD-LEADER/PABLO ALCALÁ

PRECEDING RIGHT: Patrick Patterson scored during the first-half of the Morehead State game. LEXINGTON HERALD-LEADER/PABLO ALCALÁ

BELOW: Shane Bowman wore a Kentucky themed Mexican wrestling mask in the front row of the E-Rupp-tion Zone. LEXINGTON HERALD-LEADER/PABLO ALCALÁ

RIGHT: John Calipari called from the bench during the second-half. LEXINGTON HERALD-LEADER/PABLO ALCALÁ

us, credit to them," Tyndall said.

Faried's first basket came with 3:14 left in the first half. Stallworth did not get a basket until 4:46 remained in the game.

Yet Morehead State prevented the margin from reaching cartoonish proportions.

By the first TV timeout of the second half, Kentucky extended the game-long lead beyond 14 points for the first time. The Cats outscored Morehead State 11-2 inside the first five minutes of the half to take a 44-27 lead with 15:52 left.

Two baskets by Patterson keyed the run and showed his newfound versatility. On the first, he bulled inside for a putback of a missed free throw.

On the second, he streaked downcourt and took a long pass from Bledsoe for a fast-break layup.

At the 15:19 TV timeout, Patterson had a double-double with 18 points and 10 rebounds.

As Kentucky controlled the game, Bledsoe gave fans reasons to get excited. Like somebody trying to squeeze into a crowded subway car, he twisted between two defenders and flipped in a layup to put UK ahead 46-29 with 12:52 left.

Later, Bledsoe outdid himself by again getting into the lane. This time he flipped up a blind shot as he stumbled from a bump. The ball went in to put Kentucky ahead 56-39.

After a Faried dunk off a lob pass gave Morehead State a reason to believe, Bledsoe hit a jumper while being fouled.

Their play secured starting sports for Patterson and Bledsoe, Calipari said. Wall, who returns Monday against Miami (Ohio), will be a third starter.

"Then we have to get the other guys to compete," said Calipari, who felt compelled to list what he liked. "I like my team. I'm so happy John Wall will be back. And I'm happy with what I saw from Eric and Patrick.

"We'll build from there." ■

— Jerry Tipton

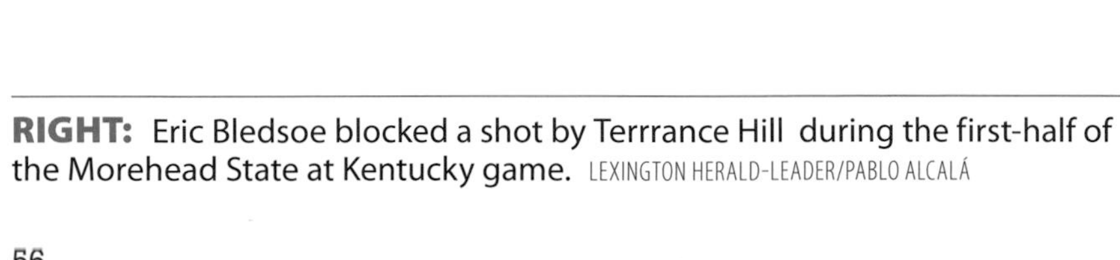

RIGHT: Eric Bledsoe blocked a shot by Terrance Hill during the first-half of the Morehead State at Kentucky game. LEXINGTON HERALD-LEADER/PABLO ALCALÁ

Wall-elujah: Freshman saves UK

Point guard hits game-winner in regular-season debut; Miami's Winbush sets Rupp record with eight threes

Kentucky's joy ride this season hit unexpected turbulence Monday night.

With Nick Winbush setting a Rupp Arena record for a visiting player with eight three-point baskets, Miami forced No. 4 Kentucky to play a possession-by-possession nail-biter.

Thanks to inside dominance and a clutch shot by John Wall, UK won 72-70.

Wall, belatedly making his highly anticipated UK debut, hit a 12-footer from the left side inside the final second to win the game.

"That's John," fellow freshman DeMarcus Cousins said. "Mr. Clutch."

But Cousins, whose double-double (10 points and 10 rebounds) came in the second half, took no chances. "I was going for the rebound," he said with a smile, "just in case."

Not to worry. Wall improvised what he intended to be a driving layup. Cut off, he rose and swished the jumper.

"John Wall is legit," Cousins said. "He's the real deal. There is no guard out there better. John just started his legacy."

When told about starting a legacy, Wall smiled a shy smile. "I don't really know what to say," he said. "I'll tell you one thing. He (Cousins) came out in the second half and got us going."

Miami, which lost at Towson on Friday, had tied the score at 70 on a Kenny Hayes three-pointer with eight seconds left. Then Wall answered. He came up one point short of becoming the third UK freshman to debut with 20 or more points. He led the Cats with 19.

Patrick Patterson and Cousins chipped in 17 and 10, respectively. Those points reflected UK's dominance inside. The Cats enjoyed a 32-12 advantage in points in the paint and a 21-8 edge in second-chance points.

Winbush led all scorers with 26 points. Overall, Miami made 15 of 26 three-point shots, which was one more than Virginia Military Institute made in winning at Kentucky early last season.

"For us to win a game when they go 15-of-26 from the three-point line, I can't believe it," UK Coach John Calipari said. "We talked at halftime, if we

LEXINGTON HERALD-LEADER » KENTUCKY.COM/SPORTS » SECTION C

SPORTS

BUSINESS, C6 DOW: 10,406.96 ▲136.49

TUESDAY, NOVEMBER 17, 2009

BELICHICK DEFENDS CALL TO GO FOR IT VS. COLTS - C5

SLAUGHTER LIGHTS IT UP IN TOPPERS' OPENING WIN - C3

Retail sales up, but economists still concerned

Cats' goals extend beyond a bowl

FOUR YEARS OF ELIGIBILITY NOT ENOUGH FOR KENTUCKY

By Chip Cosby
ccosby@herald-leader.com

Don't get the Kentucky football players wrong. The bowl-eligibility-clinching win over Vanderbilt last week was nice and all, but the Wildcats have made it clear they want much more.

The mood on the team bus following the Vandy game was subdued compared to that of 2006, when the Cats clinched bowl eligibility for the first time in seven seasons with a win over the Commodores.

"It was unbelievable elation not only among our team, but among the fan base when we got that sixth win" back in 2006, Kentucky Coach Rich Brooks said. "I think, that time, we were celebrating so long we almost came back and lost to Louisiana-Monroe. "There was no major celebration (Saturday), but what it did do was put us in position to continue what we all want to do on this football team and in this program, and that's climb the SEC East ladder while knowing we have a chance to be somewhere in the post-season."

"I remember when we won that sixth game and felt like we were on top of the world," senior offensive lineman Christian Johnson said. "You couldn't tell us nothing. Now it's not enough. We need more. We're trying to improve and get better, and we're not trying to stay in the lower or middle half of the SEC East. We want to work our way up to the top."

See UK FOOTBALL, C5

Christian Johnson said players want to get out of the SEC East's lower half.

SATURDAY
Kentucky at Georgia
When: 7:45 p.m.
TV: ESPN2

DAVID STEPHENSON | STAFF FILE PHOTO

Bobby Frankel, five-time Eclipse Award winner for outstanding trainer, died of cancer Monday at his home in Pacific Palisades, Calif. He was 68.

BOBBY FRANKEL
1941–2009

Hall of Fame trainer dies

Kentucky 72	From the box score	KentuckySports.com	Next game
Miami (Ohio) 70	■ John Wall: 19 points and 5 assists in 38 minutes ■ DeMarcus Cousins: 10 points and 10 rebounds ■ Nick Winbush: Made 8 of 10 threes, scored 26 points BOX SCORE, PAGE C4	■ Watch John Wall describe his game-winning shot. ■ View a photo gallery from Monday night's victory.	Sam Houston State (2-0) at Kentucky (2-0) When: 7 p.m. Thursday TV: FS South

Wall-elujah: Freshman saves UK

Point guard hits game-winner in regular-season debut

MIAMI'S WINBUSH SETS RUPP RECORD WITH EIGHT THREES

By Jerry Tipton
jtipton@herald-leader.com

Kentucky's joy ride this season hit unexpected turbulence Monday night.

With Nick Winbush setting a Rupp Arena record for a visiting player with eight three-point baskets, Miami forced No. 4 Kentucky to play a possession-by-possession nail-biter.

Thanks to inside dominance and a clutch shot by John Wall, UK won 72-70.

Wall, belatedly making his highly anticipated UK debut, hit a 12-footer from the left side inside the final second to win the game.

"That's John," fellow freshman DeMarcus Cousins said. "Mr. Clutch."

But Cousins, whose double-double (10 points and 10 rebounds) came in the second half, took no chances. "I was going for the rebound," he said with a smile, "just in case."

Not to worry. Wall improvised what he intended to be a driving layup. Cut off, he rose and swished the jumper.

"John Wall is legit," Cousins said. "He's the real deal. There is no guard out there better. John just started his legacy."

When told about starting a legacy, Wall smiled a shy smile. "I don't really know what to say," he said. "I'll tell you one thing. He (Cousins) came out in the second half and got us going."

Miami, which lost at Towson on Friday, had tied the score at 70 on a Kenny Hayes three-pointer with eight seconds left. Then Wall answered. He came up one point short of becoming the third UK freshman to debut with 20 or more points. He led the Cats with 19.

Patrick Patterson and Cousins chipped in 17 and 10, respectively. Those points reflected UK's dominance inside. The Cats enjoyed a 32-12 advantage in points in the paint and a 21-8 edge in second-chance points.

lose, don't let it be from three."

Miami made five of 10 three-point shots in the second half.

A wild first half saw Kentucky fall behind by 18 points before rallying to within three, 39-36 at halftime. And three-point shooting fueled UK's rally. Darnell Dodson, who went to the bench to make room for Wall in the starting lineup, made three three-pointers in the final six minutes.

That flurry keyed an 18-3 UK run in the final 6:50 of the half.

Three-point shooting propelled Miami to a 36-18 lead with 7:01 left. The Redhawks made eight of their first 10 shots from beyond the arc. Four straight three-point baskets put Miami ahead 36-18.

Winbush led the way. The junior forward from Shaker Heights, Ohio, made six of six three-point shots in an 18-point half. He made three of five Friday in Miami's loss at Towson.

Winbush came into this season billed as a good shooter. But he failed to show a good shooting eye last season, when he made 34 percent of his threes, just 39 percent of all shots and 50 percent of free throws.

That wasn't the Winbush who torched Kentucky.

"That's the most fun I've ever had playing basketball in my life," Winbush said.

Although Winbush finally missed (a three-point shot from the right side in the second half's first two minutes), Miami eased ahead 45-38 with less than 16 minutes left.

Kentucky finally tied it on a freak play. A Miami player cut to the basket and tried to

ABOVE: Patrick Patterson scored late in the second half as the University of Kentucky beat Miami (Ohio) in Rupp Arena.
LEXINGTON HERALD-LEADER/CHARLES BERTRAM

RIGHT: Coach John Calipari talked with John Wall. LEXINGTON HERALD-LEADER/CHARLES BERTRAM

take a pass. Somehow, the ball popped out and went across halfcourt. That's where Wall scooped it up and drove unmolested to a high-rising dunk.

That tied it at 52 with 7:57 left. That marked the first time since 11:55 of the first half that the Cats did not trail.

Kentucky scored its first 18 points of the second half on plays in the paint or free throws off drives.

When the heretofore invisible Darius Miller swished a three-pointer from the left corner, UK led 57-52 with 7:04 left. That matched the Cats' biggest lead.

But Miami did not crack, thanks in part to a clutch three-pointer by Hayes, who made it in front of his bench while being fouled by Wall. The four-point play killed any thoughts of Kentucky pulling away.

"We wanted to be David tonight," Winbush said, "and I think we could have done it." ■

— Jerry Tipton

RIGHT: John Wall hit the game-winning jumper as the University of Kentucky defeated Miami (Ohio) in Rupp Arena. LEXINGTON HERALD-LEADER/CHARLES BERTRAM

BELOW: John Wall was congratulated by fans as he left the court. LEXINGTON HERALD-LEADER/CHARLES BERTRAM

ABOVE: John Wall celebrated as he left the court following his game-winning jumper against Miami (Ohio) in Rupp Arena. LEXINGTON HERALD-LEADER/CHARLES BERTRAM

November 16, 2009

Wall shows he can live up to hype

Freshman displays his faults and his brilliance

MARK STORY

HERALD-LEADER SPORTS COLUMNIST

The legend of John Wall only grows. Ghosts of Gardner-Webb hung heavy in Rupp Arena Monday night. Massive underdog Miami (Ohio), fresh off a loss to Towson, had ridden blistering three-point shooting to a 70-70 standoff with mighty Kentucky.

As the game clock ticked toward zero, Wall — the lavishly hyped UK freshman point guard playing in his first "real" college basketball game — raced down court with the basketball.

"I was kind of nervous," Wall would say later. "Under six seconds to go. I knew I had to try to make a play."

When the clock dropped under two seconds, the 6-foot-4 North Carolina product rose from the floor just left of the lane and launched a 15-footer.

Bottom.

Rupp Arena so loud, it was literally vibrating from the noise.

Kentucky 72, Miami 70.

If you wondered how in the world Wall could ever live up to the hoopla surrounding his college hoops debut, I'd say that was a rather dramatic answer.

"He's fast, and he's good, and he just hit a big time shot," said Miami guard Kenny Hayes (whose own big-time shot, a trey with six seconds left, had tied the game at 70).

Deadpanned Charlie Coles, the venerable Miami Coach: "John Wall, he's pretty good."

Wall's heroics came at the end of a night when, judging by the Kilimanjaro-high expectations he faces, he was good, not great.

The final numbers: A team-high 19 points on 4-for-9 shooting. His five assists were balanced out by five turnovers.

Still, Wall's first game after completing an NCAA-mandated suspension of two contests (one exhibition; one real game) turned out to be a teachable moment.

The specter of VMI filled Rupp when Kentucky fell behind 36-18 with 7:04 left in the first half on one of Nick Winbush's six first-half three-pointers. With UK clearly needing a boost, Wall said, he briefly reverted to high school form.

"In high school, you get behind 18, you try to get it back yourself," he said. "I was trying that, trying to do too much, which you can't do in college."

That is exactly what Kentucky Coach John Calipari told him during a trip to the bench.

"I just watched for a couple of minutes, then I told him I was ready to go back," Wall said. "In college, you can't do things just yourself. I guess that was my lesson learned."

Still, Wall showed flashes of the ability that has many touting him as the No. 1 overall pick in the 2010 NBA draft.

Late in the first half, he used his quick hands to wrest the dribble away from Miami's Hayes, then batted the ball out of bounds off the RedHawk's leg.

Early in the second, Wall put a sick crossover dribble on Hayes, beat him into the lane and got fouled going up for a shot.

Late in the contest, when, stunningly, every possession counted, he penetrated into the lane, and dropped a slick pass off to fellow freshman DeMarcus Cousins for a layup that put UK ahead 69-67.

"I had five turnovers, and I took a couple of bad shots," Wall said. "Overall, I thought I played good. I can do better."

In the big picture, UK is clearly a work in progress. A team with a new coach installing a new system and six new players should be just that.

Calipari marvelled that his freshman-heavy squad survived on a night when it fell behind by 18 against a foe that would finish hitting a white-hot 15-for-26 from three-point range.

"We needed this," Calipari said. "I was ecstatic that we got down 18 points. I wanted to see what we were made of."

The game's ending certainly showed what Wall is made of.

Said Wall: "It shows I have the confidence to make shots at the end of tough games."

Pretty nice way to begin living up to the hype. ■

Cats' rout leaves room for doubt

'We're setting ourselves up for failure,' Calipari says

CANCUN, Mexico — A television timeout with 6:43 left and your team ahead by 22 points. That seemed like a time to think about the beach and a post-game beverage.

Yet Kentucky Coach John Calipari could be heard throughout the Galactic Ballroom re-enacting the Big Bang by shooting angry radiation at his team.

"I'm not worrying about the score," he said after UK beat Cleveland State 73-49 in the Cancun Challenge semifinals on Tuesday. "I'm worrying about playing the right way."

This clearly wasn't it.

Calipari tried to jump-start UK early by inserting his best blue collar player, Ramon Harris.

By halftime, with the Cats dominating around the basket yet stuck in an eight-point game in part because of turnovers, Calipari previewed his late-game tirade with some jalapeno-hot rhetoric.

"He said anything, whatever comes off the top of his head, cuss words or not," John Wall said. "… We thought we'd walk through the game and not play hard."

Calipari got a response in the second half when UK outscored Cleveland State 38-22.

The UK coach set a tone by benching All-America candidate Patrick Patterson 64 seconds into the second half after Patterson limped to the bench.

Afterward, Calipari seemed to question his big man's willingness to play with pain, and he wondered about the toughness of his entire team.

"If you're limping, you come out," Calipari said about Patterson. "Let somebody else play. All of a sudden, we're up 16, 18. I then just said, if that's what the deal is, we'll just stay where we are, and you rest your ankle."

UK broke open the game with a 19-4 run early in the second half. Cleveland State made only two of its first 14 second-half shots. But

what concerned Vikings Coach Gary Waters was disparity in fouls. When the foul totals reached seven on his Vikings and none for UK not yet four minutes into the second half, Waters got the referees' attention and pointed repeatedly to the scoreboard.

Beyond giving Kentucky free throws, Waters said, the fouls diluted his team's intensity.

"It's hard to play when everybody's in foul trouble," he said, "and they became very tentative."

Pushing around UK? Just our style, Waters said.

Ditto for forcing turnovers with in-your-face defense. The UK backcourt's tender years and turnover-prone play wasn't coincidental.

Waters saw UK's physical play around the basket as telling. With Cleveland State not getting much inside, the Vikings made 26.6 percent of their shots. Most memorably, star guard Norris Cole drove and then turned his back to the defender and flipped up a wild shot that had no chance of going in the basket.

"Norris usually drives and penetrates

PRECEDING: Kentucky's Patrick Patterson, right, and DeMarcus Cousins went up for a rebound in the first-half as Kentucky played Cleveland State in the Cancun Challenge in Cancun, Mexico. LEXINGTON HERALD-LEADER/MARK CORNELISON

ABOVE LEFT: A UK fan cheered as Kentucky played Cleveland State. LEXINGTON HERALD-LEADER/MARK CORNELISON

ABOVE RIGHT: Coach John Calipari questioned an official's call during the second-half. LEXINGTON HERALD-LEADER/MARK CORNELISON

ORTON
33
UK
BLEDSOE
24

and gets to the basket," Waters said. "That was eliminated. Then you had no interior scoring for us."

But future opponents will be as big or bigger than UK. Opposing front lines will surely be more experienced.

Calipari saw trouble down the road.

"We started the game, again, by getting outmuscled and outhustled," the UK coach said. " … We're setting ourselves up for failure."

By allowing the opponent to set a roughneck tone, UK gives future opponents ideas.

"Every team knows to come in and throw us around," Calipari said. "Well, we're setting ourselves up for failure … I'm looking at us, and we're not right. It's a team that's not going to have success when we go into league play against better opponents."

Wall, who led UK with 15 points and six assists (and, alas, five turnovers), recoiled at the thought of opponents thinking they can push around the Cats.

"They can think that if they want to," he said. "I ain't going to be soft. I'll throw a 'bow (elbow) or two."

In this game, Calipari credited three-pointers by freshman Jon Hood and Josh Harrellson late in the half for bailing out the Cats. Between those shots, UK committed four turnovers in five trips downcourt to keep Cleveland State within striking distance.

"We got beat to every 50-50 ball," Calipari said. "We got balls jerked from our hands.

"It's more than just winning a ball game. It's playing the right way and doing things we're going to have to do against top competition to be in the game.

"If we do get it and play with great intensity, all of a sudden we can become one of those (top) teams. We just don't have any consistency right now." ■

Jerry Tipton

PRECEDING: Kentucky Coach John Calipari was not happy with Daniel Orton during a timeout in the Cleveland State game.
LEXINGTON HERALD-LEADER/MARK CORNELISON

RIGHT: John Wall slammed home two of his team-high 15 points against Cleveland State. LEXINGTON HERALD-LEADER/MARK CORNELISON

Can-do Cats conquer Cancun
Several clutch plays help UK win in OT

CANCUN, Mexico — Winning its first five games by an average of 16.2 points probably diluted Kentucky Coach John Calipari's message to play every possession with urgency.

A 73-65 overtime victory over Stanford on Wednesday night surely drove home that message.

UK needed clutch plays — and plenty of them — to win the Cancun Challenge.

Ramon Harris, whom UK listed as day-to-day before the game because of a knee injury sustained Tuesday against Cleveland State, drove for a basket in overtime and later hit a free throw with 1:27 left to put the Cats ahead 66-65.

Freshman Eric Bledsoe, who had taken only three shots earlier in the game, swished a long three-pointer with 33 seconds left to seal the victory.

Kentucky (6-0) was led by another freshman, John Wall, whose career-high 23 points and floor game led him to be named Most Valuable Player of the tournament.

Darius Miller and DeMarcus Cousins added 13 each. Patrick Patterson, who had a cortisone shot to ease the pain of an ankle sprained against Cleveland State, contributed a double-double (12 points and 11 rebounds).

Calipari noted how a coach can learn about his team and his players in a pressure-cooker game.

"I think we've got two guys who are not afraid to make plays," he said of Wall and Bledsoe. Later, the UK coach added Harris and Patterson to the freshman guards as players who won his trust.

Landry Fields led Stanford with 23 points and 13 rebounds. Jeremy Green scored 18. Each was named to the All-Tournament team, but playing 45 (Fields) and 44 minutes (Green) drained the pair down the stretch.

Stanford (3-3) missed a chance to ice the game with 9.5 seconds left. Jarrett Mann, a 53.3-percent free-throw shooter this season, missed two to keep the Cardinal lead at 63-61.

Wall was fouled on the subsequent drive. His two free throws with 2.4 seconds left tied it and made the freshman 8-for-8 from the line in this game.

With Stanford Coach Johnny Dawkins' Duke ties inducing Christian Laettner flashbacks, Drew Shiller threw a long inbounds pass to Fields. UK deflected the pass off the glass and Wall secured the loose ball.

Dawkins saluted UK's clutch play. "For a young team, they showed a lot of poise," the Stanford coach said.

Before Mann's missed free throws, Kentucky appeared to have lost the game. Cousins went to the line with 10.6 seconds left and UK trailing 63-61. It marked his first free throw since throwing up an air ball more than eight minutes earlier.

His first bounced off the front of the rim. On the second, Cousins attempted to throw it hard off the rim and go get the rebound despite Calipari's order to make the shot.

"Miscommunication," Cousins said afterward.

Mann ended up with the rebound while Calipari had a conniption fit.

For only the second time this early season, Kentucky trailed at halftime. The Cats were down 39-36 to Miami (Ohio) on Nov. 16.

Scoring primarily by Fields and Green had UK behind 38-32 at halftime. Fields and Green, the team's two leading scorers, combined for 29 first-half points.

Fields, whose double-double (25 points and 13 rebounds) propelled Stanford by Virginia in Tuesday's semifinals, scored 15 points. Fueled by 4-for-4 shooting from beyond the three-point line, Green added 14 points.

Fields had to battle a revolving door of defenders. Kentucky players who took turns guarding him included Miller, Harris, Darnell Dodson (making his first appearance since the season's second game) and Josh Harrellson.

Green set the halftime score with a jumper over Dodson with 1:18 left. Green's sharpshooting led Stanford to a 5-for-8 first half from three-point range.

Patterson, who missed the final 18:56 of Tuesday's game against Cleveland State because of an ankle injury, played six ineffective minutes in the first half. Picking up two fouls by the 14:13 mark contributed to his quiet three-point, six-minute half.

As the second half began, Kentucky went inside to Patterson. He scored from the post on the first possession and later added a dunk off either a pass or badly missed shot by Harris.

Those plays got UK within 42-40 with 16:32 left.

Kentucky finally took the lead with 6:42 left.

Behind 53-49, Miller hit a three-pointer with 7:23 left. That marked UK's first trey of the second half.

After Green missed a three-point shot, Patterson posted strong for a layup that put the Cats ahead 54-53.

A post-up by Cousins put Kentucky ahead 56-53 with 5:08 left. That lead looked large because Stanford looked tired.

When Green and Fields shot from the perimeter, the ball hit only the front of the rim. Fields twice fumbled the ball away on drives.

Stanford switched to a zone, perhaps, in part, to conserve energy. ■

— Jerry Tipton

PRECEDING: UK freshman guard John Wall went to the basket for two of his 15 first-half points in the Cats' 73-65 overtime win over Stanford. LEXINGTON HERALD-LEADER/MARK CORNELISON

RIGHT: Ramon Harris cut inside for a layup in the first-half as Kentucky played Stanford in the Cancun Challenge. LEXINGTON HERALD-LEADER/MARK CORNELISON

Cats lean on Wall

UNC rallies during guard's absence

Freshman leads 28-2 first-half run and settles Cats down the stretch

Of his many fast-break plays in the first half, one moved Kentucky freshman John Wall. He flew to the left to elude a defender and somehow contorted his body into position to bank in the reverse layup while being fouled.

As a record Rupp Arena crowd (24,468) roared in appreciation of this take-that play against North Carolina, Wall searched the stands for his mother.

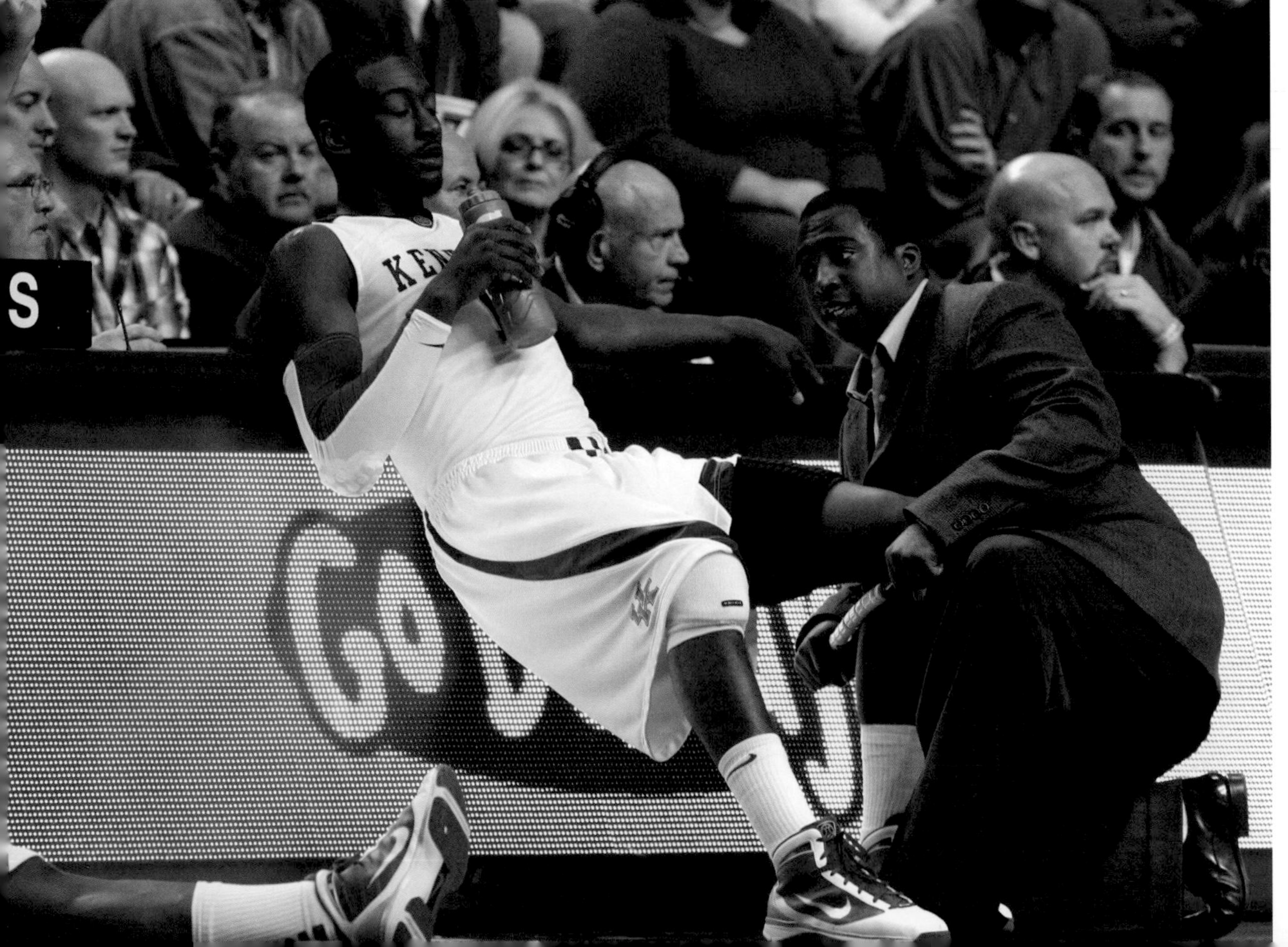

"Because it was a circus shot," he said after Kentucky's 68-66 victory Saturday, "and I was amazed it went in."

Alas, the circus left town at halftime. Cramps — not totally alleviated by an intravenous solution at halftime — reduced Wall thereafter to spectator or mere basketball mortal.

Not so coincidentally, North Carolina rallied from a 19-point first-half deficit, largely constructed by Wall, to three chances at a tying basket down the stretch against a wobbly Wall-less UK.

Wall's backup, fellow freshman Eric Bledsoe, made five of six free throws down the stretch to help UK clinch its first 8-0 start to a season since 1992–93.

LEFT: UK Trainer Chris Simmons massaged John Wall's left leg while Wall waited to re-enter the game. He headed to the locker room with cramps at the 18:46 mark and checked back in with 11:44 left. LEXINGTON HERALD-LEADER/DAVID PERRY

FOLLOWING LEFT: Kentucky's DeMarcus Cousins went up and under for a first-half basket in the North Carolina game. LEXINGTON HERALD-LEADER/MARK CORNELISON

FOLLOWING RIGHT: UK's Ramon Harris, left, congratulated Wall after Wall was fouled as he made a basket in the first-half of the North Carolina game. LEXINGTON HERALD-LEADER/DAVID PERRY

"You guys are going to say I'm crazy," UK Coach John Calipari said. "I'm happy how this played out. We had to play without John against a good team, and we had to just figure it out."

You're crazy, Cal.

This game provided 40 minutes of support for a statement made by UNC assistant Jerod Haase: Kentucky goes as Wall goes.

Wall and UK excelled in the first half. Wall had 13 points and five assists. He finished with 16 points, seven assists and three steals.

"I thought he played terrific," Calipari said. "I mean, you look at his numbers, and they were unbelievable for 32 minutes other than the seven turnovers. If he had three turnovers, then he would have played a perfect game for a point guard."

Of his catch-me-if-you-can fast-break dunk that ignited a 28-2 run, Wall said, "I think the dunk got us motivated. We started picking it up from there."

It was late in that run that Wall scored and searched for his mother. Once he spotted Frances Pulley, he raised his left hand to his temple and saluted.

"Thank you for everything she did for me," Wall said of the gesture.

With Wall at the controls, Kentucky hit three-point shots with newfound accuracy, got much the best of it around the basket and turned off North Carolina's signature fast-break attack. The Tar Heels did not have a fast-break point in the first half.

"John sort of dominated the game," said North Carolina Coach Roy Williams, who expressed surprise at the 12-0 margin in fast-break points UK enjoyed in the first half. "That was a big emphasis for us. We wanted to sprint back and cut off the easy ones."

Recently in the series, North Carolina had enjoyed the monster runs. The Tar Heels led 25-6 last season en route to a 77-58 victory in Chapel Hill.

This time, Wall's early dunk seemed to relax Kentucky. Darius Miller swished three-pointers from the left and right sides. Patrick Patterson, who led all scorers with 19 points, posted up for one basket over Tyler Zeller and took a pass from Wall for another on a fast-break dunk.

Without its transition game and inside game, North Carolina seemed helpless. When the UK lead reached 33-14, the Tar Heels had been outscored 16-2 in the paint. UNC did not get a second-chance point until the 6:25 mark.

"We weren't very patient in the first half," Williams said. "All of a sudden, Kentucky's defense became more aggressive. We panicked. We didn't get the ball inside."

UK made six of nine three-point shots in the first half. That equalled a season-high for a first half (six against Sam Houston State) and marked as many as the Cats had made in five of the previous seven games.

Even Wall, who had made only one of eight three-point shots in the last four games, made a trey.

If the first half showed the value of Wall, so did the second half. He left the floor with 18:46 left and Kentucky ahead 45-30.

Bledsoe came in and immediately walked.

Perhaps sensing vulnerability, North Carolina charged. When Deon Thompson scored while being fouled on a fast break with 16:39 left, the three-point play marked UNC's first points in transition.

On the next trip downcourt, Ed Davis scored on a banker as the trailer on the break. That reduced UK's lead to 45-38, as close as UNC had been since trailing 18-11.

UNC outscored Kentucky 20-10 in the paint over the final 19 minutes. UNC enjoyed a 14-3 advantage in points off turnovers.

LEFT: Patrick Patterson jammed home two of his game-high 19 points. He added seven rebounds to lead UK.
LEXINGTON HERALD-LEADER/MARK CORNELISON

FOLLOWING LEFT: John Wall weaved through the North Carolina defense looking to pass. Wall scored 16 points with seven assists and five rebounds despite playing just 32 minutes because of cramping after halftime.
LEXINGTON HERALD-LEADER/MARK CORNELISON

FOLLOWING RIGHT: Kentucky Coach John Calipari screamed instructions in the second-half as the Cats let much of a 43-28 lead slip away.
LEXINGTON HERALD-LEADER/MARK CORNELISON

"Let's be honest," Williams said, "it helped us with him being hurt in the second half."

The crowd roared when Wall appeared back on the court and reported to the scorer's table at the 11:44 television timeout.

But Wall was not nearly as effective. Three quick UK turnovers sent him back to the bench with 8:56 left.

Wall returned 11 seconds later, with Kentucky's lead down to 56-49.

"I was trying to fight through," said Wall, who estimated his second-half condition as 80 to 85 percent. "I still had a couple cramps."

North Carolina charged with three, 59-56.

After the charge, UNC had a wide open three-point shot to tie. Larry Drew missed. ■

— Jerry Tipton

Big stage exactly where Wall belongs
Greatness grows with each new test

JOHN CLAY
HERALD-LEADER SPORTS COLUMNIST

NEW YORK — In a crowded interview room on the ground floor of the world's most famous basketball arena, the soon-to-be (if he isn't already) most famous player in all of college basketball let slip a small smile.

You couldn't help but smile with him.

Big Apple, meet John Wall.

How can such a thin guy keep coming up so big?

How can a guy so young keep being so clutch?

He did it in his debut, making the final shot to beat Miami of Ohio. He did it Saturday against North Carolina, putting together a phenomenal first half that had the visitors back on their Heels.

He did it again Wednesday night. Bright lights. Big city. Big deal.

Not only did John Wall score 25 points in Kentucky's white-knuckler 64-61 victory over Connecticut in a whale of a game in Madison Square Garden, he scored 12 of his team's final 15 points, and 15 of its final 21.

"We rode John at the end," said John Calipari, the Kentucky coach.

There was more to learn here than the fact the Cats have a fantastic point guard, something it (and we) already knew. And for the first half, as Calipari said, "We drank the poison." Guess that would be the poison apple.

Calipari has said that with his talented but young Kentucky basketball team, it was all about the learning process.

Well then, the youthful Cats received a New York public school education.

A veteran UConn backcourt did the first-half teaching. Jerome Dyson is a wise and tough senior. He's the other No. 11, and he scored 13 first-half points. Kemba Walker is a worldly sophomore, a New York City point guard with the grit that goes with it.

And down low, the Huskies gashed Kentucky on the glass 26-14 in the first 20 minutes. The Huskies taught the Cats a thing or two.

Ah, but the Cats showed they can be quick learners. Kentucky learned how to take a punch, even on the biggest stage, the one where they used to hold all those classic heavyweight fights.

This was no Garden Party. This was bruising and tough, the second half especially, the kind of Big East basketball that Jim Calhoun's clan usually loves.

It was also the kind of game in which the person next to you turns to you and blurts out, "What a game!"

But if this were a heavyweight battle, a bantamweight won it. Wall missed the final 7:56 of the first half with two fouls. He played every minute the second half, and ended up making 10 of 16 shots from the floor, including his only three-point attempt, and he was a perfect 4-for-4 from the foul line.

Calipari was harping after the game on Wall's seven turnovers, but Cal's a coach, harping is what he's supposed to do. It's in the manual.

"Second half," said Wall, "I just tried to

do what Coach said."

Let the record show that Patrick Patterson's free throws with 11:35 left put Kentucky ahead, 41-40. But then let the record also show that it was the Wall show from there to game's end.

Twice the lithe guard got three-point plays that were huge in both time and execution.

The first came off a steal when Wall purposely slowed so that a Huskie could foul him on the layup. And he scored anyway.

The second came with all of 30.8 seconds left, after Connecticut had forged back in front, 61-60, when Wall sliced to the basket, got hit with a thud, and still muscled the ball through the nets.

And he made the free throw.

By now we're all starting to think he is from some other planet out there somewhere, but Wall is from Raleigh, N.C. Yet those were New York City kind of plays — savvy, tough, clutch, and at nail-biting, crunch time on a grand stage, the grandest they tell you around here.

"John is used to doing stuff like this," said Patrick Patterson.

We, and all of college basketball. are getting used to it, too. ■

PRECEDING: UK Coach John Calipari jumped on the sidelines during the first-half.
LEXINGTON HERALD-LEADER/CHARLES BERTRAM

LEFT: UK freshman John Wall drove the ball down the court as Eric Bledsoe (24) followed.
LEXINGTON HERALD-LEADER/CHARLES BERTRAM

BELOW: John Wall (11) and DeMarcus Cousins celebrated UK's quick start to the first-half after a UConn timeout. LEXINGTON HERALD-LEADER/CHARLES BERTRAM

Cats win big blue sprint
Kentucky breezes past Drexel, hits 2,000 ahead of Tar Heels

Kentucky became the first basketball program to reach 2,000 victories with a bimillennium mauling Monday night.

The Cats breezed past Drexel 88-44 to reach the highly anticipated goal of 2,000 victories. It came with ease after many fans — and UK Coach John Calipari — fretted that North Carolina might get to that numerical plateau first.

But UK, which improved to 12-0 to match the program's best start to a season since the Final Four team of 1983–84, made quick work of Drexel.

After 40 minutes of basketball fun, the UK team and special guests celebrated from center court with 24,354 fans (the 11th-largest crowd in Rupp Arena history).

Confetti rained down in a blue-and-white blizzard. Kool & the Gang's Celebration played in the background.

Herky Rupp, the son of program patriach Adolph Rupp, and former coach Joe B. Hall spoke to the crowd.

Then Calipari took his turn.

"We weren't part of many of the victories," he said. "But we had a job: Get across the finish line before that other blue team."

It became apparent less than four minutes into the game that Kentucky might need re-entry shields to slow down after breaking the tape.

The Cats led 15-3 with 16:10 left in the first half and piled up enough dominating plays to construct a 56-20 halftime lead.

That marked UK's highest-scoring first half of the season and the opponent's lowest-scoring half.

DeMarcus Cousins, John Wall and Patrick Patterson already had double-digit points. The cartoonish first-half UK statistics included a 27-10 rebounding advantage, a 24-6 edge in points in the paint, 12 assists and three turnovers, and Drexel's 29 percent shooting.

The rest of the evening was prelude to a coronation.

"He hit us on a bad night," Calipari said of his good friend, Drexel

Coach James "Bruiser" Flint. "That's as good as we've played."

Drexel played only one only other ranked team, Villanova. When asked to compare the Cats to 'Nova, Flint said, "I don't think it's close."

Fittingly, Cousins and Patterson led UK with 18 points. It was fitting because UK most dominated around the basket. Cousins' 13 rebounds (second most of the season) led UK's 45-22 edge on the boards.

John Wall added 16 points and seven assists.

Drexel (6-6) got 11 points from Samme Givens.

The game began with Kentucky establishing Cousins as a low-post force. He scored eight of UK's first 10 points. Six of his 14 first-half

PRECEDING: Freshman DeMarcus Cousins put in two of his 18 points as Kentucky played Drexel in Rupp Arena. LEXINGTON HERALD-LEADER/MARK CORNELISON

BELOW: John Calipari talked with point guard John Wall during the first-half. LEXINGTON HERALD-LEADER/MARK CORNELISON

RIGHT: Freshman guard Eric Bledsoe scored between Drexel's Gerald Colds (11) and James Harris. LEXINGTON HERALD-LEADER/CHARLES BERTRAM

points came on put-backs or free throws that followed attempted put-backs. Often he looked like Moses Malone: shooting, rebounding his own miss and repeating the exercise until he scored.

Patterson, who got criticized for a "soft" 21 points and nine rebounds against Austin Peay on Saturday, dunked with authority for his two baskets en route to a 11-point half.

With Kentucky in full control, the Cats turned to three-point shooting. UK made nine of 13 from beyond the arc. Those shots included DeAndre Liggins equalling a career-high of two with bombs from the left and right corners.

Ramon Harris made his first three-pointer of the season (he had been 0-for-9)."Ramon Harris knocked down a three," Flint said. "I knew we were in trouble."

The half ended with Wall punctuating the dominance with a pair of drives that moved fans out of their seats.

On the first, he eluded a defender with a behind-the-back dribble to scorer on the fast break. After a Drexel miss (the Dragons did not score in the final 2:50 and had only two baskets in the final 7:08), Wall split two defenders and laid in another basket as a third defender reached too late to contest the shot.

That gave UK its 36-point halftime lead.

Kentucky's joyride continued in the second half. The Cats scored the first 10 points to expand the lead to 66-20.

Patterson opened the run with his second three-pointer of the game, which tied a career high.

Ramon Harris completed it by making a free throw with 14:33 left. However, he missed his first free throw off the rim. That snapped a two-game streak of 31 consecutive makes for UK.

When asked if the 2,000-victory total held no significance in the national title-or-bust world of UK basketball, Calipari said, "It's hard to tell the 24,000 who stayed (that) it doesn't matter. All those things that separate us from others are important to the Commonwealth. This is one of those things that separate this program from all others." ■

— Jerry Tipton

FOLLOWING: UK celebrated its 2,000th victory. JONATHAN PALMER

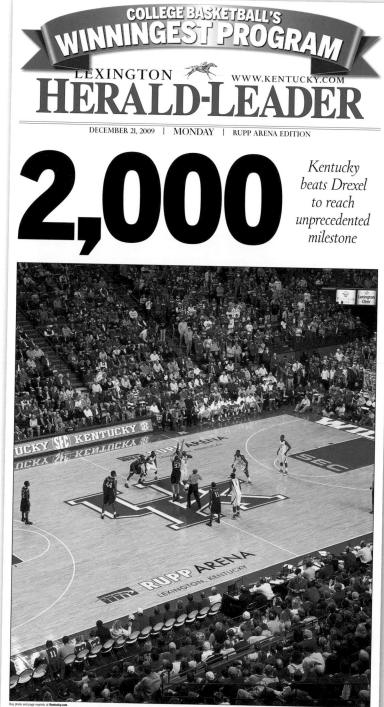

COLLEGE BASKETBALL'S WINNINGEST PROGRAM

LEXINGTON HERALD-LEADER

WWW.KENTUCKY.COM

DECEMBER 21, 2009 | MONDAY | RUPP ARENA EDITION

2,000

Kentucky beats Drexel to reach unprecedented milestone

Buy photo and page reprints at **Kentucky.com**

MARK CORNELISON | mcornelison@herald-leader.com

A packed house in Rupp Arena watched the opening tip of Kentucky's game against Drexel on Monday night when Kentucky hit the 2,000-victory mark. North Carolina sits at 1,992. Kentucky's winning percentage of 75.9 is the best in college basketball history. UK is 2,000-635-1 all-time

RUPP
ARENA
UK

December 21, 2009

UK fans celebrate a win for the ages

Young, old gather for 2,000th victory

If you didn't know better, you'd think this game was for all the marbles.

The place was packed. People were dressed up, kissing one another hello. Women brought noisemakers in their handbags.

Everybody who came through the Rupp Arena doors knew what was on Monday night's menu: A win for the record books, the bar bets and the bragging rights, and that great knowledge that you could say you were there.

On hand were 10-year-old girls like Caitlin Burdine, who got these tickets as an early Christmas present. It was just her fourth University of Kentucky game, but her daddy, Chris, was making memories.

Across a few aisles and down a few rows from Caitlin was Alta Wells, 91, who has had season tickets since her employer transferred them to her in 1956.

Truth is, Wells was a football fan first and has sat through more than her share of losing seasons. But not in this arena or the one over on Avenue of Champions. Those seasons never disappointed — especially since she was a people-watcher who, in the old arena, had tickets seven

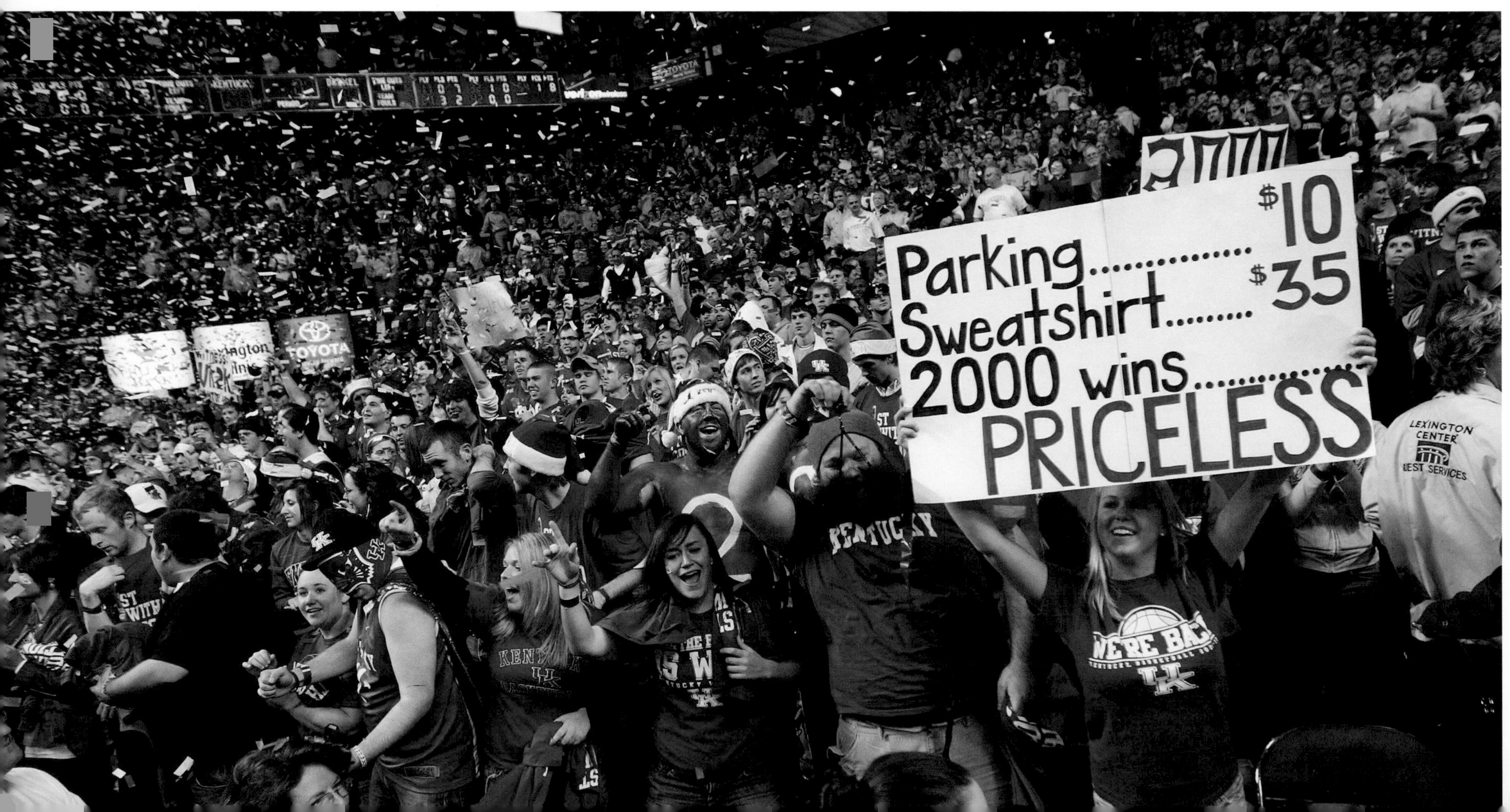

rows up from Happy Chandler, who used to like to bring politicians and Col. Harlan Sanders around occasionally.

A life is made on these special kinds of moments, Wells says, and you don't want to miss them. She says she wouldn't have missed the 2,000th victory unless the weather had kept her from driving or unless her knee, which sometimes gives her trouble when she bowls, had gone out.

William Pasco's idea was to keep it simple: Just buy Hanes T-shirts and paint a single digit — one and three nines — on each. Then, around the eight-minute timeout mark in the last half, when the cameras go swinging around the arena, he and his buds would do a simultaneous half-monty, 18-year-old chest flash.

All four guys — Pasco, Ben Horn, Josh Yeary and Andy Bessin — live in Holmes Hall, and they began standing in line at 2:30 Monday afternoon to make sure they got to the first row of the student section. They did. When the time came, they yanked up their shirts and swung them over their heads, baring their chests and the "2000" painted in bright blue.

It was not long before the moment was about to be real.

But before the blue and white confetti flew and the silver and blue streamers fell, the crowd rose. The lights got brighter. The fight song was sung by every soul in the joint.

Tradition was everywhere. And it was what mattered Monday night.

Michael Jarboe would be here if it were win No. 1,792, he says. "If it's UK basketball, I'm there. The basketball program is the reason I came to Kentucky. I got more scholarship offers from other schools, but basketball is more important than that."

Nick Tewes "body painted myself for North Carolina. I got three hours of sleep, stood in the cold in nothing else but my shorts for that game. I skipped studying for tests for a game. I've camped out for hours. I've missed a test for a students-only practice."

So, no, he wasn't going to miss this game.

And, yes, at around 9 o'clock, after John Calipari and Joe B. Hall had spoken, after some in the arena were afraid no fan would leave, Tewes was texting everyone in his cell phone book who was a Louisville fan with the same message: "In yo' face, it is now official. We are the number one program of all time."

It was sweet.

But wait — the boys in the stands were ecstatic, but they would not, they assured, be going home to burn any sofas tonight.

Sofa-burning is for March, when the college basketball world has to bow down — not just in appreciation for tradition, but in fear that Kentucky is not nearly done with it. ■

— Amy Wilson

PRECEDING: UK student Melissa Mauer held up a sign as Kentucky defeated Drexel University in Rupp Arena. LEXINGTON HERALD-LEADER/CHARLES BERTRAM

RIGHT: UK fans Andrew Strother, left, John Steele and Thomas Green painted their chests for the game against Drexel University. LEXINGTON HERALD-LEADER/CHARLES BERTRAM

December 21, 2009

2,000
Milestone belongs to Cats past and present

MARK STORY
HERALD-LEADER SPORTS COLUMNIST

The journey began Feb. 18, 1903.

Win No. 1 for the Kentucky Wildcats basketball program came by one, 11-10, over the always formidable Lexington YMCA.

On Monday night, the fascinating journey that is Kentucky basketball reached 2,000 wins first - before any other college hoops program — with an 88-44 obliteration of Drexel.

"This is for the greatest fans in the history of college basketball," UK Coach John Calipari said.

What a trek UK2K has been.

Win No. 108 (1921) came when Bill King's free throw with no time left gave Kentucky its first major tournament championship, 20-19, over Georgia in the finals of the Southern Intercollegiate Athletic Association tournament.

Win No. 489 (1946) occurred when a freshman from Louisville walked to the foul line in Madison Square Garden with his hands shaking from nerves and UK's first national tournament title hanging in the balance. Ralph Beard's foul shot beat Rhode Island, 46-45, and made Kentucky champions of the NIT.

Wins No. 557 (1948), 591 (1949), 648 (1951), 791 (1958), 1,216 (1978), 1,650 (1996) and 1,720 (1998) will always have resonance through the ages — each having made Kentucky an NCAA champion.

A series of coaching luminaries are most responsible for UK reaching 2,000 first.

Joe B. Hall completed the full racial integration of UK basketball and contributed 297 wins. Rick Pitino took Kentucky from one of its bleakest periods and returned it to national prominence while adding 219 victories.

Tubby Smith represented the commonwealth for a decade with unquestioned class, his mere presence as an African-American head coach a statement of the state's (and the South's) social progress. He delivered 263 wins.

Calipari, the first-year UK coach, says it was on his second day on the job when he began plotting. The goal: Get Kentucky to the 12 wins it needed to reach 2,000 before North Carolina could get to the 16 it required.

In his 12th game as top Cat, Cal delivered with maximum efficiency.

And, of course, there was Adolph Rupp. All the irascible Baron did for the cause of UK2K was produce 876 of the wins.

"A lot of the credit goes not only to the victories that Coach Rupp achieved but the foundation he laid for Kentucky basketball," says his successor, Joe B. Hall. "He made it easier for me … and the coaches that followed me all benefitted from the aura that surrounds Kentucky basketball. Coach Rupp built that."

The journey to 2K has featured moments around which generations of Kentuckians have spaced their lives.

Win No. 771 (1957) came when a Kentucky guard, Vernon Hatton,

LEFT: Former coach Joe B. Hall and Herky Rupp, Adolph Rupp's son, celebrated the win over Drexel. LEXINGTON HERALD-LEADER/CHARLES BERTRAM

hit a halfcourt shot as overtime expired to force Temple into a second OT. UK went on to win in three overtimes and, to this day, Hatton's heave might be the most famous shot in Kentucky history.

Win No. 1,039 (1970) was memorable in a far more significant way. When Kentucky beat Northwestern, its starting center was Tom Payne — the first African-American ever to wear the Kentucky basketball uniform.

It takes players to win games, of course, and the road to 2,000 was paved by 47 Wildcats who earned All-America honors, from Basil Hayden in 1921 to Jodie Meeks in 2009.

Yet UK2K is not just about the great players who have worn Wildcats blue.

"From 1903, every player who ever played for Kentucky has a part in this," says ex-UK guard and second-generation Wildcat Cameron Mills. "This is about the players winning the games 11-10 in the 1920s. It's about the Fabulous Five and all the great players in the 1940s and '50s. It's about my dad (Terry) and the teams in the 1960s. It's about my era (the late 1990s), and it's about the guys now. That's what makes this so cool. It's everybody's."

Amid all the winning, the road to 2,000 has featured heartbreak. The Runts fell short. In a national title-game duel of dynasties, the 1975 Cats couldn't beat UCLA. That dag-blasted Laettner hit that shot.

There's been heartache, too. Point-shaving. A year of NCAA suspension. Allegations of $50 handshakes. That infamous Emery Air Freight package.

Still, in so many ways, Kentucky basketball and its trek to 2,000 wins have been the glue that (for most) has united our often-splintered state.

"The fans are the ones I've heard talking about this," Kentucky forward Darius Miller says of UK2K. "They're the ones who told me about it, really. (Two-thousand wins) means a lot to them."

So what a thrill ride UK2K has been.

In Win No. 1,139 (1975), Kentucky defeated an unbeaten Indiana with a Final Four berth at stake. Win No. 1,580 (1994) saw the Wildcats victorious in a game in which they trailed by 31 points in the second half.

Win No. 1,979 (2009) featured a Kentucky player, Meeks, scoring more points (54) in one game than a UK Wildcat ever had.

And Win No. 2000 (2009) started with fabulous freshmen DeMarcus Cousins (18 points, 13 rebounds) and John Wall (16 points, seven assists) producing wows throughout Rupp Arena.

It ended with a blizzard of blue and white confetti and Adolph Rupp Jr. — Herky — taking the microphone in the arena named for his dad

"My father would be so proud," Rupp said.

UK2K being a milestone and not a finish line, Kentucky goes for Win No. 2,001 Wednesday against Long Beach State.

North Carolina and Kansas be warned: The race to 3,000 is on. ■

COLLEGE BASKETBALL'S WINNINGEST PROGRAM

LEXINGTON HERALD-LEADER

WWW.KENTUCKY.COM

DECEMBER 22, 2009 | TUESDAY | METRO FINAL EDITION

$1.00

2,000

Milestone belongs to Cats past and present

CHARLES BERTRAM | cbertram@herald-leader.com

During Monday's game, UK student Melissa Mauer expressed her opinion of the expected — and ultimate —outcome. **Fan story, A3**

Cruising into history books In its date with destiny, Wildcats demolish Drexel. **Sports, C1**

KentuckySports.com: See a photo slide show and video from win No. 2,000.

All-time wins

Kentucky	2,000
North Carolina	1,992
Kansas	1,980
Duke	1,885
Syracuse	1,764

On A2: Teams with the most wins in other sports

Wednesday

A full-color, 24-page special section celebrating all 2,000 of the Cats' victories.

MARK STORY
HERALD-LEADER SPORTS COLUMNIST

The journey began Feb. 18, 1903.

Win No. 1 for the Kentucky Wildcats basketball program came by one, 11-10, over the always formidable Lexington YMCA.

On Monday night, the fascinating journey that is Kentucky basketball reached 2,000 wins first — before any other college hoops program — with an 88-44 obliteration of Drexel.

"This is for the greatest fans in the history of college basketball," UK Coach John Calipari said.

What a trek UK2K has been.

Win No. 108 (1921) came when Bill King's free throw with no time left gave [illegible] tournament championship, 20-19, over Georgia in the finals of the Southern Intercollegiate Athletic Association tournament.

Win No. 489 (1946) occurred when a freshman from Louisville walked to the foul line in Madison Square Garden with his hands shaking from nerves and UK's first national tournament title hanging in the balance. Ralph Beard's foul shot beat Rhode Island, 46-45, and made Kentucky champions of the NIT.

Wins No. 557 (1948),

See STORY, A2

Buy photo reprints at Kentucky.com

MARK CORNELISON | mcornelison@herald-leader.com

As the confetti fell in Rupp Arena on Monday night, Kentucky's Patrick Patterson and his teammates found themselves tangled in streamers as they celebrated the basketball program's 2000th win, an 88-44 triumph over Drexel.

KENTUCKY

Back to Number 1

January 3, 2010 Kentucky vs. Louisville » W 71-62

Cats fight 'em off

UK closes out U of L to stay perfect as annual rivalry gets ugly

Wall steps up in second half to stop Cards

Kentucky and Louisville combined for five technical fouls, 37 turnovers and 22.6 percent three-point shooting on Saturday.

"As heated and emotional and physical, grabbing, pushing a game as I've coached in," UK Coach John Calipari said of the roller-derby action.

What UK's 71-62 victory over U of L lacked in style points it more than made up for in drama, guts and willpower.

The Rupp Arena record crowd of 24,479 could have (should have?) asked the Cats and the Cards to take a curtain call.

"Hats off to Louisville," said Calipari, who later in his post-game news conference noted the statistics that reflected UK's defensive excellence: U of L missed its first 14 shots, committed 19 turnovers and got credit for only five assists.

"And they still had a chance to beat us," Calipari said.

U of L Coach Rick Pitino, whose coaching chops were on full display, saluted Kentucky's palpable resolve.

"We thought we could win the game," he said. "But they made big plays and deserved to win."

With early UK leads of 11-1, 15-3 and 18-5 slowly ground down, Louisville got a nose in front at 42-41 with 9:51 left.

LEFT: Scratch the Wildcat got a lift in the E-Rupp-tion zone as Kentucky played Hartford, Dec. 29, 2009, in Rupp Arena. LEXINGTON HERALD-LEADER/MARK CORNELISON

RIGHT: Kentucky's Ramon Harris (5) and John Wall (11) went to the floor and took a loose ball from Louisville's Reginald Delk. LEXINGTON HERALD-LEADER/MARK CORNELISON

Enter UK freshman sensation John Wall to yet again update his storybook season. Wall hit a heavily contested driving layup, leaning back to get the shot over 6-foot-10 Terrence Jennings, to erase Louisville's only lead.

Then Wall hit a mid-range jumper that required touch and added two free throws on the next possession to ignite a 19-6 run that pointed Kentucky toward a milestone victory. The Cats improved to 15-0 to become the program's first team with that good of a start since Dan Issel's senior season of 1969–70.

Lost to many, perhaps, but not Pitino, was that until it mattered most Louisville caged Wall better than any UK opponent this season. Constantly harassed (what Pitino called mother-in-law defense in his salad days), Wall had only seven points and five turnovers until the teams hit the home stretch.

Pitino was moved to reference Michael Jordan.

"He wouldn't do his thing in the first quarter, the second quarter," the U of L coach said of Jordan. "But when the fourth quarter would come with the game on the line, he'd always make great plays.

"The tide had turned. We had momentum. … He was not having a good night. But the great thing about that young man (is) it never bothered him. He never lost focus. He stayed with it and made two killer plays (against) us."

Calipari cited how Wall did not get rattled. That was saying something since U of L shook him like a palm tree in a hurricane.

"John stayed cool and calm," said teammate Patrick Patterson, who matched Wall's 17 points.

Wall's cool reserve did crack with 9:05 left when he and U of L's Jerry Smith got hit with

TOP LEFT: Kentucky's Patrick Patterson scored over Samardo Samuels and Reginald Delk (12). LEXINGTON HERALD-LEADER/MARK CORNELISON

BOTTOM LEFT: UK freshman Eric Bledsoe went head to head with DeMarcus Cousins to calm him down, "I told him to shake it off, that we needed him." LEXINGTON HERALD-LEADER/MARK CORNELISON

ABOVE: John Wall got the crowd to roar after he drew a foul in the second-half. LEXINGTON HERALD-LEADER/PABLO ALCALÁ

FOLLOWING: Kentucky Coach John Calipari talked to his players on the sideline in the second-half. LEXINGTON HERALD-LEADER/MARK CORNELISON

UK

technical fouls.

"Coach (Calipari) said don't talk to them," Wall said. "But don't let them punk you."

As a precaution, Kentucky worked all week on playing through contact. "He didn't want to hear no excuses," Wall said of Calipari's preparation.

Five fouls, three technicals and Calipari rushing an overheated Eric Bledsoe to the bench inside the first 45 seconds suggested this would be no game for the faint-hearted.

Louisville missed its first 14 shots and didn't score a field goal until Samardo Samuels tipped in a miss with 10:53 left. That was U of L's only basket until Jerry Smith stole a Ramon Harris pass and drove to a contested layup to post his team's sixth and seventh points with 5:50 left in the half.

Until then the Cards had made only one of 19 shots.

If Kentucky (10-for-30) shot a bit better, the game might have been over. But Louisville switched to a zone after DeMarcus Cousins (18 points and 18 rebounds) had his way early around the basket.

Kentucky didn't score a basket for almost nine minutes in the first-half.

UK's turnover total climbed to 16 with more than 12 minutes left in the second-half. That helped Louisville take its only lead. Jennings' free throw put the Cards ahead 42-41 with 9:51 left.

Then Louisville hit the Wall.

"The egos with young people today are so out of whack," Pitino said. "He (Wall) just relaxed. Did his job. We're turning him over. He didn't get frustrated. His demeanor (was), it's OK. The game will be on the line and I'll show my greatness."

Perhaps hidden among all the turnovers, missed shots and flares of temper, Kentucky showed its quality.

"If your team is good, you'll win an ugly game," Calipari said. "That's when you know you're all right." ■

— Jerry Tipton

January 3, 2010

Lots of guts, glimpses of glory
Rivalry results in rough and ugly basketball

JOHN CLAY
HERALD-LEADER SPORTS COLUMNIST

In the days leading up, the message never changed.

Don't budge.

Don't give an inch.

"Don't let 'em punk you," said John Wall.

That was John Calipari's admonition to his team, in practice, in meetings, even when his Kentucky basketball team walked onto the floor of Rupp Arena on Saturday for the opening tip of the most hyped UK-U of L game in years.

"(Coach) knew they were going to be aggressive," said Wall, Kentucky's outrageously gifted freshman guard. "If we let them punk us, they still had a chance to win the game — but they probably would have won it if we weren't going to be aggressive."

Such was the survivor scenario of Kentucky's highly charged if poorly played 71-62 win over arch rival Louisville, a game that was more a demonstration of smashmouth basketball than heavenly hoops.

The ugliness some feared might greet Rick Pitino's first trip to Rupp after his summer revelation of personal transgressions never materialized — there were no signs, no posters, and just a brief "Karen Sypher, Karen Sypher" cheer from the upper deck — but was replaced by the rudeness on the floor.

This was a game high on emotion, low on execution.

It reminded you of so many Super Bowls, with all the great hype, and then, not much good football.

There wasn't a whole lot of pure basketball here. Louisville missed its first 14 shots. After coming into the game shooting 42.2 percent from three-point range, Kentucky ended up making just two of 14 from beyond the arc, missed eight of its first 14 free throws and committed 18 turnovers.

There were five technical fouls called, and not one of them on the coaches.

"Rivalry game," said Pitino when asked about the physical play.

But there was a downright beautiful stretch of 83 seconds, after Louisville scrapped its way to a 42-41 lead, when John Wall came out of the shadows to score six straight points.

Afterward, Pitino said it reminded him of Michael Jordan and Kobe Bryant, the way Wall failed to get frustrated and then succeeded when it counted most.

After Terrence Jennings' free throw put the visitors up 42-41, Wall scored on a drive with 9:31 left. Then he hit a jumper with 8:38 remaining. When he made two free throws at the 8:08 mark, UK was up five. When Perry Stevenson scored off a pretty Eric Bledsoe assist, the home team was up seven and in control.

"He wasn't having a good night," said Pitino, "but the great thing about that young man is it never bothered him, (he) never lost focus, stayed with it and made two killer plays."

But hadn't that been Calipari's message all along? Fight through the frustration. Play

PRECEDING LEFT: Kentucky's DeMarcus Cousins secured a rebound between three Louisville players for one of his 18 boards. LEXINGTON HERALD-LEADER/MARK CORNELISON

PRECEDING RIGHT: Kentucky guards Eric Bledsoe and John Wall talked during a free throw as they played U of L. LEXINGTON HERALD-LEADER/MARK CORNELISON

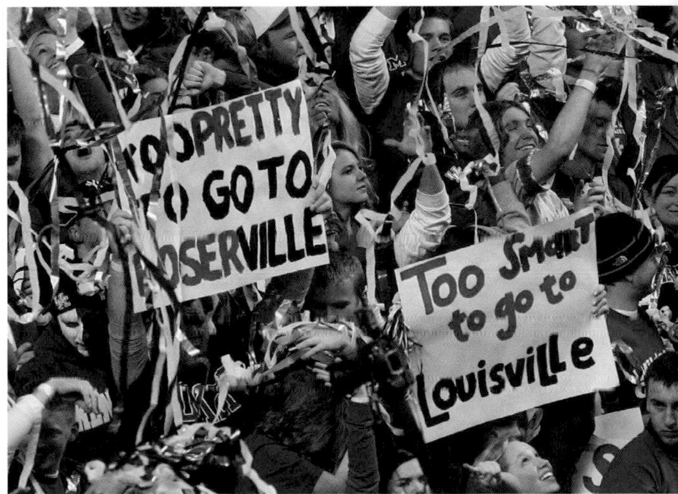

RIGHT: Wildcat fans brought signs to support their team. LEXINGTON HERALD-LEADER/MARK CORNELISON

through the bumps.

After all, Cal knows Pitino, and vice versa. It wasn't by accident that in his meeting with the media on Friday, the current UK coach kept mentioning "bumping and grinding," and "kneeing" and "hipping" and "riding" when talking about the defense used by the former UK coach.

"We went through this thing called a gauntlet," said Wall, "of where you're getting beat up when you're driving the ball and getting pulled, because we knew these guys were going to play tough."

In fact, in the first minute, the two teams were too jacked up. Brushing against each other. Trash talking. So charged up was Bledsoe, the freshman had to be yanked by Calipari seven seconds into the contest for trash-talkingw.

Then just 45 seconds after the opening tip, a savage scramble for the ball resulted in technical fouls on Louisville's Jared Swopshire and Reggie Delk, plus, after a view of the replay, an added tech on DeMarcus Cousins for forearming Swopshire in the neck while the two were on the floor.

"Just going for a loose ball," shrugged Cousins, who ended up with 18 points and 18 rebounds in 26 minutes.

"Did you see how the game was played?" said Calipari. "There were things, grabbing, kicking, grabbing, punching, eyeball-dragging, fish-hooks, nose drags. There was everything in the game."

Everything but basketball, you could argue.

Except, if you were a Kentucky fan, those sweet 83 seconds. That's all the basketball the Cats needed. ■

January 12, 2010 | Kentucky vs. Florida » W 89-77

Cats finally deliver the depth Cal desires

Dodson, Orton, Miller step it up in Florida win

GAINESVILLE, Fla. — Eric Bledsoe took advantage of the opportunity when Florida concentrated — quite sensibly — on containing national player of the year candidate John Wall.

Darnell Dodson, who missed all eight shots he took in the previous two games, hit a clutch three-pointer with the game on the line inside the final five minutes.

LEFT: John Wall, left, hugged the game's leading scorer, Eric Bledsoe, after the final horn at Florida. LEXINGTON HERALD-LEADER/DAVID PERRY

FOLLOWING: UK's Darnell Dodson, center, had the ball knocked loose by Florida's Ray Shipman, left, as he drove on Erik Murphy. LEXINGTON HERALD-LEADER/DAVID PERRY

Daniel Orton grabbed a career-high nine rebounds (one more than he had in the previous four games combined).

Darius Miller dunked for the first time this season, a wondrous sight that moved Coach John Calipari to raise both hands to his face in a gesture of mock amazement.

In beating Florida 89-77 Tuesday night, Kentucky showed the kind of quality depth that Calipari had said turns aspirations of greatness into reality.

Of course, steady Patrick Patterson provided his routinely busy statistical line: 15 points, seven rebounds and two steals.

And DeMarcus Cousins continued his curious habit of contributing more and more as the game unfolded (10 of his 13 points came in the second half).

With Orton joining the frontcourt production, Kentucky was dominant inside. The Cats outscored Florida 50-28 in the paint.

"Their speed and size and length after a period starts to wear our team down," Florida Coach Billy Donovan said. "Just because of our lack of depth."

The Gators, notably thin up front since the Al Horford-Joakim Noah days, gave up 90 points in the paint the last two games (against UK and Vanderbilt).

Calipari referred to Orton as "probably the difference in the game."

In one telling sequence, Orton blocked three straight shots. That helped the freshman from Oklahoma City equal the career-high four rejections he had against Sam Houston State.

"If he does the things he did today, it's hard to beat us," Calipari said, "because he went in and blocked every ball."

Calipari said he hugged Orton for delivering what the coach has been urging.

"You are the difference in the team," the UK coach said he told Orton. "The other guys are what they are. You are the guy."

In this game, there was a large list of contributing guys.

With Florida concentrating on Wall, UK needed someone such as Bledsoe to emerge.

"What Billy (Donovan) said was, 'We're going to make the game hard for John and make others make plays,' " Calipari said.

For stretches, Bledsoe brought the ball up court. If the opportunity existed — and it did more than once — he drove pretty-as-you-please to a layup.

"Everybody was going to John," Bledsoe said of the defenders. "It left a lane open for me to go to the hole and shoot layups."

After the game, a reporter noted that Bledsoe had big scoring games in UK's two trips to hostile environments. He scored 23 points at Indiana in December, UK's only other game on an opponent's court. To that, he added a career-high 25 at Florida.

"When the television lights come on, it seems that kid steps it up," Calipari said of Bledsoe. "He's a freshman. He has no idea what he's doing, and he goes for 25."

Calipari noted that Bledsoe's grandmother came from Birmingham, Ala., to watch the game.

"We've got to have her travel with us, I guess," the UK coach joked. "She better be at Auburn when we play this weekend."

Donovan acknowledged that Bledsoe's play foiled the idea of concentrating on Wall. The Florida coach noted the difference in scouting via video and seeing Kentucky in the flesh.

"When Wall's coming up the floor 100 mph, Bledsoe's resting," he said. "When Bledsoe's coming up the floor 100 mph, Wall's resting. It's like a two-headed monster when they're continually coming at you off the dribble."

Dodson had made more than one three-point basket only once since the North Carolina game on Dec. 5.

With UK wobbling early, he hit a three pointer to steady the Cats. Then with a 15-point lead gone and the teams tied at 72 going into the final five minutes, Dodson followed Patterson's go-ahead post-up basket with another three pointer.

"Darnell going in and making that shot showed me a ton," Calipari said. "That means I can go to him when I see things dying." ■

— Jerry Tipton

January 12, 2010

Determination despite drama

UF got back in it, but UK showed 'will to win'

JOHN CLAY

HERALD-LEADER SPORTS COLUMNIST

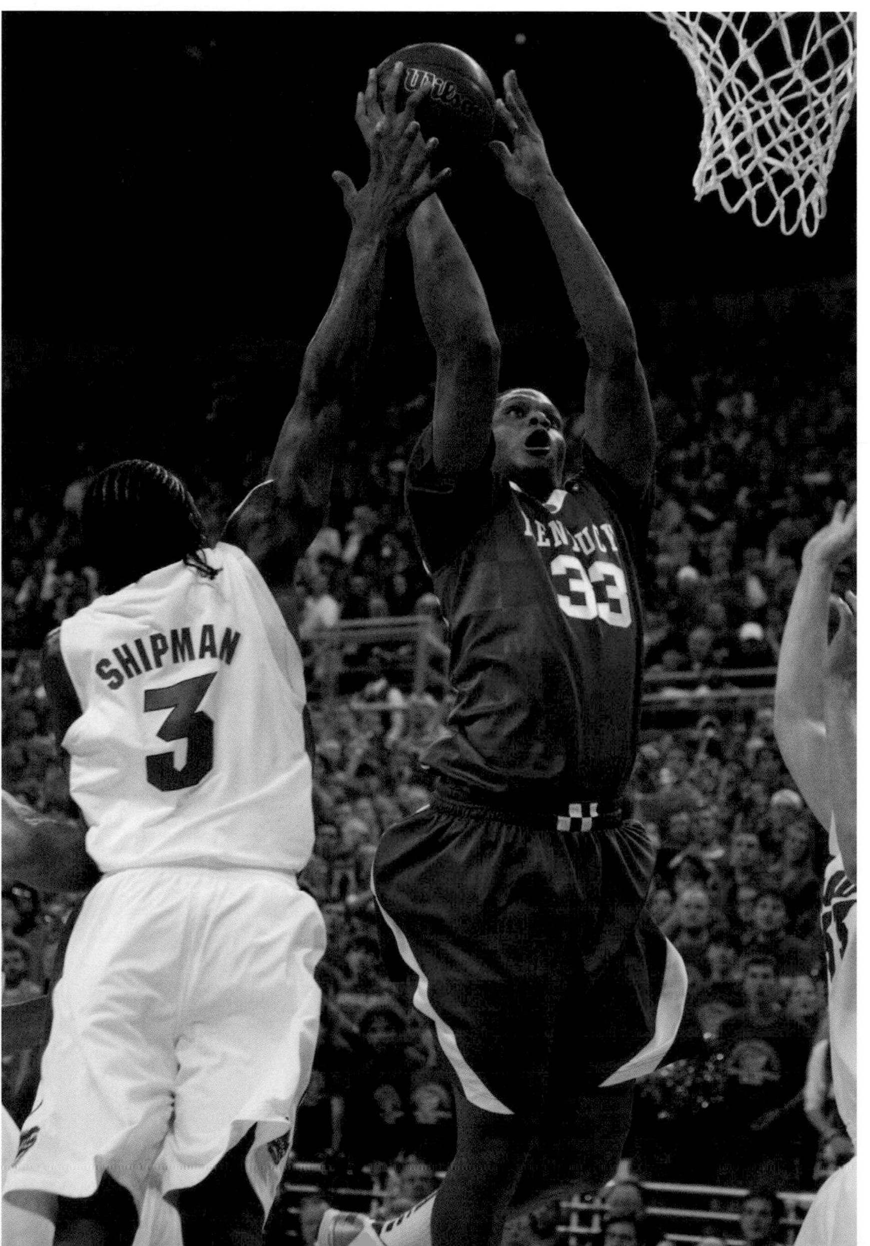

GAINESVILLE, Fla. — You could call them the drama kings, the way this young Kentucky team hasn't yet learned to put a foot on the opponent's throat. Maybe it gets bored when it gets ahead. Maybe it needs a challenge.

But so far, anyway, when the challenge arises, drama turns to domination.

"Will to win," said John Wall.

Win, indeed.

Here's the thing: Kentucky is 2-0 in the SEC.

Florida, for the first time ever under Billy Donovan, is 0-2.

The Cats beat the Gators 89-77 in the O-Dome on Tuesday night in what could be described as a loud, ragged, fun, uneven basketball game, in which the visitors appeared to be in control, up 15, not quite midway through the second half.

Only it turned into just what UK Coach John Calipari lamented about on Monday, that one of these days his young guys were going to mess around with a lead and get caught from behind.

Florida caught 'em all right, roaring back behind tiny guard Erving Walker, who helped pull Donovan's club even at 72 with 5:14 remaining.

The Rowdy Reptiles, with their wigs, their John Wall and DeMarcus Cousins signs, and their "Refined Rowdy Reptiles" T-shirts, went nuts.

"We get up 15 and all of a sudden we're tied," Calipari said afterward. "At some point this season we've got to get people down and keep them down. Or we're going to lose games. And you'll go on a run of not

LEFT: UK's Daniel Orton was challanged by Florida's Ray Shipman (3) in the first-half. LEXINGTON HERALD-LEADER/DAVID PERRY

FOLLOWING: UK Coach John Calipari talked with leading scorer Eric Bledsoe during a break in the action in the second-half.
LEXINGTON HERALD-LEADER/DAVID PERRY

only losing one but losing two, three and four."

Ah, but Kentucky had a little guard of its own. Eric Bledsoe finished with a career-high 25 points. And after Patrick Patterson made a hook, missed the free throw and the Cats came up with a scramble, Bledsoe buried a killer three-pointer with 3:57 left.

A little over a minute later, Bledsoe hit another three to make it 82-73.

For all intents and purposes, that was the ballgame. You could see Florida's shoulders slump. The Gators have quick, darting guards but little underneath the basket. They battled the taller, better Cats inside, but you never got the feeling that Florida had the advantage underneath.

Kentucky, meanwhile, has guys who rise to the challenge. John Wall was good, but not John Wall good. (He did score UK's final seven points.) Bledsoe was great.

The freshman scored 15 points the first half. He added 10 more in the second and points at the best times. He was 10-for-13 from the floor.

It's no coincidence that two of Bledsoe's best games this year have come at Indiana and now at Florida. The kid doesn't back down from a challenge.

"Everybody's going to try and come at us, try to beat us," Bledsoe said. "That's going to be any team we play, so we're just going to have to play through it."

UK shot 58.8 percent in the second half and made five of 11 three-pointers.

"We've just got to figure out how we can tap into that," said Calipari of the closing stretch, "and say, 'This is who we have to be and how we have to play.'"

Meanwhile, Florida shot 38.2 percent, but maybe the Gators were distracted by the Lane Kiffin-to-USC news. As soon as Kentucky appeared to close the deal for good, Gator Nation filed quickly out the door to grab a bit of SportsCenter, no doubt, and dream of Florida staff members busily calling Tennessee recruits.

Kentucky has their stars. They're young. They're learning. Conference play is different. Conference road games are intense. And just because you're up 15 in the second half of a game in Gainesville, doesn't mean it's game-set-match.

But when it comes to decision time, the Drama Cats, er, Kings, rule. ■

January 18, 2010

A million ways to help

'Hoops for Haiti' telethon makes quick work of generosity

University of Kentucky men's basketball coach John Calipari and his undefeated team raised more than $1 million in about five hours Sunday afternoon at a "Hoops for Haiti" telethon.

"I've been saying for months that the Big Blue Nation is full of 'crazies,'" Calipari said. "But after Sunday's outpouring of support, I can call everyone something else: compassionate and generous. ... It was beyond my wildest dreams."

Calipari emceed the show on WKYT-TV while players manned the phones. The coach said he has been telling the young men, whose team is 18-0, to be humble when things are going good.

Calipari pulled together the telethon in less than two days, reaching out to several leaders and agencies for help.

Red Cross officials said Sunday they knew of no other coach or athletic team hosting a telethon.

"Our response to this tragedy will make a difference," said Terry Burkhart, CEO of the Bluegrass Chapter of the American Red Cross.

Fans, other coaches, celebrities and business figures called in to pledge $525,000. A group called Cal's Pals for Haiti — led by Lexington businessman Royce Pulliam and including Calipari — will provide an additional $500,000. An eBay auction will continue through Tuesday, so an official total won't come until later.

By Sunday night, the bid for dinner for six at Calipari's Richmond Road home with UK fan Ashley Judd stood at $11,600. The leading bid for two-on-two hoops with former UK players Scott Padgett and Tony Delk was $1,825.

The phone lines were jammed all afternoon, and Calipari called on many famous friends.

Gov. Steve Beshear appeared on the telethon, bringing $1,000 from the personal donations of his office staff. Former UK coach Tubby Smith and sports commentator Dick Vitale each called and donated $1,000 during on-air interviews.

University of Texas basketball coach Rick Barnes and Cincinnati Bengals coach Marvin Lewis also called. They talked to Calipari on the air and made donations.

Syracuse basketball coach Jim Boeheim pledged $5,000. Former UK player Nazr Mohammed gave $10,000 to bring the total from callers' pledges to more than $500,000.

Alliance Coal CEO Joe Craft, a driving force behind UKs state-of-the-art practice facility, donated $100,000.

Calipari and his wife, Ellen, gave $25,000.

In a videotaped message, Judd explained to viewers that even small donations would provide safe drinking water for families in Haiti.

She will be providing her personal chef for the Calipari dinner.

Patrick Patterson said an older man who donated $200 began crying on the phone, calling Patterson "a great ambassador" for UK basketball.

He also said a female caller was in shock that he'd answered the phone. "She couldn't talk," he said.

Eric Bledsoe said he answered phones non-stop for 90 minutes. As the donations mounted Sunday, he gained a new appreciation for fans. "I was thankful," Bledsoe said.

In an interview with the *Herald-Leader*, Calipari said he decided to pursue the telethon idea after Pulliam, CEO of the Lexington-based Urban Active health clubs, called him Friday morning and said he had cried after seeing the victims in Haiti, and wondered what they could do to help.

Calipari said he in turn called Wayne Martin, general manager at WKYT, who also had been approached by United Way of the Bluegrass and the Red Cross.

The Red Cross is immediately sending all the proceeds to Haiti. "It's going to where it's supposed to go," Calipari told viewers.

As the telethon wound down, Calipari told viewers: "The blue dust is everywhere across the nation." ■

— Valarie Honeycutt Spears

FOLLOWING: Coach John Calipari did an impression of John Wall during the "Hoops For Haiti Telethon" at the WKYT-27 studios. MATT GOINS

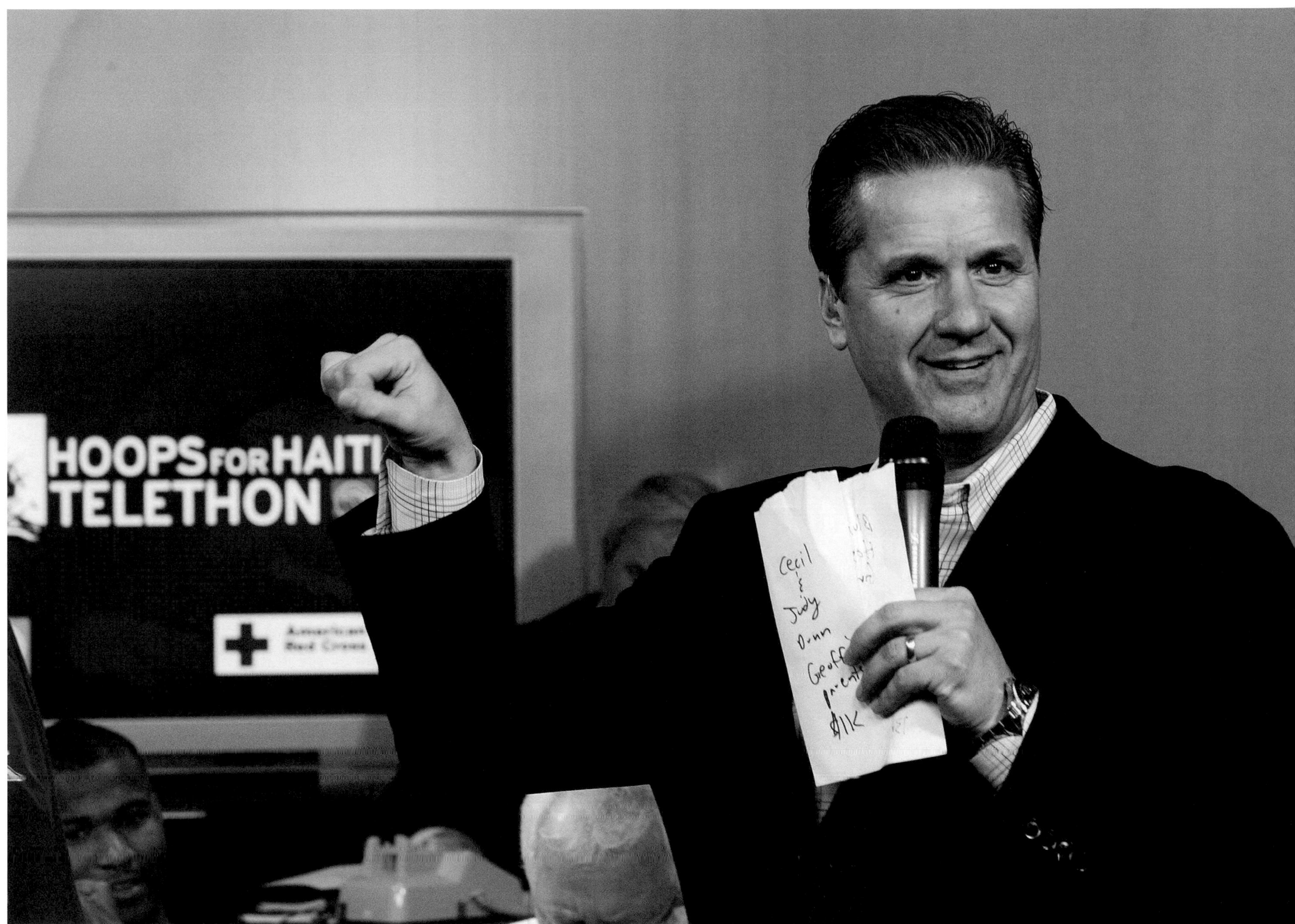
HOOPS FOR HAITI
TELETHON

January 26, 2010

Cats No. 1 and loving it

Calipari, Cats welcome rare ranking, detractors

As illogical as it sounds, Kentucky big man DeMarcus Cousins took an us-against-the-world stance last week when asked about UK's likely ascension to No. 1 in The Associated Press media poll. Illogical because on Monday the Cats became the first unanimous choice for No. 1 this season.

"It shows the world we really are No. 1," Cousins said when it became obvious Kentucky would be No. 1. "I mean, people already are saying we don't deserve it. ... Some people saying we're the third-best team."

Citing "just stuff I heard," Cousins suggested that many detractors pick at Kentucky.

"They hate us," he said. "They hate the fact we're doing big things. Everybody's saying we're good, but we're not able to do anything because we're so young. We're the last undefeated team, but we're so young.

"So much of it is backfiring in their faces, and they don't know how to handle it."

Kentucky achieved its first No. 1 ranking since the final wire service poll of the 2002–03 season. UK became the first unanimous No. 1 since North Carolina received every first-place vote last season in the pre-season poll and then the first seven of the regular season.

The Cats are also the unanimous No. 1 pick in the ESPN/USA Today coaches poll, receiving all 31 first-place votes.

After Kentucky solidified its claim on No. 1 by beating Arkansas 101-70 last weekend, Coach John Calipari noted the slings and arrows that might come. In his post-game news conference, he all but predicted criticism of UK's schedule (as of late Sunday night, collegerpi.com rated UK's schedule the 84th toughest in the nation). The UK coach urged critics to write disparaging things. "It kind of inspires us," he said.

Calipari also said the top ranking was an honor and not a burden.

When he spoke Monday about reaching No. 1, Calipari embraced the Cats reaching the lofty goal. "They wanted to be No. 1, which is a good sign," he said.

But the UK coach acknowledged the challenges that come with the top ranking.

"Now we're trying to teach them what it means being No. 1," he said.

Calipari spoke to the players Sunday night about the "obstacles" and "distractions" that come with being No. 1: increased media requests and demand for tickets; more people who want to be associated with a winner.

"Now all of a sudden a guy not very good looking becomes just a beautiful young man," Calipari said. "He goes from homely to just a hunk. And you can't figure it out."

The UK coach saluted his "pretty level-headed group." He noted how the Cats rose to the occasion against North Carolina and Louisville, and again against Arkansas when the No. 1 ranking was at stake.

But Calipari suggested an expectation of a highly charged team in every game was unrealistic.

"They're not machines and not robots," he said. "They're going to have bad nights. They're going to have flat nights. Let's just hope it's against an opponent we can beat anyway."

Calipari is no stranger to a No. 1 ranking. His Memphis team in 2007–08 was No. 1 five straight weeks. His Massachusetts team held the No. 1 ranking for nine weeks in 1995–96.

But this time is different.

"They were all veteran teams," Calipari said Saturday of his experience with highly ranked teams. "(Memphis) had been to the Elite Eight the year before.

"(UK) was an NIT team and a bunch of children. But they're very good children."

Kentucky first carries its No. 1 ranking into a game at South Carolina Tuesday night.

Calipari made no promises about how easy the crown will rest on UK's collective head.

"How will they respond?" he said. "I have no idea, and neither do you. But we're going to find out." ■

— Jerry Tipton

January 26, 2010

Cats' history at No. 1

Kentucky has finished the regular season ranked No. 1 in the Associated Press poll eight times but only once since 1978. UCLA has also finished No. 1 eight times, Duke seven times and North Carolina six.

The last time UK finished the regular season No. 1 was 2003, which is also the last time UK was ranked No. 1. That was the only week UK was ranked first that season.

Before 2003, UK had not been ranked first since 1996.

UK won the national title in 1998, but it was not ranked higher than fourth that year.

UK has won six national titles since the poll started in the 1948–49 season. In four of those years, UK was ranked No. 1 at some point during the season. The 1998 champs finished the season ranked No. 5. The 1958 championship team finished the year ranked No. 9.

UK has been ranked No. 1 at least one week in 16 different seasons, counting the preseason poll. In five of those years, the ranking was for only one week. ■

— Jerry Tipton

LEXINGTON HERALD-LEADER

WWW.KENTUCKY.COM

Life + Health, B1: A Somerset toddler has recovered after H1NI flu almost killed her

City | Region: Witness says checks were sent to Nighbert by mistake » **Sports:** Barnette must play well if the LCA girls are to win another All-A title

JANUARY 26, 2010 | TUESDAY | METRO FINAL EDITION | $1.00

CATS ASCEND TO NO. 1

UK a unanimous pick: Kentucky takes over the top spot in the Associated Press men's basketball poll for the first time since 2003.

The Cats will defend the No. 1 ranking Tuesday night when they travel to South Carolina to play the Gamecocks. **Page C1**

TONIGHT

Kentucky at South Carolina

When: 9 p.m. **TV:** ESPN

Mark Story: Could losing a game be a plus?

Some members of the 1995-96 UK team weigh in on whether these unbeaten Cats would be better off with a loss before the NCAA Tournament. **Page C1**

CHRIS WARE | staff

It's a blur: SEC TV picture quality draws complaints

Southeastern Conference basketball viewers aren't happy with what they're seeing. **Page C4**

Online: Kentuckysports.com

■ John Clay will blog live from Tuesday's game.

■ Look for a photo slide show after the game.

Even before the AP rankings came out, a congratulatory sign was placed in the median Monday in front of Coach John Calipari's house on Richmond Road.

CHARLES BERTRAM cbertram@herald-leader.com

Bank wants receiver for Zayat stable

TOP THOROUGHBRED OWNER DENIES INSOLVENCY, INABILITY TO CARE FOR HORSES

By Janet Patton

jpatton1@herald-leader.com

Ahmed Zayat was the leading Thoroughbred racehorse owner in North America in 2008 and breeder of Pioneerof the Nile, which finished second in the Kentucky Derby last year.

Fifth Third Bank has asked a federal judge to take over the racing stable of top Thoroughbred owner Ahmed Zayat, saying he might not have enough cash to feed and care for the horses.

A hearing has been set for Feb. 8.

The bank, which alleges Zayat owes more than $34 million, said it is necessary to appoint a receiver, an independent caretaker to protect the horses, which were used as collateral for the loans.

In the meantime, the bank asked U.S. District Judge Karen K. Caldwell to force Zayat to allow them to inspect the horses and his business operation. The bank said it is prepared to maintain and care for the horses until the case is resolved.

The bank, in a Jan. 4 request, said Zayat has disclosed that from 2006 through 2009, Zayat Stables lost almost $65.5 million and is expecting a cash-flow deficit of nearly $3 million this year.

The bank said Zayat claims to have lost

See ZAYAT, A2

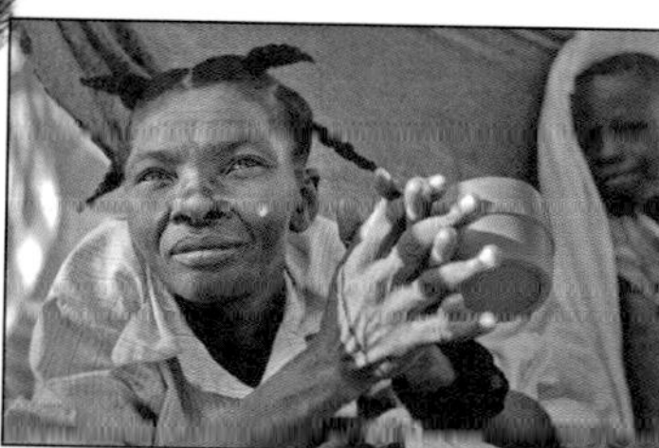

RAMON ESPINOSA | ASSOCIATED PRESS

A Haitian woman held a cup as she sat in a makeshift refugee camp in Port-au-Prince on Monday She is one of tens of thousands left homeless by the Jan. 12 earthquake.

Haitians continue to search for their dead: 'I need the body'

January 27, 2010

Hail from the chief

Obama lauds Hoops for Haiti effort, team's success

COLUMBIA, S.C. — What started as an effort to raise money for Haiti earthquake relief led to the University of Kentucky basketball team being thanked via telephone by President Barack Obama on Tuesday.

And it was clear the nation's No. 1 ranking basketball fan knows the nation's top-ranked team well.

Obama and the Wildcats participated in the phone call in Columbia, where UK played South Carolina on Tuesday night. The call was to thank the team for raising more than $1.3 million through its Hoops for Haiti telethon last week.

"I think this is just a great testament to each of you individually, is a great testament to your program, and is a great testament to Kentucky," Obama said. "It shows a lot of character. Some of you are going to be going on to the NBA. Some of you are going to be doing other things in your lives. I hope that spirit of doing for others continues."

The call came a little after 1:30 p.m. to a phone in the media room at Colonial Life Arena. Coach John Calipari sat at the table with junior Patrick Patterson next to him. The other players stood next to them.

The phone rang. Calipari looked around then pushed the button.

A cheerful voice on the other end of the line said: "Hi, it's Katie Duncan calling for President Obama."

Calipari hesitated a second, then smiled and said, "OK?"

The room laughed.

After about 30 seconds, a familiar voice came on the line.

"Well, man, I am honored to speak to the No. 1 team in the country, a few days after it happened," Obama said.

Calipari thanked Obama for the call, mentioning the importance of the Hoops for Haiti program. Then he told the president he had a few players who wanted to speak to him. First was Patterson.

"Hey, Patrick!" Obama said.

Patterson thanked the president "on behalf of the team for what you're doing for the whole country." He said how much the Hoops for Haiti program meant and added how much Obama's leadership inspired them. Obama thanked Patterson in return.

At that point, Calipari jumped back in and said freshman John Wall wanted to speak. "Hey! What's going on All-Star!" Obama said. "I've been watching you."

More laughter from the room, eliciting a sheepish grin from Wall.

Wall then invited Obama to a game in Lexington, and "maybe a game of H-O-R-S-E."

Obama was ready:

"I'm not gonna play H-O-R-S-E with you. I don't want to lose, and then you'll have bragging rights for a long time. But what we might do is have a little scrimmage. And I'm gonna make sure that you're on my team. If you're on my team, and Patterson ... I'm gonna book it up so I've got a chance."

Finally, freshman DeMarcus Cousins told Obama he hoped to see him at the end of the season.

"You know, the way you guys are going, that may happen," Obama said, referring to a potential championship visit to the White House.

Then the president turned serious. "Obviously, everybody admires the great team you have," he said. "Everybody admires the dedication on the court, the athleticism on the court. It's just fun to watch you guys. But the main reason I'm calling is for you in the middle of the season to take the time to do something like this for people that you don't know."

Then Obama put U.S. Rep. Ben Chandler, D-Versailles, on the phone, offering up similar congratulations. But Obama couldn't resist just a little more basketball talk, asking who the Wildcats played next. Calipari answered that they were on the road at South Carolina.

"All right, well I think you should be all right," he said. (He was wrong. About 10 hours later, South Carolina handed UK its first defeat.)

Calipari winced, while there was more laughter in the room. The president went on.

FOLLOWING: Patrick Patterson, left, Coach John Calipari and John Wall each spoke with President Obama when he called from the White House. THE STATE/ERIK CAMPOS

"But there is that tendency once you get to be No. 1 to start to let down a little bit. And it is a tough place to play. So you guys stay focused. I expect to see you guys in the championship game at some point. And again, congratulations on the great work you guys did."

Obama said goodbye, and Calipari and the players exhaled.

A few minutes later, the team was still absorbing the moment. As he walked offstage, Calipari said he was more nervous during the call than during a timeout. Wall said he was "still nervous."

"Extremely inspiring," Patterson said. "Not only does he know us on the basketball court, but obviously he knows us off the basketball court for what we did for the people of Haiti. It feels extremely good to know that he admires us and also that he respects us." ■

— Seth Emerson, *McClatchy Newspapers*

'A great lesson'
Calipari: You don't spell 'learn' without an 'L'

When he coached Kentucky's team, Rick Pitino likened losing to fertilizer. From such stuff, teams can grow stronger and healthier.

John Calipari sounded much the same note after South Carolina upset visiting UK 68-62 Tuesday night. Disappointing as it was to see dreams of an unbeaten season dashed and a seven-years-in-the-making No. 1 ranking immediately tarnished, it could be an "L" of a way to improve.

"It's a great lesson," the UK coach said. "... A lot of times, until you take an 'L,' they don't want to believe you, especially with how young we are."

Meanwhile, South Carolina rode a proven Cat-killer in fifth-year senior Devan Downey and a well-executed game plan to the program's first victory over a No. 1 team. The seeds of this upset also included the Gamecocks' stunning ability to rebound with the previously dominant UK front line, surprising contributions from heretofore nondescript players, an inspiring sellout crowd and, Calipari suggested, Kentucky's false sense of confidence.

"We've had this happen in other games where we're just good enough at the end to win it, anyway," the UK coach said. "For our team, this is what happens when you have young guys think you're going to win it in the last minute of the game."

Kentucky players had plenty of reasons to believe they'd win again in the final reel. That worked against Auburn, Florida, Georgia, Louisville, Stanford, Connecticut, North Carolina, Sam Houston State, Miami (Ohio), etc., etc.

"We've done that all year," Calipari said. "We may have been undefeated, but we were lucky to be undefeated."

This time, South Carolina never stopped outhustling Kentucky, as reflected in a 44-40 rebounding advantage and the Cats getting about half of what Calipari considers the normal "hustle points."

As Calipari saw it, Kentucky's irresistible urge to show its undeniable talent also got in the way of winning.

"This is what happens to a young team," he said. "We weren't really listening to how we're trying to execute down the stretch. We're trying to make hero plays. We had layups we were trying to make fancy."

None was more nakedly obvious than Darnell Dodson's miss on a breakaway dunk. Kentucky trailed 51-49 with less than six minutes left when the sophomore in his first season on the Division I level made a steal, but then lost control of the ball as he rose for a

planned one-hand slam.

"On national TV," Calipari said of the ESPN-heightened embarrassment factor for Dodson. "Probably not a good feeling right now. These are all lessons. This isn't an AAU game. It's not a pickup game. You make the play. There's no degree of difficulty. Just make the play. And we had a degree of difficulty."

Calipari made sure not to single out Dodson as the lone culprit. Quite the opposite. The UK coach said he asked each player after the game to reflect on ill-advised impulses to showboat or relax.

"I want you to think of one or two plays you tried to make a fancy play," he said he told the players. "(Or) you stopped playing. You didn't block out."

Even in the blowout of Arkansas last weekend, the Cats saw big leads as an invitation to entertain: Ahead 34-13, DeMarcus Cousins launched a three-pointer in hopes of his second basket from beyond the arc this season; ahead 46-23 and then 50-23, Eric Bledsoe went on flights of fancy.

No harm done at home against an Arkansas team playing its second game in three days.

South Carolina, which plotted to stay close and then take its chances with arguably the best point guard in the Southeastern Conference, fed off such lapses.

Calipari noted how UK's big men stood flat-footed as Downey came off screens for scoring opportunities.

"Instead of being in a (defensive) stance," the UK coach said. "… Now, all of a sudden, our big guys are screeners, too."

In other words, UK's big men got in the way of any teammate wishing to contest Downey's shot.

PRECEDING: South Carolina's Devan Downey and UK's DeAndre Liggins went for a loose ball in the first-half. It was ruled a held ball with possession going to UK.
LEXINGTON HERALD-LEADER/CHARLES BERTRAM

LEFT: DeMarcus Cousins battled South Carolina's Sam Muldrow for a rebound. LEXINGTON HERALD-LEADER/CHARLES BERTRAM

Downey, smart as well as quick, seized on the moment. "I told Coach at the end of the game, let's just run ball screens," he said.

Because of injury (Dominique Archie) and dismissal (Mike Holmes), South Carolina cannot afford the luxury of fancy plays. Coach Darrin Horn, the former Tates Creek High School star, called the Gamecocks "more of a game-plan type of team."

Calipari saluted Horn's plan, which called for milking the shot clock and then giving Downey the ball on offense. Defensively, the Gamecocks stressed getting back in transition to force Kentucky to play in half-court sets. Once there, South Carolina guarded Cousins one-on-one in the low post rather than double-teaming and having to rush outside the lane to cover his passes out of traps.

Horn acknowledged the risk. He called Cousins, who equaled a career high of 27 points, "unguardable" and "the best I've seen in 15 years of coaching."

LEFT: John Wall kept the ball from going out of bounds as Kentucky played the University of South Carolina in Colonial Life Arena in Columbia.
LEXINGTON HERALD-LEADER/CHARLES BERTRAM

BELOW: DeMarcus Cousins talked to John Calipari in the second-half.
LEXINGTON HERALD-LEADER/CHARLES BERTRAM

FOLLOWING: The UK bench watched the last 2 minutes of the South Carolina game. LEXINGTON HERALD-LEADER/CHARLES BERTRAM

But, Horn added, you have to make decisions on what to try to take away from Kentucky.

While lamenting his team's play, Calipari did not want to detract from South Carolina's performance.

"They made us play the way we played," he said of the Gamecocks. "I'm not taking anything away from them. They deserved to win."

Not that the UK coach absolved his players of responsibility. He suggested some players might be trying to justify the hype surrounding their arrival at Kentucky by attempting memorable plays.

"I keep trying to tell them, you've got nothing to prove," Calipari said. "Just go play ball. You don't have to prove you're this (and) you're that."

Junior All-America candidate Patrick Patterson was strangely subdued: four shots and five points in 35 minutes. When asked if Patterson could have done more to lead his youthful teammates, Calipari said, "I would hope so. But we had our chances to win even with him playing that way."

No doubt, those chances will come again and again. Perhaps the defeat will help the Cats to make the most of those chances. ■

— Jerry Tipton

Calipari pushes all the right buttons
Dodson, Liggins take full advantage of opportunity

JOHN CLAY
HERALD-LEADER SPORTS COLUMNIST

About five minutes remained in the second half Tuesday night at South Carolina when the Cats' Darnell Dodson had a breakaway jam in the open court that would have tied the score with the host Gamecocks. Only Dodson missed it.

"I rushed it," said the sophomore on Friday.

Flat-out missed it.

"They're still giving me a hard time," said Dodson.

You might not think that a player who missed a wide-open dunk in what turned out to be the first loss of the season, and earned the head coach's wrath in the process — "Make the play!!!!" said John Calipari — would go from reserve to starter the next game.

"That's the great thing when you're the head coach," said Calipari on Saturday, with a smile. "You can make those kind of decisions."

This was a good decision. Starting for Eric Bledsoe, Dodson scored 16 points in 18 minutes, second to DeMarcus Cousins' 21 points, in Kentucky's 85-72 win over Vanderbilt in Rupp Arena.

The same player who missed the point-blank jam on Tuesday went 5-for-10 from the floor, and 4-for-8 from behind the three-point line.

"I loved the way Darnell shot the ball," said Calipari.

Here was another good decision: Giving reserve DeAndre Liggins 25 minutes, as the sophomore scored nine points, grabbed four rebounds and nailed an important three with 12:10 left in the game when Vanderbilt was making a run.

"The big shot was DeAndre's three," said Calipari. "That was a courage shot."

There were several shots of courage for a team that ended up making 12 of 23 three-pointers, a success rate of 52.2 percent.

The previously slumping Patrick Patterson hit three threes. John Wall, fresh off a poor shooting game at South Carolina, hit a couple of triples. Down the stretch, Dodson nailed a pair of threes — one at the 6:32 mark, the other at the four-minute mark — that kept the Commodores at bay.

"What were they, 29 percent in league play going into the game?" asked Kevin Stallings, the Vanderbilt coach.

Indeed, the Cats made just 29.7 percent beyond the arc in their first five SEC games. They were 3-for-12 in Columbia on Tuesday. They were a deceiving 10-for-33 from behind the line in the rout of Arkansas last Saturday. They were 2-for-14 against Georgia.

"When they make the correction, you hope it isn't against you," said Stallings. "Unfortunately, it was."

Calipari didn't expound on why he made the switch to Dodson from Bledsoe. And when the second half began, Bledsoe was back in the starting five, this time in place of Darius Miller, who after a career-high 18-point performance against Arkansas last Saturday has failed to score in the past two games.

PRECEDING: DeMarcus Cousins slapped high fives with fans as he came on the court. LEXINGTON HERALD-LEADER/MARK CORNELISON

BELOW: Kentucky coach John Calipari talked to his team during a technical foul shot. LEXINGTON HERALD-LEADER/MARK CORNELISON

RIGHT: UK's Darnell Dodson hit this three in the first-half. LEXINGTON HERALD-LEADER/DAVID PERRY

BELOW: UK's DeMarcus Cousins, center, smiled in the first-half as he was sent to the free throw line. At left is Daniel Orton and at right is Darius Miller. LEXINGTON HERALD-LEADER/DAVID PERRY

RIGHT: Darius Miller looked to pass out of trouble as Kentucky played Vanderbilt. LEXINGTON HERALD-LEADER/MARK CORNELISON

FOLLOWING LEFT: UK's DeAndre Liggins drove on Vandy's Brad Tinsley in the first-half. LEXINGTON HERALD-LEADER/DAVID PERRY

FOLLOWING RIGHT: Kentucky Coach John Calipari was all over DeMarcus Cousins as he came to the bench with foul trouble. LEXINGTON HERALD-LEADER/MARK CORNELISON

"Darnell always gives us a big lift when he's in the game," said Wall. "The main thing coach tells him is to get better on his defense. Coach told him if he plays defense like he plays offense, he'd never come off the floor."

Liggins was the one who added some defensive bite Saturday. He did a nice job helping on Vandy guard Jermaine Beal, who coming off a 25-point effort at Tennessee, made just six of 14 shots. Plus, Liggins made a couple of shots. "If I have the open shot, I'll shoot the open shot," he said.

In the dribble drive, many of those shots come from the wing. Miller is obviously struggling there. Bledsoe slipped at South Carolina, going just 2-for-7 from the floor. Saturday's benching appeared to help his cause. The freshman contributed 13 points and seven rebounds.

"Whoever wants that time, get in there and play," said Calipari. "Again, today I thought there were five or six shots that we passed on, and then we ended up taking a worse shot as the clock went down. I appreciate their unselfishness, but we've got guys that are capable shooters. You've got to let it go."

It helps when it goes in. ■

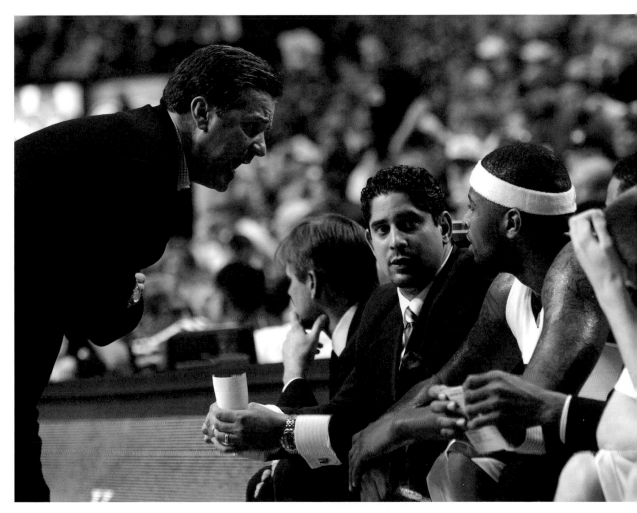

Bledsoe plays hero in Wildcats' drama

Guard beats Vols' zone with clutch threes

JOHN CLAY
HERALD-LEADER SPORTS COLUMNIST

The day started with *College GameDay* and ended with the Bledshow.

Kentucky beat Tennessee 73-62, but after 22,000 screaming UK fans packed Rupp Arena to watch ESPN's studio show Saturday morning, the main attraction Saturday night turned into more of a drama.

Like most good TV dramas, you need some conflict, with a bit of a cliff-hanger, and a crowd pleasing hero.

The conflict: Tennessee's surprise 3-2 zone defense.

The cliff-hanger: Could Kentucky find a zone buster?

The hero: Eric Bledsoe.

John Wall's swift sidekick had made just two of his previous 19 three-point attempts until all of a sudden Bledsoe drained important back-to-back threes to give the host Cats some separation, turning a nervous four-point margin into a 66-56 cushion.

The freshman finished with 16 points, hitting five of nine shots from the floor, including three of six from behind the three-point line.

"Eric just showed so much courage in what he did and how he played," said UK Coach John Calipari.

"Show" being the operative term of the day, starting with ESPN's *College GameDay*, featuring Rece Davis, Hubert Davis, Jay Bilas and Digger Phelps, and a record crowd of crazies filling Rupp just to set another record.

Of course, if Digger is in the house, you know Kentucky is going to win.

Not that this was a no doubter, mind you. Those who thought/hoped the *GameDay* momentum would carry the Cats to an easy vanquishing of the Vols were disappointed. This was no Big Blue blowout.

Give Bruce Pearl the credit for that. The Vols coach, the man in the orange jacket, threw a surprise 3-2 zone at the Cats. "To tell you

---

SPORTS

LEXINGTON HERALD-LEADER » KENTUCKY.COM/SPORTS » SECTION C

SUNDAY, FEBRUARY 14, 2010 ★

LEX. CATHOLIC BOYS KNOCK OFF NO. 1 SCOTT CO. - C7

ST. XAVIER WINS 22ND STRAIGHT SWIM TITLE - C8

Kentucky 73
Tennessee 62

Beyond the box score
Eric Bledsoe: After 2-for-19 slump, hit 3 straight threes
Guards: Wall, Bledsoe had 31 of UK's 43 2nd-half points
Late run: Trailing 52-50, UK went on 20-4 run
BOX SCORE, PAGE C4

KentuckySports.com
■ Go to John Clay's blog to watch post-game interviews.
■ Read Jerry Tipton's blog for updates on UK basketball.

Next game
Kentucky at Mississippi St.
When: 9 p.m. Tuesday (ESPN)
Records: UK 24-1 (9-1 SEC); Mississippi St. 18-7 (6-4)

MICHAEL SOHN | ASSOCIATED PRESS
Tony Benshoof of the United States used his gloves to slow himself at the finish during a luge training run. He was the first to test the course since Friday's fatal crash.

Impact of luger's death felt day after

MEN'S STARTING POINT CHANGED TO LIMIT SPEEDS

By Tom Withers and Tim Reynolds
Associated Press

WHISTLER, British Columbia — Someone had to be first, and it was Tony Benshoof.

Overlooking a labyrinth that claimed the life of one of his competitors a day earlier, Benshoof, the top U.S. medal hope in men's luge, drew a breath of mountain air, secured the visor over his face and dropped down this elevator shaft of ice not knowing what to expect.

He glided to the bottom, slower but safer. And that's all that mattered.

The Olympic sliding track, slightly modified to make it less perilous and more than 5 mph slower for racers, reopened Saturday less than 24 hours after Georgian luger Nodar Kumaritashvili died in a horrifying crash not likely to

See OLYMPICS, C10

Winter Olympics coverage: More stories, Sunday's TV highlights and the medal count. **Page C11**

Cats corner Vols

Bledsoe hits two big three-pointers to bail out Cats

Buy photo reprints at Kentucky.com
MARK CORNELISON | mcornelison@herald-leader.com
Kentucky freshmen John Wall, left, and Eric Bledsoe celebrated a UK run with a jumping chest bump Saturday. Both guards came up big in the second half to send the Cats to a win over No. 12 Tennessee.

FELLOW FRESHMAN WALL LEADS UK WITH 24 POINTS IN WIN OVER UT

By Jerry Tipton
jtipton@herald-leader.com

Eric Bledsoe found the soft spot in Tennessee's surprising zone defense and had his best scoring game in a month as Kentucky beat the Volunteers 73-62 Saturday night.

Bledsoe, who had missed his previous 11 three-point attempts by midway through the first half, led Kentucky to victory with his second-half sharpshooting. Bledsoe's three-pointers from the right and left corners fueled a 20-4 breakout that finally put away 12th-ranked Tennessee.

Bledsoe's 16 points marked the most he's scored since getting 25 at Florida on Jan. 12. He had been 8-for-28 from beyond the arc against Southeastern Conference teams before finding his spot in the corners.

Tennessee's 3-2 zone, which marked a radical departure from the Vols' preferred man-to-man, left the corners open.

"It's not that we weren't guarding Bledsoe," Tennessee Coach Bruce Pearl said. "They'd been reluctant to shoot the corner three. So we were playing off it a little. It's a risk you take. Obviously, he made us pay."

Tennessee's zone helped hand DeMarcus Cousins his first game with less than 10 points since North Carolina on Dec. 5. Having scored 10 or more points in 16 straight games and in all but two games this season, Cousins fell short, in part, because he made only one of eight free throws. He did grab 12 rebounds.

Kentucky improved to 24-1 overall and 9-1 in the South-

See UK, C4

the truth," said Calipari, "we weren't ready for it."

So gears were grinding the first 20 minutes. Tennessee is not a bad defensive team in any defense. Pearl's zone gave Kentucky trouble. UK shot just 35.7 percent the first half, including just 2-for-9 behind the three-point stripe. Halftime score: Kentucky 30, Tennessee 29.

It was nip-and-tuck through the first part of the second

BELOW: Kentucky's DeMarcus Cousins supported his teammates from the bench. Cousins struggled with Tennessee's zone defense. LEXINGTON HERALD-LEADER/MARK CORNELISON

RIGHT: Kentucky's Eric Bledsoe put in a layup after stealing the ball from Tennessee's Bobby Maze. Bledsoe finished with 16 points. LEXINGTON HERALD-LEADER/MARK CORNELISON

half, as well. UT's backup point guard, the 5-foot-9 Melvin Goins, stood tall, sinking threes, scoring on backdoors, keeping the Rupp Arena crowd chewing its nails. The Vols led 52-50 with 10:12 remaining.

As the clock ticked down, Tennessee started to lose its grip a bit. Playing hurt, Wayne Chism did a fade route. Scotty Hopson, playing under the weather, struggled to reach double figures. Goins took a heat check, finally missing shots.

Kentucky seized the (Game)day. In a 20-4 run that turned a 52-50 deficit into a 70-56 lead, the dynamic duo of Bledsoe and Wall accounted for all but two of those points. Bledsoe scored 10. Wall scored eight.

Yet the biggest six came when Bledsoe drained those successive threes that seemed to drain the juice out of the Big Orange.

"Those were big shots," admitted Pearl.

It was pout night for Big Cuz. Frustrated without flow, DeMarcus Cousins could never really rock the rim. "We got too many guys still acting like freshmen, because they are," Calipari said.

But even veteran Patrick Patterson, while more aggressive, ended up with just 10 points and seven rebounds.

It was DeAndre Liggins who provided another big lift with seven points, four rebounds and four assists. And at the under-four-minute TV timeout, Calipari provided the sophomore with an impromptu chest-bump.

"He's as valuable to our team as anybody right now," said Calipari.

And Bledsoe?

"I told him if he wasn't shooting, I'm taking him out," Calipari said.

By game's end, Tennessee was the team taken out.

Kentucky, said Pearl, "is finding ways to win."

Finding heroes. ■

FAR LEFT: Kentucky's DeAndre Liggins helped an official make the offensive foul call after he drew a charge in the second-half Saturday. Liggins had seven points and four assists. LEXINGTON HERALD-LEADER/MARK CORNELISON

LEFT: John Calipari coached Patrick Patterson before Kentucky regained its lead in the second-half. LEXINGTON HERALD-LEADER/PABLO ALCALÁ

Cats in the clutch

'We kind of reached out and grabbed one,' Calipari says
Three players have double-doubles in overtime victory

STARKVILLE, Miss. — Mississippi State showed remarkable fortitude in the face of setback after setback Tuesday night.

That only served as a consolation prize as Kentucky beat the Bulldogs 81-75 in overtime.

With a Humphrey Coliseum record crowd of 10,788 and an ESPN audience watching, State had to shake off its best player, Jarvis Varnado, playing only five minutes after halftime and fouling out.

Already shorthanded, the Bulldogs played without leading scorer Ravern Johnson, who was suspended for what Coach Rick Stansbury called "attitude detrimental to the basketball team."

Yet, State led 67-60 with three minutes to go in regulation. Playing its third game in six days, State wilted.

"Unbelievable effort," Stansbury said. "We had no subs left. Absolutely nothing left in the tank."

Kentucky, which improved to 25-1 overall and 10-1 in the Southeastern Conference, again showed its will to win.

UK Coach John Calipari lamented his team's mistakes down the stretch and said of the Bulldogs, "They should have won the game. We kind of reached out and grabbed one."

LEFT: Coach John Calipari questioned an official's call as Kentucky played Mississippi State. LEXINGTON HERALD LEADER/MARK CORNELISON

RIGHT: John Wall went up high to block the shot of Dee Bost in the second-half. The UK freshman had 18 points, 10 rebounds and eight assists. LEXINGTON HERALD-LEADER/MARK CORNELISON

BELOW: DeMarcus Cousins, who had 19 points and 14 rebounds for Kentucky, went up to block a shot by Barry Stewart. It was one of 12 UK rejections. LEXINGTON HERALD-LEADER/MARK CORNELISON

FOLLOWING: Kentucky's Patrick Patterson pulled down one of his five first-half rebounds. The junior had 19 points and 10 rebounds. LEXINGTON HERALD-LEADER/MARK CORNELISON

Seeking to break a 67-67 tie, State called time with 30.4 seconds left in regulation.

Eric Bledsoe's tight defense left Barry Stewart nothing but a doubleclutched airball from three-point range as UK denied a pick-and-roll, a play that State got great mileage out of all night.

Kentucky scored the first three points of overtime, the final two courtesy of a blocking call on freshman Romero Osby (and not a charge or walk on Patrick Patterson).

The Cats took the lead for good on a John Wall threepoint play in the lane. That put UK ahead 75-72 with 1:31 left.

After Osby missed a threepointer, a late whistle gave Stewart his fifth foul and sent Wall back to the line. Wall made one free throw to put UK ahead 76-72 with 44.6 seconds left.

When asked about the late whistle, Stansbury said, "Oh (shoot)."

A moment later he added, "On the road. On the road. Damn, you don't get those calls."

But Kentucky did.

"Kentucky, that's why they're Kentucky," Stansbury said. "They find ways to be whatever they are."

Dee Bost, who scored a career-high 32 against Auburn last weekend, led State with 22 points. State fell to 18-8 overall and 6-5 in the SEC.

Despite the presence of Varnado, Kentucky dominated the boards. Four of UK's 12 first-half baskets came off second- or third-chance opportunities. The Cats had nearly as many offensive rebounds (11) as Mississippi State had rebounds (14). UK enjoyed a 52-35 rebounding edge.

After Varnado went to the bench for a rest with 8:25 left (his first rest in two games), Wall scored seven straight points to help UK take a 25-20 lead. He finished the half with 11 points.

For the game, Wall was one of three Kentucky players with double-doubles.

The freshman guard nearly finished the game with a triple-double with his 18 points, 10 rebounds and eight assists.

Patterson and DeMarcus Cousins both had 19 points for UK. Cousins added 14 rebounds and Patterson 10 boards.

A drive by Bost, who had nine first-half points, got Mississippi State within 32-29 at halftime.

Inside the first three minutes of the second half, the game seemed to turn decisively Kentucky's way.

Varnado picked up his second, third and fourth fouls in a 33-second span. He fouled defending Cousins on the low post, then twice more trying to prevent a Patterson layup.

"I can't say what I really think, so I'll be politically correct the best I can," Stansbury said when asked about the fouls. "Jarvis has to be more disciplined. (But) the fourth and fifth fouls were nicky-pick fouls. Both of them."

To the bench with 17:43 left went Varnado, the SEC's leading rebounder (12.0 rpg) and the nation's fifth-most prolific rebounder.

Instead of crumbling, State made a charge. Kodi Augustus, who had made only one of eight three-point attempts in the last three games, hit his second of his career-high four to put the Bulldogs ahead 40-38. The lead grew to 42-38 on a Bost fast-break layup, prompting a UK timeout with 16:21 left.

The teams locked into a test of wills, forging four tiesin the next six minutes.

Another put-back, this time by Cousins, put the Cats ahead 53-51 with 10:50 left.

Kentucky's lead was 58-54 when Varnado returned at the television timeout with 7:41 left. He made his presence known by scoring five straight points to help put State ahead 61-58.

Then unbelievably, Varnado reached in against Daniel Orton trying to rebound Stewart's missed three-point shot.

His fifth foul put Varnado on the bench for the final 5:08.

State again proved resilient. When Bost made two free throws with three minutesleft, Kentucky faced its largest deficit of the game, 67-60.

Kentucky showed its own resolve. A three-pointer by DeAndre Liggins (his seventh in the last six games) and a fastbreak layup by Bledsoe broughtthe Cats within 67-65.

After a UK timeout, Patterson tied it with another basket from the right baseline with 39.3 seconds left.

Those were the last points of regulation.

Kentucky's Patrick Patterson pulled down one of his five firsthalf rebounds. The junior had 19 points and 10 rebounds. ■

Febuary 18, 2010

Mississippi State apologizes for fans' behavior after game

Mississippi State Athletics Director Greg Byrne apologized to Kentucky Athletics Director Mitch Barnhart and Coach John Calipari on Wednesday for the behavior of Mississippi State fans who threw water bottles and debris on the floor near the end of UK's 81-75 overtime win Tuesday night.

In his weekly letter on the Mississippi State athletics Web site, Byrne wrote:

"ESPN color analyst Jimmy Dykes said the university received a 'black eye' last night, following our overtime loss to Kentucky. Because of the actions of a few, we embarrassed ourselves on national television and damaged the university's name. … The post-game events, in which some of our fans threw items on the playing floor, were totally unacceptable."

Byrne served as an associate athletics director at UK under Barnhart.

"From my time at Kentucky, I certainly understand the passion the fan base has for college basketball," Byrne said in a phone conversation Wednesday. "It doesn't matter which team comes in here to play, we want to represent the university in a first-class manner."

Byrne said he called Calipari after the game to express his regret over what happened.

Meanwhile, SEC Associate Commissioner Charles Bloom said the league did not plan to take any disciplinary action against the school. ■

— John Clay

Wildcats indebted to Tennessee for wakeup call
Hopson relishes beating his home state

MARK STORY
HERALD-LEADER SPORTS COLUMNIST

KNOXVILLE — Kentucky, you might want to send a fruit basket to Bruce Pearl.

Tennessee beat UK 74-65 Saturday before a raucous 21,124 in Thompson-Boling Arena. In doing so, Pearl and his Volunteers probably did John Calipari a major favor.

Badly outhustled early, UK sleepwalked through the first half of this noon start and found itself down by 19, 54-35, with a little more than 14 minutes left in the game.

Roughly 12 minutes of playing time later, the expected brilliance of John Wall (seven straight points to launch a comeback) and some welcomed toughness from Darius Miller (three huge pressure baskets) helped Kentucky (27-2, 12-2 SEC) tie the score at 65.

"When it went 65-65, I thought we were winning," Calipari said later. "There was no question in my mind, we were winning this game."

From the season's second game at Miami (Ohio) right through UK's stirring late game work in Starkville and Nashville earlier this month, dodging late bullets has been the Cats' M.O.

In a sport whose champion is picked in a wild and- woolly, one-and-done tournament, that's a dangerous pattern with which to get comfortable.

On Saturday, the Rocky Toppers made UK pay.

This time, it was Tennessee (21-7, 9-5) that made the pressure plays, especially Hopkinsville product Scotty Hopson.

The former University Heights Academy star set up Tennessee's go-ahead bucket at 1:34 when he caught DeMarcus Cousins on a defensive switch, drove past him into the lane and threw a nifty pass to J.P. Prince for a layup.

With 38 seconds to go, Hopson delivered the dagger by burying a three-pointer for a 70-65 UT lead.

"It feels great," Hopson said, smiling ear to ear, of being the hero in a defeat of the home-state university he spurned.

While I'm not usually an advocate of "the good loss," I think this one was a lesson Kentucky needed before March Madness.

That was also Calipari's post-game spin.

"Look, I wanted to win the game," the Kentucky coach said. "But this is a great learning experience for our team."

Lesson One: If UK is to attain the lofty aspirations that the Kingdom of the Blue has for it, it cannot afford to slumber into games as it did Saturday.

After Kentucky scored the first four points, Tennessee unleashed a stunning 18-0 run. The Volunteers flat outworked the Cats early on, as evidenced by a 17-7 rebounding advantage at the second TV timeout.

Because UK played a 9 p.m. game Thursday against South Carolina and faced a noon tip Saturday, Calipari skipped the normal

LEFT: Of his team's laid-back attitude against Tennessee, UK Coach John Calipari said afterward, "If you lose, you lose. Where do we eat?". LEXINGTON HERALD-LEADER/MARK CORNELISON

FOLLOWING: UK's John Wall scored between Bobby Maze (3) and Wayne Chism, right, on one of many off-balance drives. Wall scored nine points during a 30-11 second-half run. LEXINGTON HERALD-LEADER/MARK CORNELISON

KENTUCKY
11
KENTUCKY
54
TENNESSEE
20
TENNESSEE
3
TENNESSEE
32

pre-game shoot-around (which he second-guessed afterwards).

But Cousins said the short turnaround time and break from normal pregame routine were no excuse for Kentucky being left in the starter's gate.

"We've played afternoon games before," the UK center said, shaking his head. "We just came out low energy and they came out and hit us in the mouth."

Wall said that Calipari told his team to imagine the consequences of starting an NCAA tournament game as poorly as the Cats did in Knoxville.

"Our season would be over," Wall said. "I think that's getting through to everyone."

Lesson Two: It would be nice if somebody in Kentucky blue could start hitting some outside shots.

Tennessee often had two men, one in front, one behind, on Cousins when the ball came inside.

As a result, Kentucky perimeter shooters had vast expanses of open prairie from which to fire.

Yet UK shot 2-for-22 from three-point range. It is now 27-for-125 in its last seven games from deep.

Said Wall: "I think it's a confidence thing. We hit them in practice. But the key for us down the stretch, (is) making shots when they give it to us."

A trip through UK basketball

history tells us a late season loss is hardly fatal to a deep March run. Kentucky's five most recent Final Four teams and their last non-NCAA tourney defeats: 1998 (Feb. 14); 1997 (March 2); 1996 (March 10); 1993 (Feb. 24); 1984 (Feb. 27).

It could well be that losing on Feb. 27, 2010, means Kentucky is more likely to still be playing basketball during the season's final weekend.

Said Calipari: "This was a great lesson. Losing like this will wake us up. This is not a bad thing. This is a good thing."

On second thought, maybe Bruce Pearl would prefer candy. ■

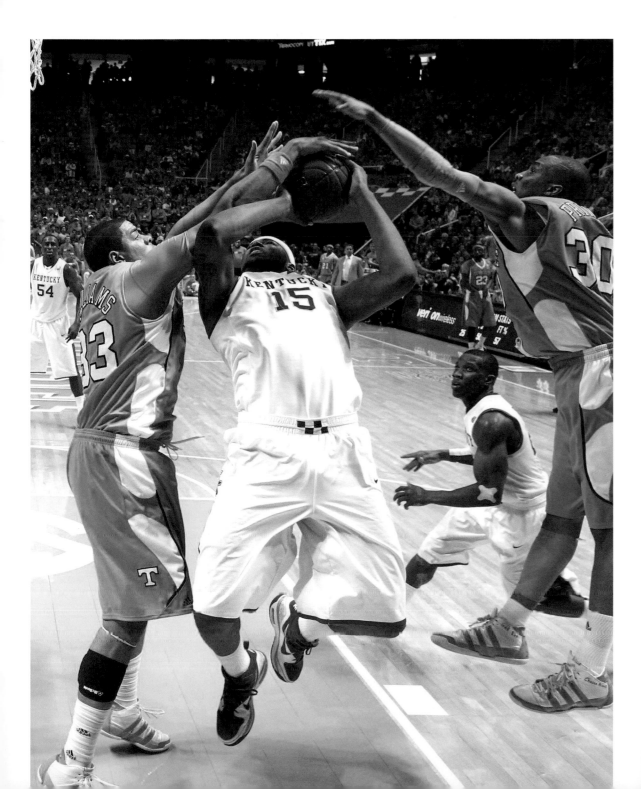

PRECEDING LEFT: Eric Bledsoe passed around Tennessee's Wayne Chism (4) after getting cut off under the basket. LEXINGTON HERALD-LEADER/MARK CORNELISON

PRECEDING RIGHT: Kentucky was down by six when Darius Miller shot an off-target three-pointer with 3:54 left in the game. LEXINGTON HERALD-LEADER/MARK CORNELISON

LEFT: Kentucky's DeMarcus Cousins got hit by Brian Williams, left, and J.P. Prince on his way to the basket as Eric Bledsoe got into position for a loose ball. No foul was called. Cousins had 15 points and 14 rebounds for his 10th double-double in 12 games. LEXINGTON HERALD-LEADER/MARK CORNELISON

BELOW: Kentucky's John Wall yelled at his teammates during a late second-half timeout. LEXINGTON HERALD-LEADER/MARK CORNELISON

115
ALABAMA
44

SEC Tournament

March 12, 2010 Kentucky vs. Alabama » W 73-67

It's Wall Good

With Cats off-kilter, freshman sparks 2nd-half rally

NASHVILLE — Quit obsessing about the shaky three point shooting, Kentucky Coach John Calipari lectured reporters repeatedly this season. UK's fortunes rest with defense and rebounding.

A 73-67 victory over Alabama in the Southeastern Conference Tournament on Friday showed that when the Cats defend and rebound like they shoot three-pointers, it helps to have John Wall.

"John makes the game a whole lot easier," big man DeMarcus Cousins said of his fellow freshman. "When the ball's in his hands, you know something fantastic is going to happen."

Wall's flair for the fantastic fueled a 21-5 second-half breakout that propelled Kentucky into the SEC Tournament semifinals against Tennessee on Saturday. With everyone in Bridgestone Arena surely knowing what was coming, the SEC Player of the Year drove not once, not twice, but three straight times to scores that snuffed what looked like an upset in the making.

"John Wall put his team on his back," said Alabama guard Mikhail Torrance, who had the unenviable task of defending Wall and the SEC's leading scorer, Devan Downey, the last two days. "He's fast. I mean, the hype is real."

A slow start and poor rebounding effort put Kentucky behind for all but two of the game's first 26 minutes. Increasingly, Cousins looked to Wall to come to the rescue.

"I was telling John the whole game: Just take

LEFT: John Wall avoided Alabama's Tony Mitchell and Chris Hines (44) for a shot in the first-half. LEXINGTON HERALD-LEADER/DAVID PERRY

RIGHT: Coach John Calipari talked to his team in a second-half timeout. LEXINGTON HERALD-LEADER/MARK CORNELISON

over," Cousins said. "Nobody can guard him. And that's what he did."

On the third of his three straight driving layups, Wall scored with his left hand while being bumped. When a foul was called, Wall strutted like a gunfighter who had just shot down his rival.

The three-point play put Kentucky ahead 43-42 with 13:51 left. That was the Cats' first lead since 8-7. A moment later, Eric Bledsoe got into the act with a driving layup that made it 45-42, prompting an Alabama timeout.

The multiple drives were no accident. Necessity moved UK's coaches to order more aggressive moves to the basket.

"Attack the basket, and see what else happens," Perry Stevenson said in describing the call to drive. "Taking jump shots, obviously, wasn't working for us."

Kentucky, a 30-game winner for the first time since 2002–03, made only one of 13 three-point shots. Nine came in a first half during which the Cats played into Alabama's hands.

"The game plan was to make them a jump-shooting team," Torrance said.

Wall, who made five of eight free throws in the final minute to seal the victory, led Kentucky with 23 points. Patrick Patterson added 20.

Bledsoe scored 10.

Torrance led Alabama with 20 points. JaMychal Green had 14 and Tony Mitchell 10.

For only the third time against an SEC team, Kentucky trailed at halftime. The two others came at Tennessee in the last game with a noon tip-off and against Georgia in the league opener on Jan. 9.

Alabama led 35-30 at thebreak, in part because of a 26-16 rebounding advantage. Alabama also worked the high-post screen again and again to create scoring opportunities.

"It looks like teams are trying to do that to us all year," Stevenson said. "I guess since Cancun."

Several of Torrance's 11 first-half points came offdrives created by a teammate's screen at the top of the key. "He was going left," Calipari said. "We had worked and said, he's not going to go left. And he went left."

Meanwhile, Darnell Dodson made the Cats' only three, a jumper from the left wing with 1.8 seconds left to set the halftime score.

"Just a horrible first half,"Cousins said. "The effort wasn't there. We just played bad.

"We weren't doing our job. At the beginning of the game, we weren't doing what we're good at. That's rebounding and getting the boards."

Cousins, who was held scoreless in the first half and finished with just two field goals, all but promised a better performance on Saturday. "The next game should be better," he said.

Meanwhile, just in case, Wall will be around.

When someone asked whether one player could stay between Wall and the basket, Cousins said the answer would be no "if two are in front of him."

To which, someone said, how about three defenders?

"Maybe," Cousins said. ■

— Jerry Tipton

LEFT: Self-proclaimed Cal's Gals Kay Burgess, left, Linda Elam, Pat Phipps and Mandy Elam, all of Barbourville, posed for photos outside Bridgestone Arena before UK played Alabama in Nashville. LEXINGTON HERALD-LEADER/MARK CORNELISON

FOLLOWING LEFT: DeMarcus Cousins was called for a foul after he made contact with Mikhail Torrance. LEXINGTON HERALD-LEADER/MARK CORNELISON

FOLLOWING RIGHT: Alabama's Chris Hines (44) lost the ball between UK's Patrick Patterson and Perry Stevenson. LEXINGTON HERALD-LEADER/MARK CORNELISON

ALABAMA
2
15
KENTUCKY
11
VANDERBILT

OLE MISS
54
ALABAMA
44
21
EASTERN
ENCE

March 12, 2010

Semifinally, we get Cats-Vols III

Fans, players want to see deciding game

JOHN CLAY
HERALD-LEADER SPORTS COLUMNIST

NASHVILLE — In this particular tournament at this particular time, Saturday's semifinal is the dream matchup.

Kentucky vs. Tennessee.

"It's the game everyone wanted to see," said Volunteers senior J.P. Prince after Tennessee beat Mississippi 76-65 in Friday's second quarter final.

"Their fans will be en route here," said UT's Scotty Hopson, overlooking the fact that much of the Big Blue Nation packed Bridgestone Arena on Friday for UK's 73-67 win over Alabama. "Our fans will be here.

"I love playing in games like this," said Hopson.

After all, Hopson is fromKentucky, a star for University Heights in Hopkinsville before signing with the Vols. And when Tennessee beat Kentucky 74-65 in Knoxville on Feb. 27, Hopson celebrated by mimicking the"John Wall Dance." Catch any flak from back home for that? "A little bit," said Hopson. "Not much." Then he dropped his headso you couldn't see his shy, and revealing, smile.

It was Kentucky that dropped its head that day in Knoxville, digging a deep hole early, rallying to tie the game at 65-all with two minutes left, only to fail to score the rest of the way. It was sweet revenge for Tennessee, which lost to Kentucky at Rupp before a *College GameDay* crowd on Feb. 13. Now comes the rubber match.

Through the first 23 minutes of Kentucky's quarterfinal game with Alabama — the day's first quarterfinal — it looked as if there might not be a rematch. And then, just like that, it was as if there was an announcement: We now return to your regular- scheduled program.

The Cats scored on 10 consecutive possessions. The first five were drives. Eric Bledsoe started the victory parade to the rim. Then bam-bam-bam, Wall strung together three straight blow-bys for buckets, adding an and-one to the third trip. Next, Bledsoe scored off yet another rocket ride to the rim. By the time Alabama finally managed a stop, a 40-34 deficit had turned into a 55-45 Kentucky lead.

"Pick and roll," said Wall.

The Tide got rolled.

Only here's the thing: When you're Kentucky and you're driving to the basket, the rim is right where it's supposed to be, right there at the center of the backboard.

When you're Kentucky and you're shooting threepointers, that rim seems to be a moving target.

The Cats were 1-of-13 from behind the arc on Friday. That's 7.7 percent. That's the worst a Kentucky team has shot the three since Tubby Smith's 2005–06 clubmade just two of 27 three-pointers for 7.4 percent in a 79-53 loss to Indiana at the old RCA Dome.

Unlike then, Kentucky didn't lose on Friday. And maybe John Calipari is right. Three-point shooting, or the lack of three-point shooting accuracy, won't beat his team come (real) tournament time, even if it has shot 24.3 percent from behind the arc over its last 10 games.

But you also have to wonder if those "gaps" that Wall found in the Alabama defense allowing him to get to thebasket will be there in the next three weeks, when the Cats play better teams.

Say, a Tennessee.

The thing about Saturday's game is that it is not at UK's Rupp Arena or UT's Thompson-Boling Arena, but at a, um, neutral site.

"It's gonna be a packed crowd," said Prince. "I saw a lot of blue in there. I'm excited to play (Saturday)."

"Well, we are in Nashville, Tennessee, and we're going to try to defend our territory," said UT coach Bruce Pearl. "And I understand thatwe've got some wonderful visitors from the north that are probably — they rival Tennessee as the greatest basketball fans in the country."

Wonderful visitors?

"No," said Pearl, "I've got obviously tremendous respect for their program and great admiration."

And the fans got what they wanted. ■

BIG CUZ, HE CAN

Cousins dominates after three so-so games Kentucky advances to SEC title game

NASHVILLE — After three subpar games, DeMarcus Cousins re-emerged as a beast on Saturday.

Meanwhile, Tennessee's best big man, Wayne Chism, got in early foul trouble and spent much of the game standing at the end of his bench smoldering.

That glaring contrast reflected a game that went all Kentucky's way as UK won 74-45, which marked Bruce Pearl's most lopsided loss in five seasons as Tennessee coach. With the victory, Kentucky advanced to the Southeastern Conference Tournament championship game for the first time since 2005.

"Coach has been on me a lot about my energy level and just my effort," said Cousins, who had not reached double digits in points or rebounds the last three games. "I tried to come out with a high energy. It showed today."

His UK teammates seemed to feed off Cousins' 19 points and 15 rebounds. That helped UK reach its goal of setting a tone early. Instead of falling behind 18-4 like they did in Knoxville two weeks ago, the Cats never trailed. Never took a step back, either.

"They out-toughed us," UT big man Brian Williams said. The Vols (25-8) came unglued at times in the face of a relentless Kentucky defense. UK held Tennessee scoreless the final 6:11 of the first half. When UT's one sustained charge reduced the lead to 45-39, UK yielded only one basket in the final 9:27.

"We didn't run our offense," Williams said. "They didn't do nothing to make us not run the offense. We forced things. We got frustrated. We didn't keep our cool."

Cousins, a player whose ability to keep cool has been questioned (four technicals this season), was the big man in control of his emotions and the game this time.

The tone was set in the first three minutes when J.P. Prince drove to the basket. Cousins appeared to be moving as he tried to take a charge. The call was a charge.

Prince saw that call reflecting how the referees inhibited the Vols. "They were

RIGHT: DeMarcus Cousins pinned the shot of Tennessee's Cameron Tatum on the board for one of his two blocks. LEXINGTON HERALD-LEADER/MARK CORNELISON

letting them be a little more physical than we were," he said.

Coincidentally or not, Cousins played freely thereafter. The only time he got sidetracked was when he picked up a technical foul late in this game that oozed ill will. He pounded a balled fist into an open hand and appeared to make threatening remarks to Tennessee's Melvin Goins. But television replays showed that Goins had elbowed Cousins in the groin. The Tennessee player was given a technical foul and a flagrant foul, which resulted in his ejection.

Cousins acknowledged making threatening remarks to Goins. When a reporter suggested he had kept his cool, Cousins said, "Not really. I blurted some things out."

By then, thanks a lot to Cousins and the defensive effort, only thefinal score mattered.

Defensively, the strength being counted upon to propel UK deep into the NCAA Tournament, the Cats held Tennessee to a season-low 19 points in the first half and 45 points for the game. The Vols came into the game averaging 79.5 points.

Cousins led the way with 11 firsthalf points and might have been pushing 20 in the half had he made his free throws. He made only seven of 17 in the game, and that included an air ball."We all have our little bloopers," he said. "I believe I was rushing on my free throws. I'll see if I can work on that." Realizing what he said, Cousins added, "I will work on that."

Cousins, who hadn't scored double-digit points since the game in Knoxville on Feb. 27, enjoyed a bit of good fortune. Twice he picked up loose balls at the basket and dunked. But Cousins also played perhaps his most active game defensively. He tapped the ball away from the fastbreakingPrince in one sequence and later simply ripped the ball away as Scotty Hopson drove to the basket.

It got so bad for Tennessee that the Vols did not see Pearl hold up one finger, signalling to take the last shot in the half. Instead, Goins drove against pressure and threw up a nochance flip shot.

The Vols got within 45-39. Then the game shifted dramatically. Patrick Patterson

LEFT: Official Doug Sirmons moved the Cats off the court after a double technical foul was called on DeMarcus Cousins and Melvin Goins. LEXINGTON HERALD-LEADER/MARK CORNELISON

FOLLOWING: Eric Bledsoe signaled after hitting a long-range three-pointer in the second-half. LEXINGTON HERALD-LEADER/DAVID PERRY

dunked off a John Wall feed, Chism took a quick three-pointer and Eric Bledsoe swished one of his five three-pointers to ease the tension.

Tempers boiled over when a UK foul sent Chism's headband flying. As the referees registered the foul, Chism stood face to face with Wall. Meanwhile, Prince and Daniel Orton exchanged angry looks.

The refs called technicals on Orton and Chism.

As for the basketball, the baskets by Patterson and Bledsoe began a 13-2 run to put the Vols away. ■

— Jerry Tipton

March 13, 2010

No sense defusing it, we refuse to believe it
Vols, rubber match: it's always big deal

NASHVILLE — In the days preceding the march to Music City, John Calipari tried to act like the SEC Tournament didn't matter.

It mattered.

It mattered Saturday because it was Kentucky - Tennessee, a rubber match between border rivals with emotional coaches and trash talking players and dueling passionate fan bases.

It mattered because both teams wanted the same thing.

"We both wanted to win," said Patrick Patterson.

Even the head coach?

"Don't let Coach Cal fool you," said DeMarcus Cousins, smiling.

So because it mattered, Kentucky played as if it mattered greatly, as if its life depended on it, turning in one of the best defensive performances it has mustered in this or many other years, thrashing the trash talking Volunteers 74-45 in the semifinals of the SEC Tournament at Bridgestone Arena.

Yes, the previously off target Cats made eight of 22 three-pointers, and Cousins awoke from his three-game slumber to score 19 points and grab 15 rebounds.

Yes, John Wall was John Wall once again, scoring 14 points and dishing out nine assists.

But it wasn't Kentucky's offensive firepower that burned the Big Orange.

"Defense and rebounding win championships," said Tennessee Coach Bruce Pearl afterward, "and they play the best defense of any team in our league."

Up just 45-39 with 9:27 remaining, Kentucky proceeded to hold the Vols to one field goal the rest of the way. That was a Kenny Hall dunk with 4:39 left after UK had extended its lead to 58-41. That's it. One field goal.

"It was a real struggle to score against them," Pearl said. "It required a tremendous amount of energy to get open and to get good looks. And we just didn't have it."

Kentucky didn't let Tennessee have it.

"If we play defense like we did today and we're making shots, it's going to be tough for any team to beat us," said Wall.

If Kentucky plays like it matters, it's tough for teams to beat the Cats. And despite the fact that this was just a conference tournament semifinal, each team saw two of its players pick up technical fouls.

It got to the breaking point when Tennessee's backup mini-guard Melvin Goins purposely hit the 6-foot-11 Cousins where it really, really hurts.

Goins was ejected for the flagrant foul, of which Cousins said, "I don't know what was going on with that." And why did Cousins retaliate by pounding his fist into his hand and mouthing off?

"I blurted some things out," said Big Cuz.

If it didn't matter, why did the normally mild-mannered Daniel Orton get into it with his own coaches on the bench to the point where he was told to return to the locker room and had to be tracked down by Scott Padgett?

"Everyone just got caught up in the moment," said Orton afterward.

This was an afternoon where, in a supposedly neutral-site arena, whenever the Tennessee band struck up Rocky Top, the Kentucky fandom, which occupied at least 70 percent of the seats, drowned out the song with thunderous chants of "Go Big Blue! Go Big Blue!"

Hearing something like that, in an atmosphere like Saturday's, sometimes can change your priorities.

"For us to play here and finish so we keep that (No. 1) seed is important," said Calipari afterward.

"Here's what's more important: When I see a building full of blue fans, who paid a lot of money for the tickets — $500, $1,000 probably, people that could not afford to pay a $500 or $1,000, they're taking their vacation in Nashville, Tennessee, to watch our team play. Well, then, you kind of feel you owe it to them to give your best shot."

Because it mattered Saturday, Kentucky gave its best shot. ■

RIGHT: John Wall, center, and DeMarcus Cousins cut off Melvin Goins' path to the basket. Goins later was ejected for hitting Cousins in the groin LEXINGTON HERALD-LEADER/MARK CORNELISON

MUSIC CITY MAGIC

Cousins' buzzer-beater helps Cats rally for SEC title

NASHVILLE — Kentucky trailed Mississippi State by five with less than 90 seconds left in the second half. The scent of UK's miracle comeback at Starkville last month hung heavy in Bridgestone Arena.

Could Kentucky rally and beat State again, this time in the Southeastern Conference Tournament finals?

Daniel Orton didn't think so.

"I thought we'd lost," Orton said. "I'm not going to lie to you. I was thinking of moving on, getting back and watching the Selection Show."

Orton was wrong.

In a game strangely — and dramatically — reminiscent of the victory at State, Kentucky rallied to win 75-74 in overtime to claim its 26th SEC Tournament title.

Even with the familiarity of Kentucky's ability in the clutch and State's aching frustration as another game (and an NCAA Tournament bid) started to slip away down the stretch, it was hard, as announcer Al Michaels might say, to believe in miracles again.

"We're not supposed to win," said DeMarcus Cousins, whose putback of an airball at the buzzer sent the game into overtime. "Out of all the wins we've had, this is probably our luckiest one. I mean, we're not supposed to win that game."

Kentucky, which takes a 32-2 record and No. 1 seed into the NCAA Tournament this week, trailed 62-57 with less than 90 seconds left.

After Patrick Patterson's putback reduced the deficit to three with 1:23 left, destiny seemingly took control.

"The Good Lord willing, He didn't want us to win," point guard Dee Bost said. "He's got a plan for everything. That's just how it went."

Jarvis Varnado, a force inside with 18 points, nine rebounds and five blocks, opened the door by missing two free throws with 1:06 left.

With the lead still three, State inbounded the ball with 43.1 seconds left. Darnell Dodson deflected the inbounds pass enough to prevent Barry Stewart from a clean catch. John Wall reached between Stewart's legs, grabbed the bobbled ball and drove the baseline for a layup.

The door opened wider when Dee Bost missed the front end of a one-and-one with 27.4 seconds. When Wall showed he was human and missed a 12-footer in the lane, Stewart's two free throws restored a three-point margin with 8.2 seconds left.

Up three in the final seconds kicked in a favorite water-cooler debate: Do you foul intentionally to prevent a tying three-pointer?

LEXINGTON HERALD-LEADER » KENTUCKY.COM/SPORTS » SECTION C

SPORTS

RACHEL ALEXANDRA'S LOSS DOOMS DUEL WITH ZENYATTA

PLUS ALL THE LATEST FROM THE KENTUCKY DERBY TRAIL - HORSE RACING, PAGE C6

MONDAY, MARCH 15, 2010

SEC TOURNAMENT

Kentucky (OT) 75

Mississippi St. 74

From the box score

Youth! Freshmen Wall, Cousins, Bledsoe scored all 11 UK points in OT
Ball security: UK's nine turnovers were its fewest since Dec. 29
Close call: Sunday's game included 12 ties and 20 lead changes.
BOX SCORE, PAGE C4

Inside

■ Not much practice makes perfect on UK's missed free throw. **C5**
■ Turner, Ohio State rout Tubby, Minnesota for Big Ten title. **C5**

KentuckySports.com

■ Keep tabs on the next crop of Cats at ukrecruiting.bloginky.com.
■ Check out photo galleries from the tournament.

Next game

NCAA Tournament first round
Kentucky vs. E. Tennessee St.
When: Thursday, time TBA
Where: New Orleans **TV:** CBS-27

MUSIC CITY MAGIC

COUSINS' BUZZER-BEATER HELPS CATS RALLY FOR SEC TITLE

By Jerry Tipton
jtipton@herald-leader.com

NASHVILLE — Kentucky trailed Mississippi State by five with less than 90 seconds left in the second half. The scent of UK's miracle comeback at Starkville last month hung heavy in Bridgestone Arena.

Could Kentucky rally and beat State again, this time in the Southeastern Conference Tournament finals?

Daniel Orton didn't think so.

"I thought we'd lost," Orton said. "I'm not going to lie to you. I was thinking of moving on, getting back and watching the Selection Show."

Orton was wrong.

In a game strangely — and dramatically — reminiscent of the victory at State, Kentucky rallied to win 75-74 in overtime to claim its 26th SEC Tournament title.

Even with the familiarity of Kentucky's ability in the clutch and State's aching frustration as another game (and an NCAA Tournament bid) started to slip away down the stretch, it was hard, as announcer Al Michaels might say, to believe in miracles again.

"We're not supposed to win," said DeMarcus Cousins, whose putback of an airball at the buzzer sent the

See UK, C4

SECTION D: A 20-PAGE NCAA TOURNAMENT PREVIEW

COMING TUESDAY: THE SECOND PIECE OF THE LIFE-SIZE DEMARCUS COUSINS PHOTO

DAVID PERRY | dperry@herald-leader.com

Buy photo reprints at **Kentucky.com**

UK's John Wall tackled fellow freshman DeMarcus Cousins before Ramon Harris piled on after Cousins' putback tied the game and

MARK CORNELISON | mcornelison@herald-leader.com

John Wall and his teammates held up the Southeastern Conference Tournament trophy Sunday. Wall had 17 points, nine assists, six rebounds, five steals and one big three-pointer.

Even against a UK team that made only one trey in beating Alabama in Friday's quarterfinals, ranked 10th among 12 SEC teams in three-point accuracy in league play and 133th nationally?

Mississippi State Coach Rick Stansbury answered, yes.

Stewart fouled Eric Bledsoe with 4.6 seconds left. Adding fuel to the debate, it was Stewart's fifth foul, removing one of State's four players with a double-digit scoring average and its best perimeter defender.

Bledsoe made the first, then missed the second on a high-arcing attempt that bounced to the right of the rim. Patterson could not retrieve the rebound, which went toward the right corner. Wall grabbed it, waited for one defender to fly by before launching a three over Bost.

"I hit John on the arm," Bost said. "The ref didn't see it."

LEFT: DeMarcus Cousins put back a missed jumper (by John Wall, not pictured) with .01 on the clock to tie the game 64-64 . LEXINGTON HERALD-LEADER/DAVID PERRY

BELOW: Kentucky super fan Ashley Judd covered her head with a pom-pon during regulation when it looked like Kentucky might lose. LEXINGTON HERALD-LEADER/MARK CORNELISON

FOLLOWING LEFT: John Wall held up three fingers on each hand after he hit a three-pointer in the overtime period. LEXINGTON HERALD-LEADER/MARK CORNELISON

FOLLOWING RIGHT: John Wall and his teammates held up the Southeastern Conference Tournament trophy. LEXINGTON HERALD-LEADER/MARK CORNELISON

But State could not securethe airball. Saying he thought time would expire, Vanardo did not try for the rebound. DeMarcus Cousins got the ball and scored at the buzzer to send the game into overtime.

Asked if he'd foul Bledsoeagain given the outcome, Stansbury said, "Absolutely. We would foul every time in that situation, up three. If you're asking me if I knew they were going to miss the free throw and get it back, would I have done it? No.But, you know, I'll take those chances every time."

After his putback, Cousins retreated downcourt and, surprisingly, saw Wall rushing toward him and embracing him so hard the two UK players slid into the front row of media seating.

"John didn't know, he thought we won," Cousins said. "He almost

killed me. I thought John broke my nose."

Wall only bloodied Cousins'nose. Wall wounded State mortally in overtime. He scored eight of UK's 11 points in the extra period. None were more memorable than an off-balanced three-pointer from the left wing with 27.6 seconds left to put the Cats ahead 74-69.

"It wasn't pretty, but it went in," Orton said of the only three-pointer Wall made. "I was shocked. I couldn't believe he made it."

Given all the big shots andbig plays Wall's made this season, the shot had a replay quality to it. But the fabulous freshman put this clutch victory ahead of earlier dramatic victories over, say, Stanford, Connecticut or, of course, at Mississippi State.

"In those games, we had time to come back," he said. "This one, it was right down to the wire." ■

— Jerry Tipton

March 14, 2010

SEC Championship Wildcats savor their victory

Growing up fast

Freshman-heavy team has hard work ahead

MARK STORY

HERALD-LEADER SPORTS COLUMNIST

One must be able to ace exams to succeed in college. The NCAA Tournament Selection Committee has potentially set up a doozy of a series of final examinations for John Calipari and his kiddie Cats.

For Kentucky to make it back to the Final Four for the first time since 1998, the freshman-heavy Wildcats are facing graduate-school-level tests.

As the No. 1 seed in the East Region, Kentucky should be in scant danger ofbecoming the first top seed ever to lose to a No. 16 when it faces East Tennessee State Thursday in New Orleans.

After that, the exams John Wall, DeMarcus Cousins and Co. must pass to get to Indianapolis figure to be downright grueling.

Big Test No. 1: Texas Talent. When and if Kentucky makes round number two, the foe likely to be waiting is Texas (which will be favored to eliminate Wake Forest in round one).

That's the same Texas that rose to No. 1 in the country in January. The same Texas that was considered to be one part of a Big Three with Kansas and Kentucky when it came to the most physically gifted teams in the country.

Since those heady days, Rick Barnes' Longhorns have stumbled badly, losing nine times since Jan. 17.

Chemistry issues and shaky point guard play have messed with Texas. Still, this is a roster with both size (6-foot-10 behemoth Dexter Pittman) and star power (senior forward Damion James; hotshot freshman Avery Bradley).

For the Longhorns, beating Kentucky would represent a chance to redeem their lost season in one dramatic swoop.

Big Test No. 2: Tempo. If UK wins its first two, it is almost certain Kentucky will face in the round of 16 a team capable of slowing the pace and forcing the fast-dancing Cats to survive a slow waltz.

Whether that opponent is No. 4 seed Wisconsin, No. 5 Temple or No. 12 Cornell almost doesn't matter.

20-PAGE NCAA SECTION

D2: CATS HAVE TOUGH BATTLE IN EAST, HOME TO TEXAS, WEST VIRGINIA, TEMPLE AND NEW MEXICO

D10-11: LOUISVILLE AND MURRAY STATE MATCHUPS D16-19: EACH REGION'S TEAM-BY-TEAM BREAKDOWN

LEXINGTON WWW.KENTUCKY.COM

HERALD-LEADER

MARCH 15, 2010 | MONDAY | METRO FINAL EDITION | $1.00

SEC CHAMPION WILDCATS SAVOR THEIR VICTORY

GROWING UP FAST

MARK CORNELISON | mcornelison@herald-leader.com

Buy photo reprints at Kentucky.com

Patrick Patterson jumped onto his teammates' backs to celebrate as Kentucky defeated Mississippi State in overtime 75-74 in the SEC Tournament championship Sunday in Nashville.

FRESHMAN-HEAVY TEAM HAS HARD WORK AHEAD

One must be able to ace exams to succeed in college. The NCAA Tournament Selection Committee has potentially set up a doozy of a series

becoming the first top seed ever to lose to a No. 16 when it faces East Tennessee State Thursday in New Orleans.

After that, the exams John Wall, DeMarcus Cousins and Co. must pass

FIRST AND SECOND ROUNDS OF THE 2010 NCAA DIVISION I MEN'S BASKETBALL TOURNAMENT.

Where: New Orleans Arena, New Orleans, La.

When: Thursday, March 18 through Saturday, March 20

General public ticket cost: $198 each; limit, 8 per household

Sports, C1: Cats pull out an overtime win that is just short of miraculous.

Online coverage

Watch video and a slide show of

My guess is that it will be Atlantic 10 Tournament champ Temple. Coach Fran Dunphy's Owls are allowing only 56 points a game, have a victory over Villanova, and have a crafty backcourt featuring Ryan Brooks and Juan Fernandez. For a team like Kentucky that is playing two freshman guards, this would not be an easy matchup.

Big Test No. 3: Big East grit. If seeds hold, Kentucky's foe in the region finals would be big, bad Bob Huggins and West Virginia.

To my eye test, the Mountaineers were more deserving of a No. 1 seed than one of the teams (Duke) that got one.

WVU enters the Dance on a wave of momentum after riding a week of clutch shooting by Da'Sean Butler to the Big East Tournament championship.

With the 6-7 Butler joined by 6-9 Devin Ebanks and 6-8 Kevin Jones, WVU has a rugged front line that is among the best in the country.

The Mountaineers (27-6) are about as tested as a team can be. They enter NCAA play with victories over Ohio State, Villanova and Georgetown (two) on their résumé.

Of course, Huggins' record as an NCAA Tournament coach is spotty at best. This, however, may be the best team he's coached since the 2000 Cincinnati team whose season was marred by Kenyon Martin's pre-NCAA tourney broken leg.

Kentucky (32-2) enters its "final exam" off its near-miraculous overtime escape against Mississippi State in the finals of Sunday's SEC Tournament.

Was winning in such a way — sending the game into overtime with a deliberately missed foul shot that led to the game-tying bucket a millisecond before the final horn — a positive sign of tournament toughness?

Or will it leave the youthful Cats with a false sense of security going into the only tournament that actually matters? Time will tell.

If the "tests" turn out as projected and Kentucky passes them all to return to college basketball's final weekend, the Cats will have shown one thing beyond any doubt:

They can do advanced work. ■

TOP: Eric Bledsoe put in two of his 18 points on a drive. Bledsoe later intentionally missed a free throw, paving the way for DeMarcus Cousins' put-back right before the end of regulation. LEXINGTON HERALD-LEADER/MARK CORNELISON

BOTTOM: DeMarcus Cousins pleaded his case to Coach John Calipari as Kentucky played Mississippi State. LEXINGTON HERALD-LEADER/MARK CORNELISON

302
303
304
FOREST
NCAA
33
KENTUCKY
54
ETSU
5
KENTUCKY
NCAA

March 18, 2010 | Kentucky vs. East Tennessee State » W 100-71

Cats leave no doubt in a rout

Bledsoe's eight threes put NCAA foes on notice

NEW ORLEANS — Kentucky mocked all the concern about being too young or too inexperienced or too something for the one-and done pressure of the NCAA Tournament on Thursday.

Looking every bit like the No. 1 seed in the East Region and a national championship contender, UK put a men-against-boys whipping on 16th-seed East Tennessee State 100-71.

Kentucky (33-2) assumed a 10-point lead less than seven minutes into the game, expanded the margin to 30 late in the first half and breezed into Saturday's second-round game against Wake Forest.

East Tennessee State (20-15) hoped to stay close and rattle Kentucky. UK wanted to crush the Bucs' spirit quickly and decisively. "We did a good job of that today," Daniel Orton said.

As the first half ended with Kentucky ahead 54-26, television commentator Will Perdue turned to scouts from Wake Forest sitting behind him and asked, "Get anything out of that?"

Much laughter ensued as Kentucky reached the century mark in points for the 12th time in NCAA Tournament play. That hadn't happened since a 101-

LEFT: Daniel Orton dunked as the University of Kentucky played East Tennessee State in New Orleans Arena. LEXINGTON HERALD-LEADER/CHARLES BERTRAM

RIGHT: Lyndsay Lemon, left, and her mom Melodye Lemon, who live in both Kentucky and Louisiana, cheered UK from a sea of Texas fans.
LEXINGTON HERALD-LEADER/CHARLES BERTRAM

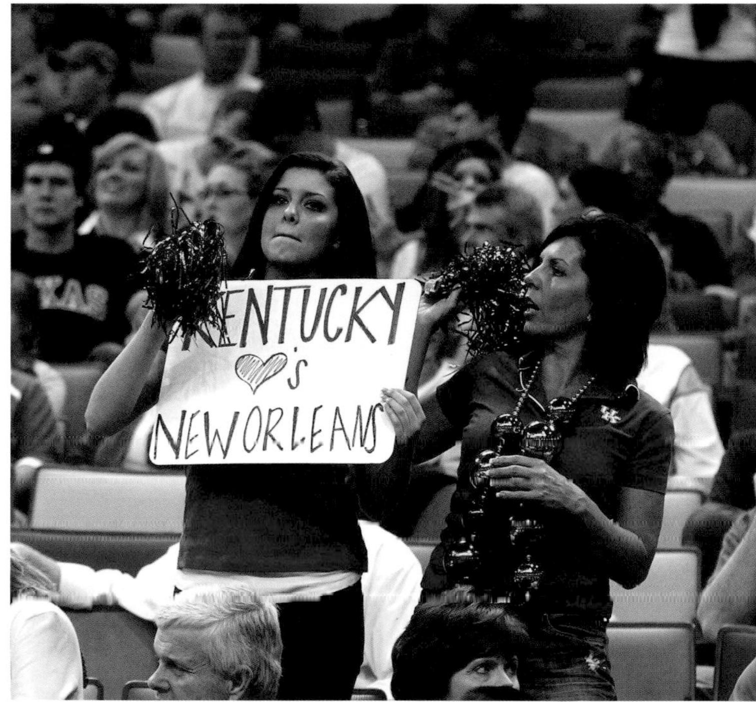

70 victory over Utah en route to the 1996 national championship.

This one was a true laugher. The first half was like a relay race with UK players passing a you-be-the star-for-a-while baton to one another.

Junior forward Patrick Patterson had it first. Making good on his stated intention to make the most of his first NCAA Tournament game, he scored 11 of Kentucky's first 21 points. Patterson's back to-back dunks put the Cats ahead 21-10 early.

When he went to the bench for a rest at the 13:24 mark, Patterson's 11 points marked as many as he'd scored in eight earlier games this season. He finished with 22.

"Pretty much everything I thought I'd be," he said of his belated NCAA Tournament debut. "Definitely a lot of fun."

Then Eric Bledsoe took a turn.

LEFT: Patrick Patterson slammed one of his four dunks that helped power the University of Kentucky to victory.
LEXINGTON HERALD-LEADER/CHARLES BERTRAM

BELOW: Coach John Calipari talked with Patrick Patterson and John Wall.
LEXINGTON HERALD-LEADER/MARK CORNELISON

FOLLOWING: DeMarcus Cousins tried to wish in a Mark Krebs jumper in the final minute. LEXINGTON HERALD-LEADER/MARK CORNELISON

Bledsoe made eight of nine three-point attempts to break Tony Delk's UK record for an NCAA Tournament game. He finished with a career-high 29 points.

Patterson likened Bledsoe's sharpshooting to Jodie Meeks' 54-point game at Tennessee last season.

"Pretty close to Jodie," Patterson said. "I didn't know Eric could shoot like that."

The fourth of Bledsoe's three-pointers, which left him one shy of a career high, put Kentucky ahead 40-16 with 6:32 left in the half. His eight treys equaled the fourth-highest total for a UK player.

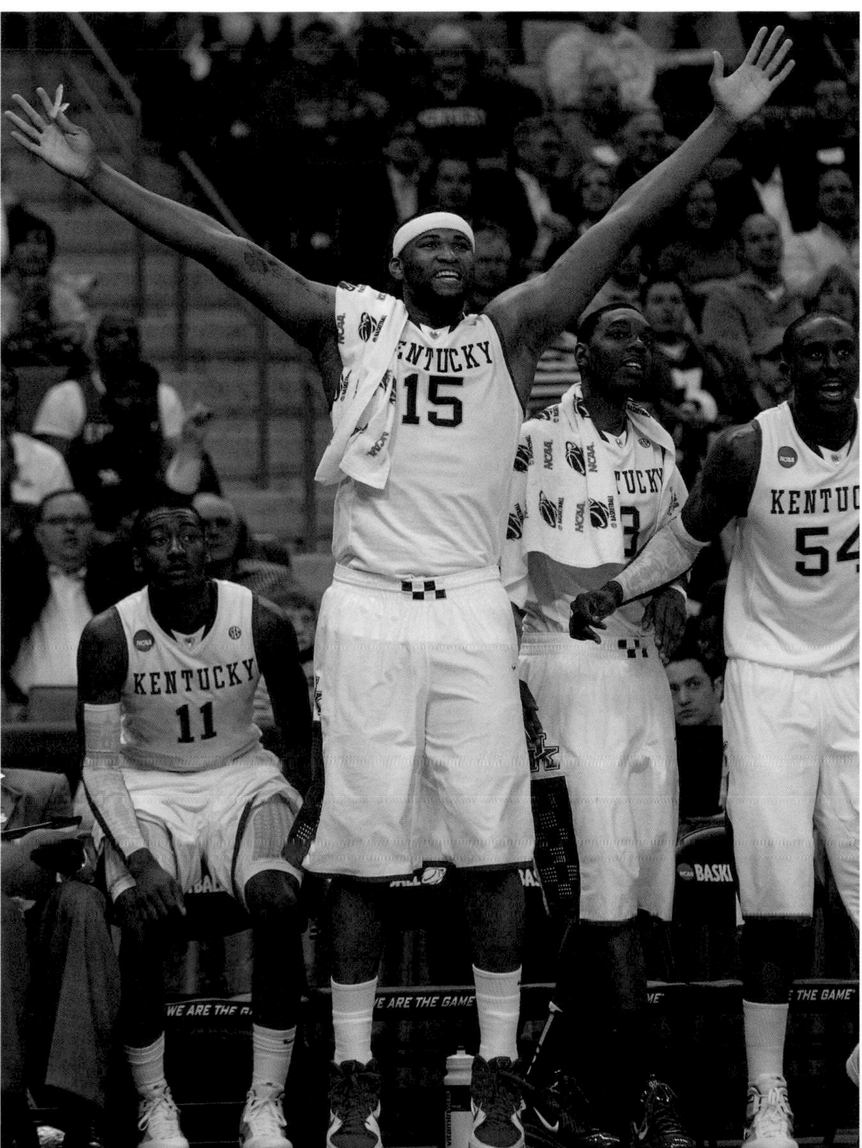

Orton took center stage late in the half. He scored eight points and grabbed seven rebounds in nine minutes. But it was his one assist that seemed most memorable.

Orton dribbled down on the fast break and threw a lob that appeared to be a bit too high. But Patterson leaped high enough to grab it and stuff it through. That marked the third UK dunk in less than a minute.

Ramon Harris punctuated Kentucky 's highest scoring half since putting up 57 in the first half against Arkansas on Jan. 23. Harris, whose last three-pointer came in that Arkansas game, put up a shot that appeared to wedge between the basket and the glass before dropping through. That improbable three put Kentucky ahead 54-24with 1:08 left.

The Cats finished with a season-high 15 three-pointers and breathed life into Coach John Calipari's oft-stated contention that Kentucky rolls when it makes perimeter shots.

When asked what UK could do by shooting like this consistently, DeMarcus Cousins smiled and said, "I believe this tournament would be real easy."

The Cats settled for a 54-26 halftime lead.

John Wall, the hero so often this season, didn't have to make any clutch plays Thursday. He quietly amassed seven assists in 11 first-half minutes. He finished with 11 assists, his highest total since the school-record 16 against Hartford.

Into the second half, the onslaught continued unabated. Bledsoe hit three more treys before the first television timeout.

When Wall hit the first of his three three-pointers, which equaled his career high, the shot gave Kentucky a 72-35 lead with 15:51 left. That was UK's 11th trey. Matching or surpassing the season high — 14 against Hartford — seemed inevitable, as had victory an hour or so earlier.

Wall made UK's 14th three pointer in style. He banked it in from near the top of the key.

After mocking the thought of freshmen freezing on the big stage, Orton added a thought sure to chill future UK opponents in this tournament.

"We all keep a pretty cool head," he said. "It's a pretty average day for us." ■

— Jerry Tipton

March 19, 2010

Bledsoe comes out firing like Delk

Tip from coach Tony leads freshman to 29 points, gives UK a dangerous new dimension

MARK STORY

HERALD-LEADER SPORTS COLUMNIST

NEW ORLEANS — Before his first NCAA Tournament game ever, Eric Bledsoe sought counsel from his own personal Yoda.

Tony Delk, star of Kentucky's 1996 NCAA champions and current UK coach in training, told the freshman from Alabama that the first tourney game is the hardest one.

"Because you don't know what might happen," Bledsoe said. "He said you're always nervous, but you've got to get it out of your system and, after that, it's easy."

If the NCAA Tournament gets any easier for Bledsoe, well, UK will have to immediately hang his jersey in Rupp Arena's rafters.

Here in the Big Easy, the 6-foot-1 freshman came out hotter than a Remoulade Sauce. Bledsoe drained nine of 11 shots, including 8-for-9 three pointers to score a career-high 29 points.

With Bledsoe leading the way, Kentucky looked every bit how a No. 1 seed and aspiring national champion should,blasting No. 16 East Tennessee State by a 100-71 score that wasn't, actually, that close.

One of the knocks on UK entering the Dance, of course, is the erratic nature of its outside shooting.

Bledsoe, in some ways, has been the poster person for that.

In the 14 games that started with the Arkansas contest in Rupp Arena and ended with Alabama in the first game of the Southeastern Conference Tournament, Bledsoe shot a horrid 9-for-46 from three-point range.

Yet, in addition to shooting one of the best deliberately missed free throws in college basketball history, Bledsoe heated up in the final two games in Nashville.

He came into the sparsely filled New Orleans Arena for Thursday night's game having made seven of his prior 12 three-point attempts.

Yet that was nothing compared to the long-range strafing he launched on ETSU.

UK was already up 29-14, when Bledsoe nuked any thoughts that the Cats were going to be challenged or upset as many favorites were on the first day of the 2010 NCAAs.

In a 3:14 stretch, No. 24 drained a trey from the right wing; he made a steal and took it in for a layup; he buried another trey from the right wing; then hit yet another three; and, finally, he cashed in the first of two free throws.

That was a personal 12-0 run for Bledsoe.

From that point forward, there was never any tension involved for

the Kingdom of the Blue.

Just as impressively, Bledsoe came back after halftime and had a 3:13 stretch in which he scored 11 points.

"Coach told me to play defense," Bledsoe said of UK head man John Calipari, "and that when I play defense, it carries over to offense. So that's what I did."Bledsoe's long-range marksmanship was the biggest part of a 15-for-33 effort from beyond the arc by UK. Just what would it mean for Kentucky in its bid foran eighth NCAA title if the outside shots keep falling?

"We're pretty much unbeatable," answered UK big man DeMarcus Cousins.

Kentucky's overall performance certainly harkened back to the late 1990s, the modern golden era of deep NCAA tourney runs. Just as UK did back then to the San Jose States and Riders, the 2010 Cats turned their 1 vs. 16 matchup into an impressive platform of dynamic dunks, monster blocked shots and — thanks to Bledsoe — some dead-eye long-range shooting.

Said Calipari: "East Tennessee State, they hit a buzzsaw. Hopefully, we're this good. I'm not sure if we are, but we'll see if we can keep it going."

As for Bledsoe and his Yoda, maybe Delk settled the freshman down a little too well.

The eight treys Bledsoe drained Thursday night eclipsed the UK record of seven three-pointers in an NCAA Tournament game set in the 1996 national title contest by one Tony Delk.

In the Wildcats locker room after Thursday's beat down, someone asked Bledsoe whether he was going to give his counselor a hard time about that.

"I've already started," Bledsoe said. "Tony who?"

What did Delk have to say in reply?

Said Bledsoe: "He said I should have stopped at seven." ■

PRECEDING: UK freshman guard Eric Bledsoe stole the ball from East Tennessee's Justin Tubbs (3) and Micah Williams in the first round of the NCAA Tournament. LEXINGTON HERALD-LEADER/MARK CORNELISON

RIGHT: Eric Bledsoe put in a three pointer. Bledsoe's eight threes broke Tony Delk's NCAA Tournament UK record.
LEXINGTON HERALD-LEADER/MARK CORNELISON

March 20, 2010

Cousins on jerk alert vs. Wake

McFarland known for irritating opponents

MARK STORY

HERALD-LEADER SPORTS COLUMNIST

NEW ORLEANS — If this were the WWE, Chas Mc-Farland would be the "heel," DeMarcus Cousins the "face."

If it were a Batman movie, the Wake Forest senior center would be the Joker to the UK big man's Caped Crusader.

Because it is the NCAA Tournament, what McFarland represents is the ultimate composure test for Kentucky's sometimes combustible freshman center.

When UK faces off against Wake Forest in Saturday's East Regional second round, the matchup of emotionally volatile centers could be pivotal.

Will Rogers — who famously said he never meta man he didn't like — never encountered Chas (pronounced Chase) McFarland on a basketball court.

In its Feb. 22 edition, *ESPN The Magazine* featured the Wake big man with a headline that asked "why does everyone, no, really, everyone, want to take a swing at Chas McFarland?" Everywhere Wake goes on the road in the Atlantic Coast Conference, fans boo McFarland. Longtime watchers of that conference say McFarland has become part of an unholy trinity of all-time fan villains that includes J.J. Reddick and Tyler Hansbrough.

The latter two, of course, were college superstars for mega-powers Duke and North Carolina, respectively. McFarland has gotten on that list as a role player simply by being annoying.

"Everywhere we go, people yell and scream at me, tell me how bad I suck," McFarland said Friday. "But they don't boo nobodies, so I must be somebody."

In the last three years, three players playing against Wake have been ejected: all three came after incidents that involved McFarland.

"The thing that makes that kid a good player is, he plays with a lot of passion," Wake Forest Coach Dino Gaudio said of McFarland. "At times, it's bad for him because he plays with too much emotion. I tell him, at times he's, like, emotionally intoxicated. Really. It gets the better of him."

A thin, 7-foot 245-pounder not blessed with robust athleticism, McFarland sayshe has to rely on emotion, physicality and guile to have any chance to succeed in major college basketball.

"I play with a chip on my shoulder," he said.

If we polled Wake opponents, they might say McFarland also plays

LEFT: DeMarcus Cousins left the court in apparent pain at the end of the first-half as Kentucky played Wake Forest. LEXINGTON HERALD-LEADER/CHARLES BERTRAM

FOLLOWING: DeMarcus Cousins grabbed one of his eight rebounds over Chas McFarland, left, and Al-Farouq Aminu. LEXINGTON HERALD-LEADER/CHARLES BERTRAM

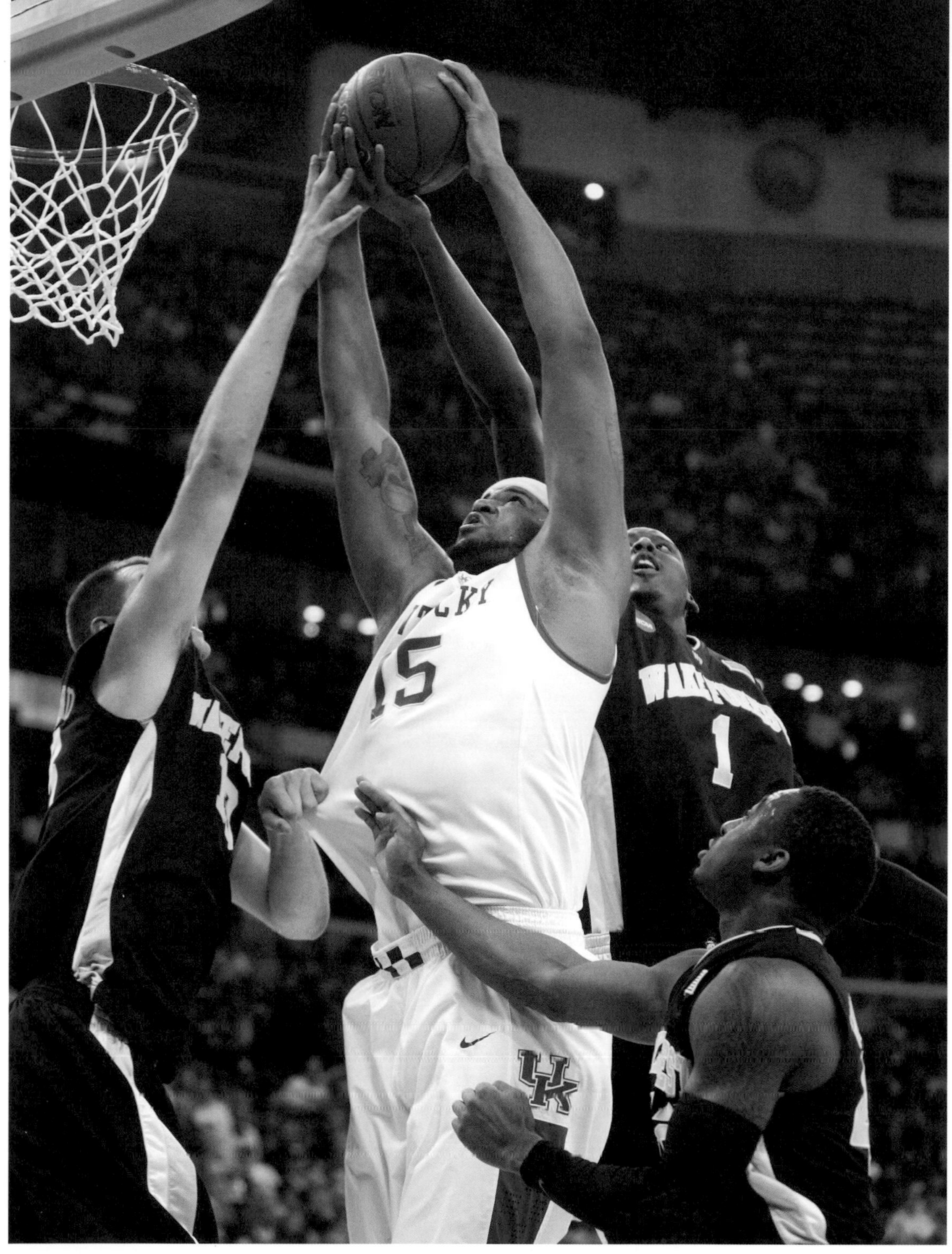

with his elbows up high. With a penchant for getting right up next to foes and yelling in their ears. And with a knack for a well-timed shove in the back.

Wake Forest star Al-Farouq Aminu says McFarland's playing style "got under the skin" of Clemson stand out Trevor Booker earlier this year and bothered Texas big man Dexter Pittman in Wake's Thursday NCAA opener.

"We'll see what happens. Hopefully, Chas can get under (Cousins') skin a little like that," Aminu said.

At 7.3 points and 7.1 rebounds a game, McFarland is a valuable player on merit. Still, it doesn't take the basketball IQ of Magic Johnson to see that if the Demon Deacons big man could get Cousins (20 double-doubles so far this season) to overreact, which team would benefit more.

UK knows this, too.

"We talked about that on the court (Friday) at practice, and we talked about that (Thursday) night after the game," said Patrick Patterson. "We know. If Chas does do that, hopefully DeMarcus will handle it in the right way."

Cousins came out of Alabama high school basketball with the reputation of a hothead. Though he has a team-high five technical fouls so far this season at UK, he's actually handled himself pretty well on the composure front.

With Kentucky's NCAA title hopes at stake Saturday, he faces the ultimate test: Chas McFarland. Is Big Cuz ready for the Big Agitator?

"I knew that question was coming," Cousins said with animation. "I'm just gonna go play basketball. I'm not going to a fistfight, I'm not going to play dirty, I'm just gonna play ball."

If he can stay calm while facing off with college basketball's No. 1 pest, Big Cuz could become known as the Big Cool. ■

Cats win big and easy
UK crushes Wake, rolls on to Sweet 16
2-game combined margin of victory is 59 points

NEW ORLEANS — In the city known as The Big Easy, Kentucky breezed past a second straight opponent and into the NCAA Tournament East Regional semifinals Saturday night.

UK dispatched Wake Forest 90-60 with a scintillating performance that resembled the first-round whipping of East Tennessee State. Pounding ETSU was one thing. But humbling a team from the Atlantic Coast Conference impressed the Cats.

"We just played out of our minds," point guard John Wall said.

"That's the best we played all year."

Foul trouble for Wake Forest's leading scorer and rebounder, Al-Farouq Aminu, helped get the rout started. But Kentucky was clicking with newfound precision and merciless consistency, and advancement to Syracuse this week became a certainty by halftime.

A crowd of 11,966 in the New Orleans Arena watched Kentucky Wake Forest (20-11) was led by Aminu with 16 points.

Kentucky, which had won its four previous games against Wake Forest (two in the NCAA Tournament), led 44-28 at halftime.

Aminu's foul trouble dramatically changed the first half. When he picked up his third foul and went to the bench at the 11:39 mark, the score was tied at 19. Thereafter, Wake Forest struggled to score, and UK enjoyed a 25-9 advantage. Wake made four of 19 shots without Aminu on the floor.

Two of those came on putbacks. The only other player with a double-digit scoring average, point guard Ishmael Smith, made one shot. Well, to be precise, he didn't make a shot. His only field goal came on a Daniel Orton goal tend.

Texas Coach Rick Barnes, whose team lost to Wake Forest in the first round, had called Smith "a one-man fast break." But Kentucky got back in transition, limiting Wake to six fast-break points in the first half.

To Kentucky's benefit, none of Aminu's three fouls inside the first eight minutes came while playing defense. Twice he grabbed DeMarcus Cousins as the UK player attempted to get an offensive rebound. The other foul came on a charge against PatrickPatterson.

Aminu seemed susceptible to foul trouble. He had fouled out of four games earlier this season and had four fouls in nine others.

Miller led the way for Kentucky.

He had made only four of 18 shots in the last four games (two of 12 from threepoint range), but he scored 16 points in the first half Saturday. That equalled his second-highest point total of the season (16 against

PRECEDING: Coach John Calipari questioned an official's call at the New Orleans Arena during the second round of the NCAA Tournament.
LEXINGTON HERALD-LEADER/MARK CORNELISON

LEFT: Eric Bledsoe sliced between L. D. Williams and Al-Farouq Aminu. Bledsoe ended up with 13 points, on 6-for-9 shooting, and five assists.
LEXINGTON HERALD-LEADER/CHARLES BERTRAM

BELOW: Darius Miller scored on a jumper between Al-Farouq Aminu (1) and Chas McFarland (13). LEXINGTON HERALD-LEADER/CHARLES BERTRAM

Hartford) and made his career-high (18 against Arkansas on Jan. 23), well within reach.

Miller made six of seven first-half shots, leaving him one shy of the career-high seven he made against Arkansas.

The former Kentucky Mr. Basketball came out hot. He scored nine of UK's first 12 points.

A post-up basket by Cousins, who had eight first-half points, gave UK the lead for good at 21-19. That started a 10-1 run that gave the Cats control.

The 44-28 halftime score marked the largest deficit Wake Forest

had faced going into the second half this season. With the Demon Deacons ranked 312th nationally in three-point baskets per game, Kentucky seemed a cinch to not just survive, but thrive and advance.

Nothing in the early moments of the second half dispelled that notion.

Wall and Bledsoe swished three-pointers. Miller equalled his career-high with a floater in the lane at the 17:38 mark.

Wake Forest called time with 16:13 left to ponder a 55-32 deficit. ■

— Jerry Tipton

PRECEDING LEFT: Darius Miller reacted to hitting a three-pointer against Wake Forest. LEXINGTON HERALD-LEADER/MARK CORNELISON

PRECEDING RIGHT: Mark Krebs went in for a basket. LEXINGTON HERALD-LEADER/MARK CORNELISON

ABOVE: The UK bench cheered after a DeMarcus Cousins dunk against Wake Forest. LEXINGTON HERALD-LEADER/CHARLES BERTRAM

15
MILLER
1
PATTERSON
54
24
UK

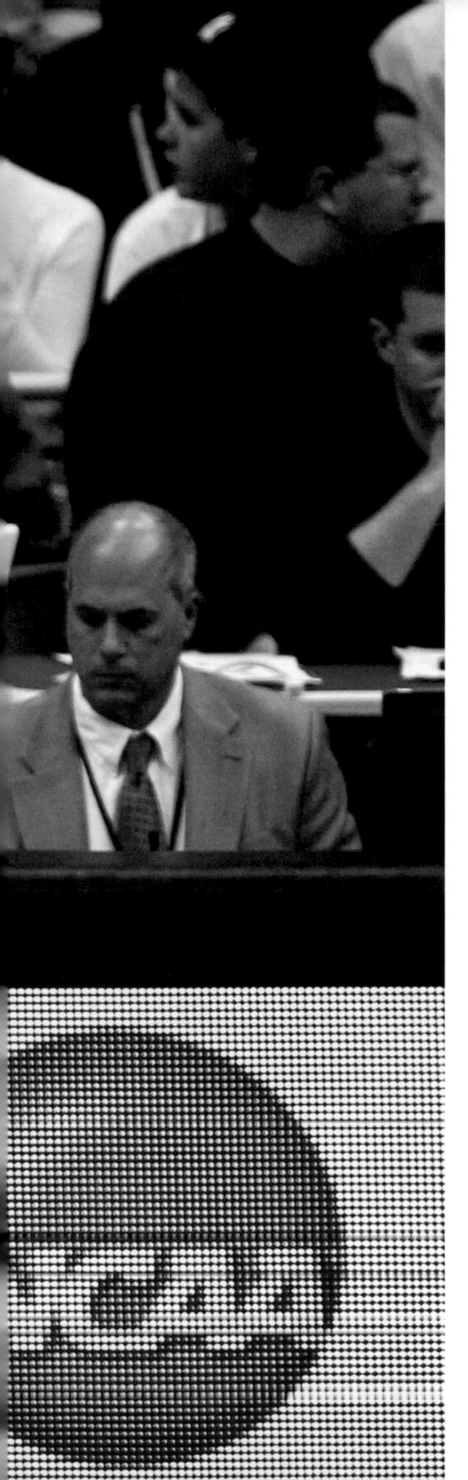

SWEET 16: CORNELL

March 25, 2010 | **Kentucky vs. Cornell » W 62-45**

Tangled up in Blue

UK lets off the gas offensively but smothers Big Red on other end

SYRACUSE, N.Y. — The dominant Kentucky which won last week's battles of New Orleans in memorable fashion did not appear here Thursday night.

In its place was the regular-season Kentucky that alternated brilliant and bumbling play.

"I guess you can say we kind of reverted back to our old ways," DeMarcus Cousins said.

But true to that familiar pattern, Kentucky's defense saved a game that could have slipped away. UK thoroughly throttled Cornell en route to a 62-45 victory that got the Cats to the NCAA Tournament East Region finals. UK will play West Virginia on Saturday.

Kentucky, which won its 35th game to match the program's most victories since the national championship season of 1997–98, held Cornell to season-lows in points and shooting accuracy (33.3 percent).

The Big Red went scoreless for more than seven minutes and, maybe more shockingly, the nation's most-accurate three-point shooters did not make a shot from beyond the arc for 23 minutes.

In that stretch, the Cats built a 16-point lead and seemed headed for a repeat of the breezes past East Tennessee State and Wake Forest last week.

"We played to maintain the lead rather than win," Patrick

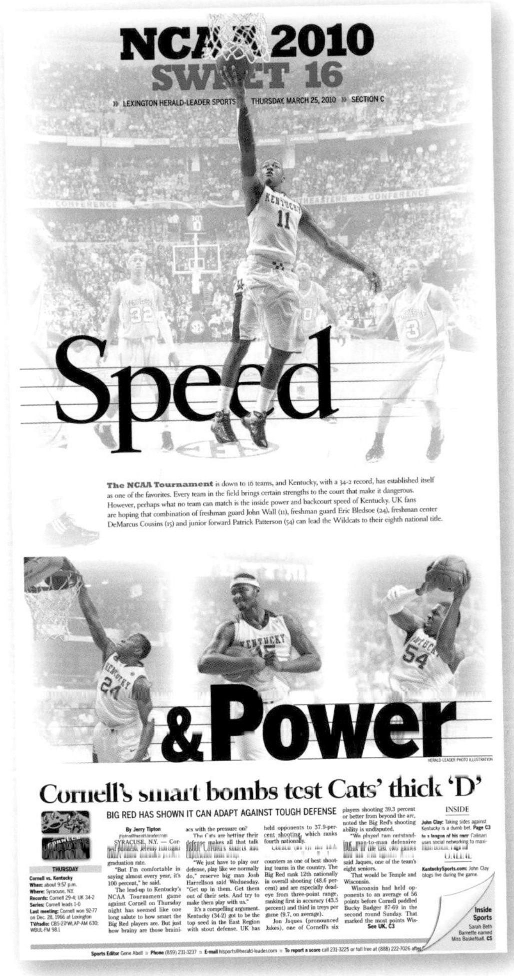

NCAA 2010
SWEET 16

» LEXINGTON HERALD-LEADER SPORTS THURSDAY, MARCH 25, 2010 » SECTION C

Speed & Power

The NCAA Tournament is down to 16 teams, and Kentucky, with a 34-2 record, has established itself as one of the favorites. Every team in the field brings certain strengths to the court that make it dangerous. However, perhaps what no team can match is the inside power and backcourt speed of Kentucky. UK fans are hoping that combination of freshman guard John Wall (11), freshman guard Eric Bledsoe (24), freshman center DeMarcus Cousins (15) and junior forward Patrick Patterson (54) can lead the Wildcats to their eighth national title.

HERALD-LEADER PHOTO ILLUSTRATION

Cornell's smart bombs test Cats' thick 'D'

BIG RED HAS SHOWN IT CAN ADAPT AGAINST TOUGH DEFENSE

By Jerry Tipton

SYRACUSE, N.Y. — Cor- [illegible] graduation rate.

"But I'm comfortable in saying almost every year, it's 100 percent," he said.

The lead-up to Kentucky's NCAA Tournament game against Cornell on Thursday night has seemed like one long salute to how smart the Big Red players are. But just how brainy are those brainiacs with the pressure on?

The Cats are betting their defense makes all that talk [illegible]

"We just have to play our defense, play like we normally do," reserve big man Josh Harrellson said Wednesday. "Get up in them. Get them out of their sets. And try to make them play with us."

It's a compelling argument. Kentucky (34-2) got to be the top seed in the East Region with stout defense. UK has held opponents to 37.9-percent shooting, which ranks fourth nationally.

[illegible] counters as one of best shooting teams in the country. The Big Red rank 12th nationally in overall shooting (48.6 percent) and are especially dead-eye from three-point range, ranking first in accuracy (43.5 percent) and third in treys per game (9.7, on average).

Jon Jaques (pronounced Jakes), one of Cornell's six players shooting 39.3 percent or better from beyond the arc, noted the Big Red's shooting ability is undisputed.

"We played two outstanding man-to-man defensive teams in the last two games [illegible]," said Jaques, one of the team's eight seniors.

That would be Temple and Wisconsin.

Wisconsin had held opponents to an average of 56 points before Cornell paddled Bucky Badger 87-69 in the second round Sunday. That marked the most points Wis-

See UK, C3

THURSDAY
Cornell vs. Kentucky
When: about 9:57 p.m.
Where: Syracuse, N.Y.
Records: Cornell 29-4; UK 34-2
Series: Cornell leads 1-0
Last meeting: Cornell won 92-77 on Dec. 28, 1966 at Lexington
TV/radio: CBS-27/WLAP-AM 630; WBUL-FM 98.1

INSIDE
John Clay: Taking sides against Kentucky is a dumb bet. **Page C3**

ONLINE
KentuckySports.com: John Clay blogs live during the game.

Inside Sports
Sarah Beth Barnette named Miss Basketball. **C5**

Sports Editor Gene Abell » **Phone** (859) 231-3237 » **E-mail** hlsports@herald-leader.com » **To report a score** call 231-3225 or toll free at (888) 222-7026

LEFT: Coach John Calipari talked to the team during a timeout as Kentucky played Cornell. LEXINGTON HERALD-LEADER/CHARLES BERTRAM

Kentucky
62

NCAA 2010
SWEET 16

Cornell
45

» LEXINGTON HERALD-LEADER SPORTS » KENTUCKYSPORTS.COM » FRIDAY, MARCH 26, 2010 » SECTION B ★

Schooled

Kentucky perseveres through sluggish second half and sends the smart kids packing. Page B2

UK freshman John Wall had eight points, eight assists and seven rebounds to help lead the Cats past Cornell and into the Elite Eight.

CHARLES BERTRAM
cbertram@herald-leader.com

BUTLER UPSETS NO. 1 SEED 'CUSE

Ex-Bryan Station standout Shelvin Mack scores 14 and the Bulldogs advance to the Elite Eight for the first time. **Page B4**

CATS SHOW THEIR SMARTS ON 'D'

John Clay says it was the "dumb kids" from UK that played the smarter game against the Ivy Leaguers of Cornell. **Page B2**

COUSINS SPELLS SUCCESS FOR UK

Mark Story says DeMarcus Cousins put his dominance on display when the Cats needed him most Thursday night. **Page B3**

NEXT GAME

Kentucky vs. West Virginia
When: 7 p.m. Saturday
Where: Syracuse, N.Y.
Records: UK 35-2; West Virginia 30-6

Patterson said of a second-half that saw Cornell close within six points of Kentucky.

"We kind of laid back," Daniel Orton said. "We got too comfortable."

Cousins came to the rescue. He delivered five of his team-high 16 points in a two minute span to ease the growing tension.

Besides getting sloppy in the second half, Kentucky made itself vulnerable by not shooting well from the three point line (2-for-16) nor the foul line (six of the first 16).

But the defense was constant. Cornell (29-5) scored a season-low for points, the previous low coming in a 48-45 victory at Princeton. The Big Red got 17 points from point guard Louis Dale. But leading scorer Ryan Wittman struggled in making only three of 10 shots and finished with 10 points.

"That's something we can't simulate in practice," guard Chris Wroblewski said of the length and athleticism that makes Kentucky's defense so good. "It's totally a different breed of team. They got their hands on basically every possession."

In taking a 32-16 halftime lead, the Cats limited Cornell to three baskets in the final 15:14 of the half. None came from the Big Red's offensive calling cards — half-court precision and three-point marksmanship. The baskets were two layups off inboundspasses by center Jeff Foote and a short floater by Dale that Orton goaltended.

Wittman made only one of four shots against a defense spearheaded by Darius Miller.

"Darius did a fantastic job on him," teammate DeAndre Liggins said. When asked if it was the best defense Miller had played this season, Liggins blurted out, "Oh, my God, yes, sir."

That defense completely stifled Cornell, which matched its season average of 12.1 turnovers with a dozen in the first half and finished with 15.

The defense helped Kentucky snuff a fast Cornell start that brought repeated roars from the vast majority of fans rooting for the local Ivy League school to upset the regional's No. 1 seed. Inside the first five minutes, that seemed plausible. Cornellmade four of its first eight shots with a three-pointer by Dale putting UK behind 10-2 with 15:14 left.

"We did a great job landing the first punch," Wroblewski said. "Unfortunately, they're a very talented team."

No one knew that Cornell would get off only 10 more shots the rest of the half.

Kentucky took the lead in telling fashion. Miller stole the ball and fed Liggins for a three-point play that put the Cats ahead 11-10 with 12:29 left. That was part of a 12-0 run that fed a pattern of Cornell turnover — Kentucky fast break that broke it open.

The Cats also sped in transition off Cornell misses. Miller got a dunk after Dale missed. Then UK separated Wittman from the ball, leading to a John Wall dunk.

Those back-to-back plays — part of Kentucky's 13-0 advantage in fast-break points — put the Cats ahead 25-16 and prompted a Cornell timeout with 2:54 left.

The timeout didn't help as Cornell went scoreless the final 4:14.

Cornell's 16 first-half points marked a drastic departure from its earlier NCAA Tournament play. In those two victories last week, the Big Red averaged 81.3 points.

Kentucky began the second half with four turnovers in its first five possessions. Cornell rallied within 40-34.

Then Kentucky got relief — and baskets — from Cousins. ■

— Jerry Tipton

LEFT: Cornell's Geoff Reeves (15) was called for a foul on UK's Patrick Patterson as Reeves and former Kentucky player Mark Coury tried to steal the ball after a Patterson rebound. LEXINGTON HERALD-LEADER/CHARLES BERTRAM

RIGHT: Eric Bledsoe scored on a drive past Cornell's Mark Coury. LEXINGTON HERALD-LEADER/CHARLES BERTRAM

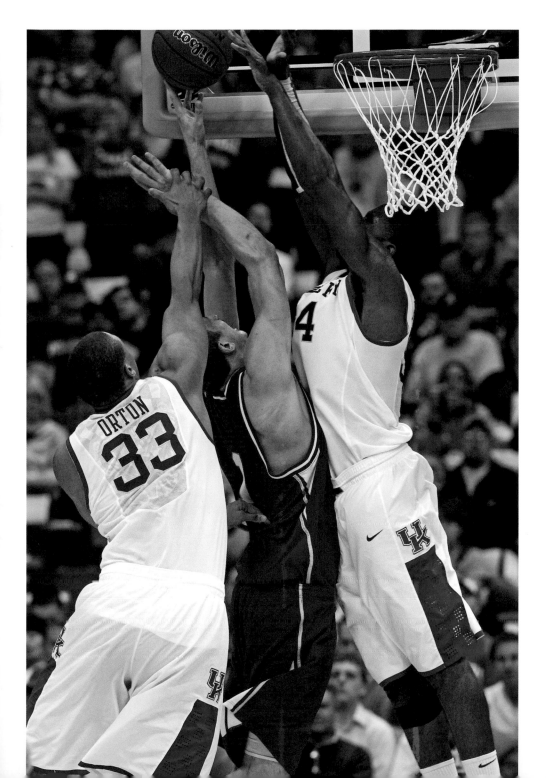

PRECEDING LEFT: Coach John Calipari yelled instructions to his team. LEXINGTON HERALD-LEADER/MARK CORNELISON

PRECEDING RIGHT: Kentucky's DeMarcus Cousins was grabbed by Cornell center Jeff Foote in the second-half. Foote was called for a shooting foul on the play. LEXINGTON HERALD-LEADER/MARK CORNELISON

LEFT: UK's Patrick Patterson, right, and Daniel Orton contested the shot of Cornell center Jeff Foote. "I thought we worked really hard at making it hard for them," UK Coach John Calipari said. LEXINGTON HERALD-LEADER/MARK CORNELISON

BELOW: John Wall, left, and DeAndre Liggins celebrated as Kentucky defeated Cornell. LEXINGTON HERALD-LEADER/MARK CORNELISON

March 26, 2010

Stingy Cats cram for final

UK dusts Big Red, braces for Mountaineers

JOHN CLAY

HERALD-LEADER SPORTS COLUMNIST

SYRACUSE, N.Y. — When it was all said and done, when Kentucky had secured a Saturday date with West Virginia in the East Regional final, one thing stood out.

The "dumb kids" sure play smart defense.

All week this NCAA East Region semifinal had been portrayed as the "smart kids" from Cornell against the "dumb kids" from Kentucky, as UK's DeMarcus Cousins put it. The knock-down shooters for the Big Red against the wildly athletic cruisers for the Big Blue. Kentucky played street ball. Cornell played smart ball.

Turned out, this late-night Thursday matchup turned into a grind-it-out, defensive oriented game, with the Cats claiming a 62-45 win over the Cinderella team from nearby Ithaca.

Success in that style should bode well for Saturday, when Kentucky meets a Bob Huggins — coached West Virginia team that loves nothing more than hand-to-hand combat, this time at 7 p.m. for a trip to the Final Four.

But if Cornell, the nation's leading three-point shooting team, was portrayed as playing brainy basketball, Kentucky was portrayed as the outrageously talented Cats. Most times, that means offense. Lots of scoring. Lots of dunks. Lots of highlights.

Instead, Kentucky showed its chops on the defensive end. Its size and length got to the Ivy League champs. After a confident 10-2 start, Cornell struggled the remainder of the first half, scoring just six more points. By halftime, Kentucky led 32-16.

Cornell turned it over twice in the first half in its win over Wisconsin last weekend. The Big Red turned it over 12 times in the first half against the Cats.

"I thought we worked really hard at making it hard for them," said UK Coach John Calipari afterward.

The Cats lost a bit of their offensive focus the second 20 minutes, but for the most part the D was still there. Cornell had made 58 percent of its shots in its first two NCAA games. It made a chilly 33.3 against the Cats. Cornell led the nation in three-point accuracy at 43.1 percent. It was a mere 5-for-21 for 23.8 percent from beyond the arc against the Cats.

It takes discipline to play that kind of defense. It takes effort, and precision, and yes, smarts. It takes the kind of stuff that doesn't show up on ESPN's Top 10.

"You've got to be a disciplined team to stay the whole shot clock," Calipari said.

"When they were coming off screens and handoffs, we tried to pressure them over," said Darius Miller. "We tried not to give them open looks. We tried to guard the three, and make them take tough twos."

The twos were tough. Ivy League Player of the Year Ryan Wittman scored 24 points in the Big Red's win over Wisconsin on Saturday. During one stretch Thursday night, Wittman went 26 minutes without a point. He ended up making just three of 10 shots, his college career now at an end.

"Sometimes you just have games like that where they don't go down," Wittman said. "(But) I don't think Wisconsin had quite the length on the perimeter that they have."

The smart kids don't look as smart when the ball doesn't go in the hole.

"That was just all talk," said Cousins after scoring 16 points and grabbing seven rebounds.

In the end, the NBA kids beat the MBA kids. Now Saturday they meet the West Virginia kids. Not kids, men. Calipari and Huggins know each other from their C-USA days. It'll be as much wrestling match as reunion. Hillbilly Heaven in upstate New York.

Defense is West Virginia's calling card. Huggins' teams rarely put up big offensive numbers, but they always make it extremely difficult for the opponent to score. That's the way Kentucky played Thursday night. ■

FOLLOWING: Kentucky took the floor against Cornell in the Sweet 16.

LEXINGTON HERALD-LEADER/MARK CORNELISON

SPALDING
CORNELL

KENTUCKY
KENTUCKY
1
KENTUCKY
33

Elite 8: West Virginia

March 27, 2010

Not where they belong

West Virginia sends Cats home one step short of Final Four

SYRACUSE, N.Y. — With its season-long quest for the Final Four one victory away, Kentucky picked a bad time to repeat its penchant to shoot poorly from three-point range and the foul line.

UK Coach John Calipari said more than once that those shortcomings wouldn't cost the Cats. But they certainly didn't help in a 73-66 loss to West Virginia in the NCAA Tournament East Regional finals Saturday.

Kentucky missed its first 20 three-point attempts en route to a 4-for-32 display of futility from beyond the arc. That marked UK's third-worst accuracy of the season.

The Cats also shot their third-worst percentage of the season from the foul line: 55.2. They made only 11 of their first 23 free throws on the way to a 16-for-29 night.

Those points were dearly missed against a veteran West Virginia team that enjoyed one of its best three-point shooting games of the season. The Mountaineers made 10 three-pointers, only the sixth time all season (and the first since Feb. 6) that they made that many in a game.

"The shoe was on the other foot tonight," said Darnell Dodson, who made two of nine attempts from three point

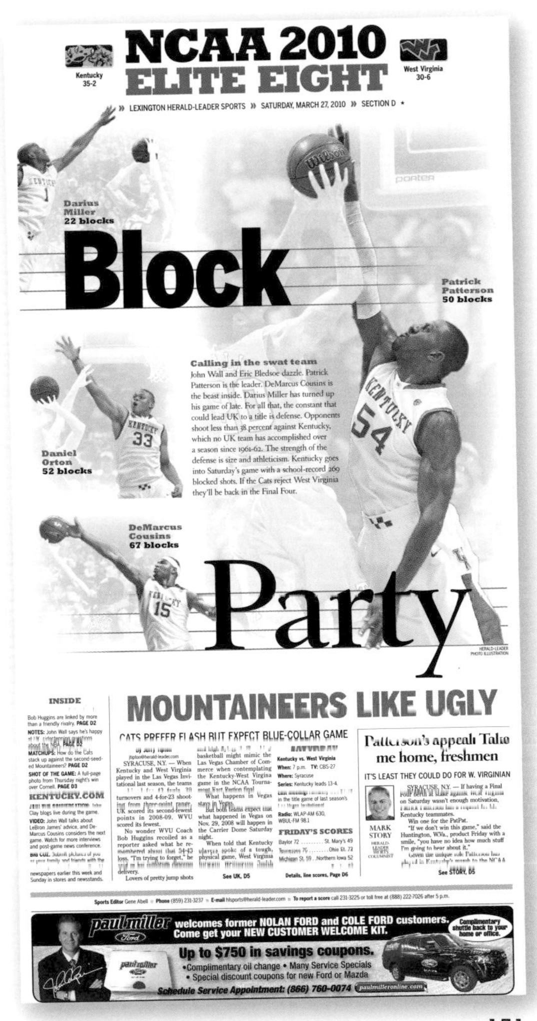

NCAA 2010 ELITE EIGHT

Kentucky 35-2

West Virginia 30-6

» LEXINGTON HERALD-LEADER SPORTS » SATURDAY, MARCH 27, 2010 » SECTION D ★

Block Party

Darius Miller 22 blocks

Patrick Patterson 50 blocks

Daniel Orton 52 blocks

DeMarcus Cousins 67 blocks

Calling in the swat team

John Wall and Eric Bledsoe dazzle. Patrick Patterson is the leader. DeMarcus Cousins is the beast inside. Darius Miller has turned up his game of late. For all that, the constant that could lead UK to a title is defense. Opponents shoot less than 38 percent against Kentucky, which no UK team has accomplished over a season since 1961-62. The strength of the defense is size and athleticism. Kentucky goes into Saturday's game with a school-record 269 blocked shots. If the Cats reject West Virginia they'll be back in the Final Four.

HERALD-LEADER PHOTO ILLUSTRATION

INSIDE

Bob Huggins are linked by more than a friendly rivalry. PAGE D2

NOTES: John Wall says he's happy [illegible] about the NBA. PAGE D2

MATCHUPS: How do the Cats stack up against the second-seeded Mountaineers? PAGE D2

SHOT OF THE GAME: A full-page photo from Thursday night's win over Cornell. PAGE D3

KENTUCKY.COM

[illegible] Clay blogs live during the game.

VIDEO: John Wall talks about LeBron James' advice, and DeMarcus Cousins considers the next game. Watch for more interviews and post-game news conference.

BIG CUE: Submit pictures of you [illegible] newspapers earlier this week and Sunday in stores and newsstands.

MOUNTAINEERS LIKE UGLY

CATS PREFER FLASH BUT EXPECT BLUE-COLLAR GAME

[illegible]

jtipton@herald-leader.com

SYRACUSE, N.Y. — When Kentucky and West Virginia played in the Las Vegas Invitational last season, the teams [illegible] turnovers and 4-for-23 shooting from three-point range. UK scored its second-fewest points in 2008-09. WVU scored its fewest.

No wonder WVU Coach Bob Huggins recoiled as a reporter asked what he remembered about that 54-43 loss. "I'm trying to forget," he [illegible] delivery.

Lovers of pretty jump shots [illegible] basketball might mimic the Las Vegas Chamber of Commerce when contemplating the Kentucky-West Virgina game in the NCAA Tournament East Region final.

What happens in Vegas stays in Vegas.

But both teams expect that what happened in Vegas on Nov. 29, 2008 will happen in the Carrier Dome Saturday night.

When told that Kentucky players spoke of a tough, physical game, West Virginia [illegible]

See UK, D5

SATURDAY

Kentucky vs. West Virginia

When: 7 p.m. TV: CBS-27

Where: Syracuse

Series: Kentucky leads 13-4.

Last meeting: [illegible] in the title game of last season's [illegible]

Radio: WLAP-AM 630, WBUL-FM 98.1

FRIDAY'S SCORES

Baylor 72	St. Mary's 49
Tennessee 76	Ohio St. 73
Michigan St. 59	Northern Iowa 52

Details, line scores, Page D6

Patterson's appeal: Take me home, freshmen

IT'S LEAST THEY COULD DO FOR W. VIRGINIAN

MARK STORY

HERALD-LEADER SPORTS COLUMNIST

SYRACUSE, N.Y. — If having a Final Four berth at stake against West Virginia on Saturday wasn't enough motivation, Patrick Patterson has a request for his Kentucky teammates.

Win one for the PatPat.

"If we don't win this game," said the Huntington, W.Va., product Friday with a smile, "you have no idea how much stuff I'm going to hear about it."

Given the unique role Patterson has played in Kentucky's march to the NCAA

See STORY, D5

Sports Editor Gene Abell » Phone (859) 231-3237 » E-mail hlsports@herald-leader.com » To report a score call 231-3225 or toll free at (888) 222-7026 after 5 p.m.

LEFT: John Calipari walked down the UK bench as his disappointed players watched the final minute of Saturday's loss to West Virginia. "We didn't get our main goal, which was winning the national championship," DeMarcus Cousins said.

LEXINGTON HERALD-LEADER/CHARLES BERTRAM

range.

Kentucky, which extended its school-record Final Four drought to 12 years, finished the season with a 35-3 record. The Cats lost in a regional final for the fourth time since their last Final Four appearance in 1998.

That UK fell so tantalizingly short of its Final Four goal hurt.

"This year definitely hurts the worst," junior Patrick Patterson said of the three season-ending losses he's experienced at UK. "We had the opportunity. We had all the pieces to do it. And we fell short against a team that played harder."

In a fitting punctuation to the season, freshmen led UK in this last game. John Wall scored 19 points. DeMarcus Cousins added 15. Patterson scored eight points in what might have been his final game for Kentucky. His 13 rebounds led UK's 51-36 dominationof the boards.

West Virginia improved to 31-6. The Mountaineers advanced to the Final Four for the first time since Jerry West led them there in 1959.

Da'Sean Butler led West Virginia with 18 points. Point guard Joe Mazzulla, pressed into the starting role when Darryl Bryant broke his foot earlier in the week, contributed17 points and a heady floor game. Kevin Jones added 13 points and Devin Ebanks had 12.

Kentucky trailed at halftime 28-26, the first deficit at intermission since facing Mississippi State in the SEC Tournament championship game two weeks earlier.

Why did UK trail in a half it led for more than 12 minutes, and by as much as seven points? To every headline writer's delight, you could say the Butler did it.

Butler hit four three-pointers to lead a WVU rally. After going scoreless for the game's first 13 minutes, he erupted for 15 points in barely more than five minutes.

That rapid-fire production erased Kentucky's 16-9 lead and put West Virginia ahead 25-20.

Butler, who injured his right (shooting) hand in Thursday's victory over Washington, missed his first five shots. He really didn't come close to scoring.

Then after the TV timeout at the 7:16 mark, Butler made up for lost time. On WVU's first possession, he hit his first three-pointer to reduce Kentucky's lead to 16-12. WVU Coach Bob Huggins casually swigged water from a jug as if knowing all was well.

Butler, who scored all 15 of his first-half points in less than six minutes, followed with three more treys. On the third, he hit from the top of the key while being fouled by Wall. The four-point play putthe Mountaineers ahead 25-20 with 2:50 to go.

Butler completed his first-half scoring by making two technical free throws. DeAndre Liggins got a technical foul with 1:37 left for apparently cursing.

Until Butler got going, West Virginia seemed determined to shoot

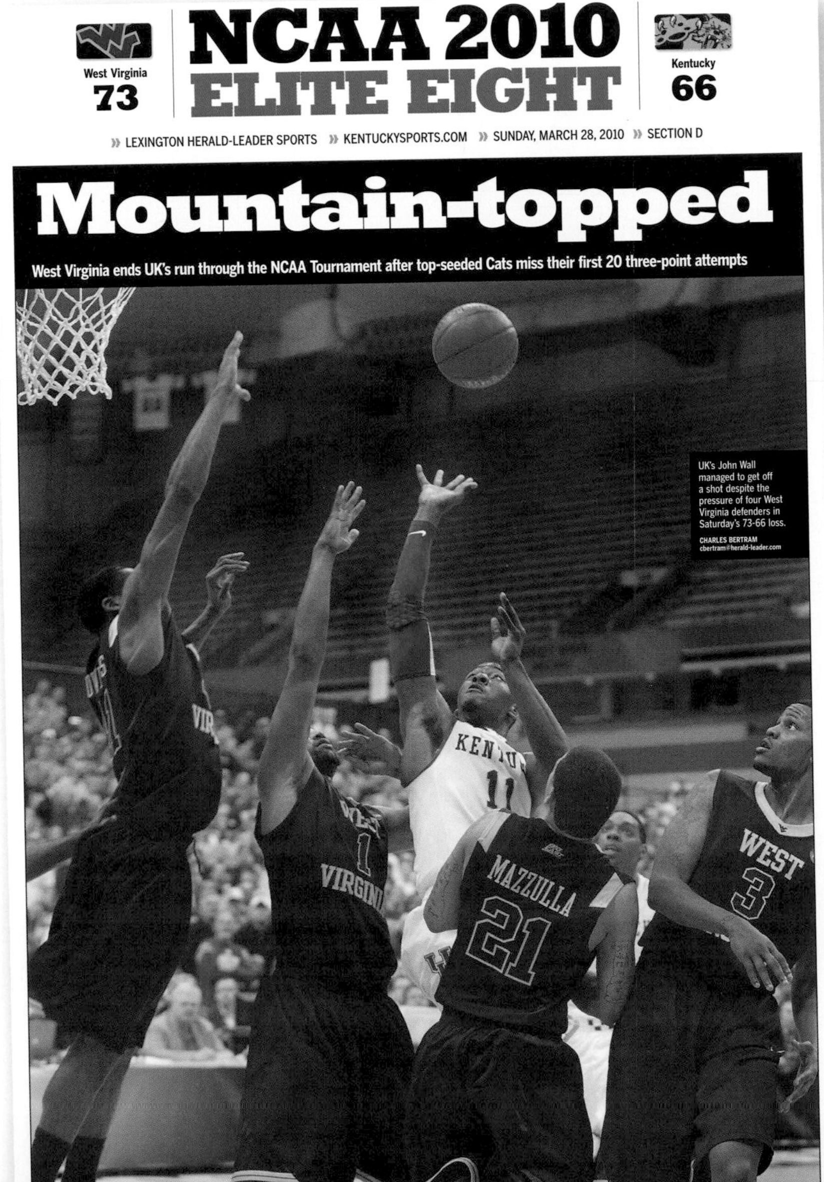

West Virginia 73

NCAA 2010 ELITE EIGHT

Kentucky 66

» LEXINGTON HERALD-LEADER SPORTS » KENTUCKYSPORTS.COM » SUNDAY, MARCH 28, 2010 » SECTION D

Mountain-topped

West Virginia ends UK's run through the NCAA Tournament after top-seeded Cats miss their first 20 three-point attempts

UK's John Wall managed to get off a shot despite the pressure of four West Virginia defenders in Saturday's 73-66 loss.

CHARLES BERTRAM
cbertram@herald-leader.com

itself out of the game from long range. The Mountaineers came into the game ranked 198th in three-point accuracy. WVU's eight first-half threes surpassed their season average of 6.8.

The Cats hurt themselves by missing all eight three-point attempts and turning over the ball 10 times.

"It definitely drains your confidence a little bit," Dodson said of the threepoint misses. "We were missing every type of way." ■

— Jerry Tipton

March 27, 2010 — Kentucky vs. West Virginia » L 73-66

Fun while it lasted

Biggest game of the year wrong time for UK's weaknesses to rear up

JOHN CLAY
HERALD-LEADER SPORTS COLUMNIST

SYRACUSE, N.Y. — In the end, Kentucky picked the biggest game of the year to play its worst game of the year.

In the end, Kentucky's wondrous freshmen, who had been so mature, so poised, played so young.

In the end, a great and wondrous season that had taken the Wildcats so far, came up short.

What was it that Bob Huggins said Friday about you had to be lucky to make the Final Four?

This Kentucky team may not have had many weaknesses, but in the East Regional finals, Kentucky was unlucky enough to have all of them laid bare in a 73-66 loss to West Virginia.

Inconsistent three-point shooting: Kentucky missed its first 20 three-point attempts and ended up 4-for-32 from beyond the arc.

"It gets a little demoralizing when you miss the shots that we missed," said UK Coach John Calipari afterward.

Spotty foul shooting: The Cats made just 16 of 29 from the foul line for 55.2 percent. "We kept missing free throws," said Calipari. "Oh my goodness."

The task of trying to win it all starting three freshmen: Huggins' older, more experienced Mountaineers got into the heads of the Cats, employing a tricky 1-3-1 zone on defense and knocking down big shots on offense.

"They outplayed us," said Calipari, "but I think there were times when our inexperience hurt us."

But then Calipari said this: "It also got us where we are today."

He's right about that. A year ago, Kentucky was losing to Notre Dame in the quarter finals of the NIT. There was no John Wall, no DeMarcus Cousins, no Eric Bledsoe, no Daniel Orton. There was a different coach.

LEXINGTON HERALD-LEADER WWW.KENTUCKY.COM

$153 of coupons inside

MARCH 28, 2010 | SUNDAY | METRO FINAL EDITION $2.00

NCAA ELITE EIGHT: EIGHT-PAGE SPECIAL SECTION INSIDE

Game Story, D2: Cats picked a bad time to start shooting poorly, missing their first 20 three-point shots.

Mark Story, D5: UK's freshman guards played like freshman guards, especially against West Virginia's 1-3-1 zone.

Game notes, D6: It was Dick Enberg's last NCAA tournament game, and he started calling them in 1961.

FUN WHILE IT LASTED

Kentucky Coach John Calipari held his head as his team's journey to the Final Four hit a dead end Saturday in Syracuse, N.Y.

BIGGEST GAME OF THE YEAR WRONG TIME FOR UK'S WEAKNESSES TO REAR UP

BY JOHN CLAY
JCLAY@HERALD-LEADER.COM

SYRACUSE, N.Y. — In the end, Kentucky picked the biggest game of the year to play its worst game of the year.

In the end, Kentucky's wondrous freshmen, who had been so mature, so poised, played so young.

In the end, a great and wondrous season that had taken the Wildcats so far, came up short.

What was it that Bob Huggins said Friday about you had to be lucky to make the Final Four?

This Kentucky team may not have had many weaknesses, but in the East Regional finals, Kentucky was unlucky enough to have all of them laid bare in a 73-66 loss to West Virginia.

■ Inconsistent three-point shooting: Kentucky missed its first 20 three-point attempts and ended up 4-for-32 from beyond the arc.

"It gets a little demoralizing when you miss the shots that we missed," said UK Coach John Calipari afterward.

■ [illegible] Cats made just 16 of 29 from the foul line for 55.2 percent.

See CLAY, A11

Butler did it

Shelvin Mack, a Bryan Station graduate, celebrated after his Butler team beat Kansas State 63-56 Saturday to advance to the NCAA Final Four. The Bulldogs won't have to travel far; the Final Four will be in Indianapolis, across town from the school. **Sports, C1.**

PAUL SAKUMA | ASSOCIATED PRESS

PHOTOS BY MARK CORNELISON

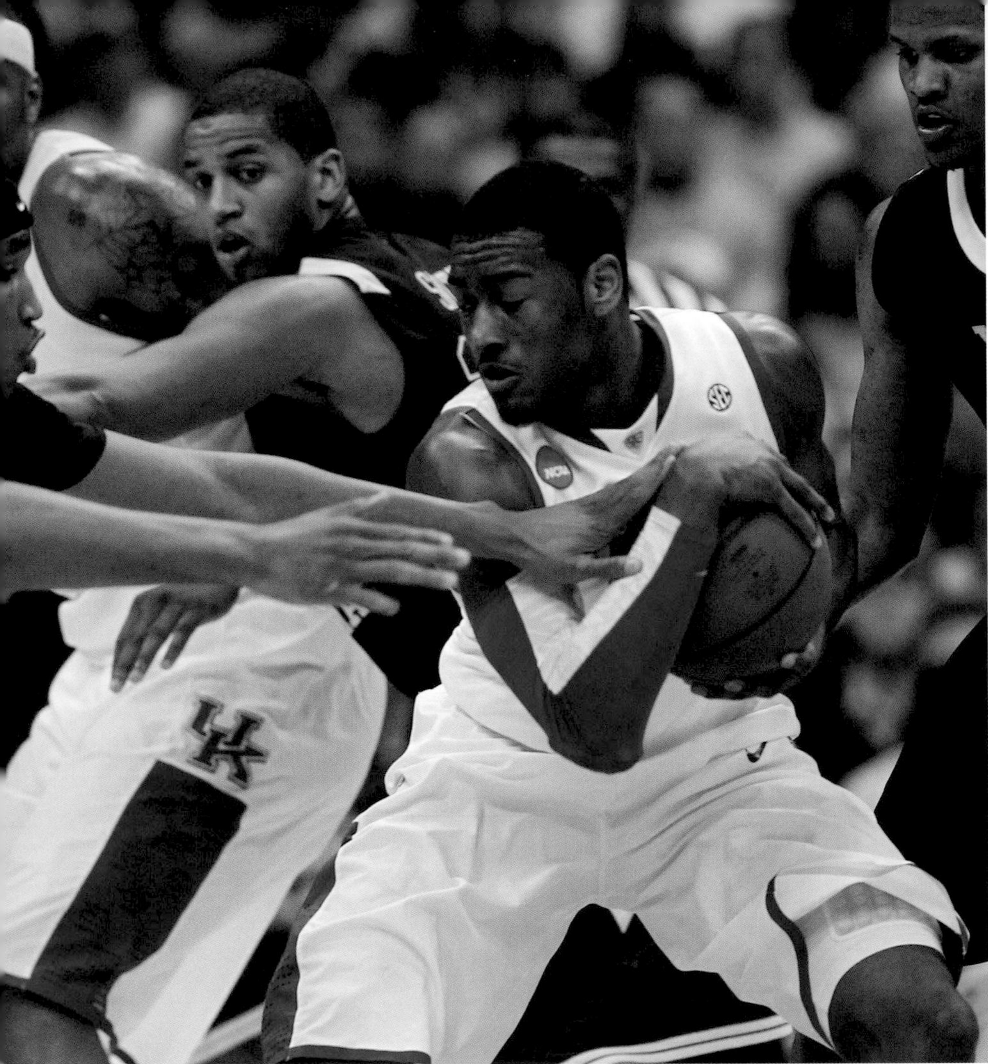

ABOVE: John Wall secured the ball in traffic as Kentucky played West Virginia. LEXINGTON HERALD-LEADER/MARK CORNELISON

RIGHT: DeMarcus Cousins muscled in a basket. LEXINGTON HERALD-LEADER/MARK CORNELISON

FOLLOWING LEFT: Coach John Calipari and assistant coach Orlando Antigua yelled at their players in the second-half. LEXINGTON HERALD-LEADER/CHARLES BERTRAM

FOLLOWING RIGHT: Eric Bledsoe sat in the locker room after UK was defeated by West Virginia in the Carrier Dome. LEXINGTON HERALD-LEADER/CHARLES BERTRAM

All that was magically swept away nearly the day Calipari took the job. He sold the program. He mended the fences. He brought in unbelievable talent. He won an SEC regular-season title, an SEC Tournament title. He attained a No. 1 ranking and a No. 1 seed. He took the program back to that seat at the head table.

Then, in the biggest game of the year, he ran up against a savvy old friend with an air tight plan.

Give Huggins credit. His 1-3-1 zone defense bothered the Cats. It

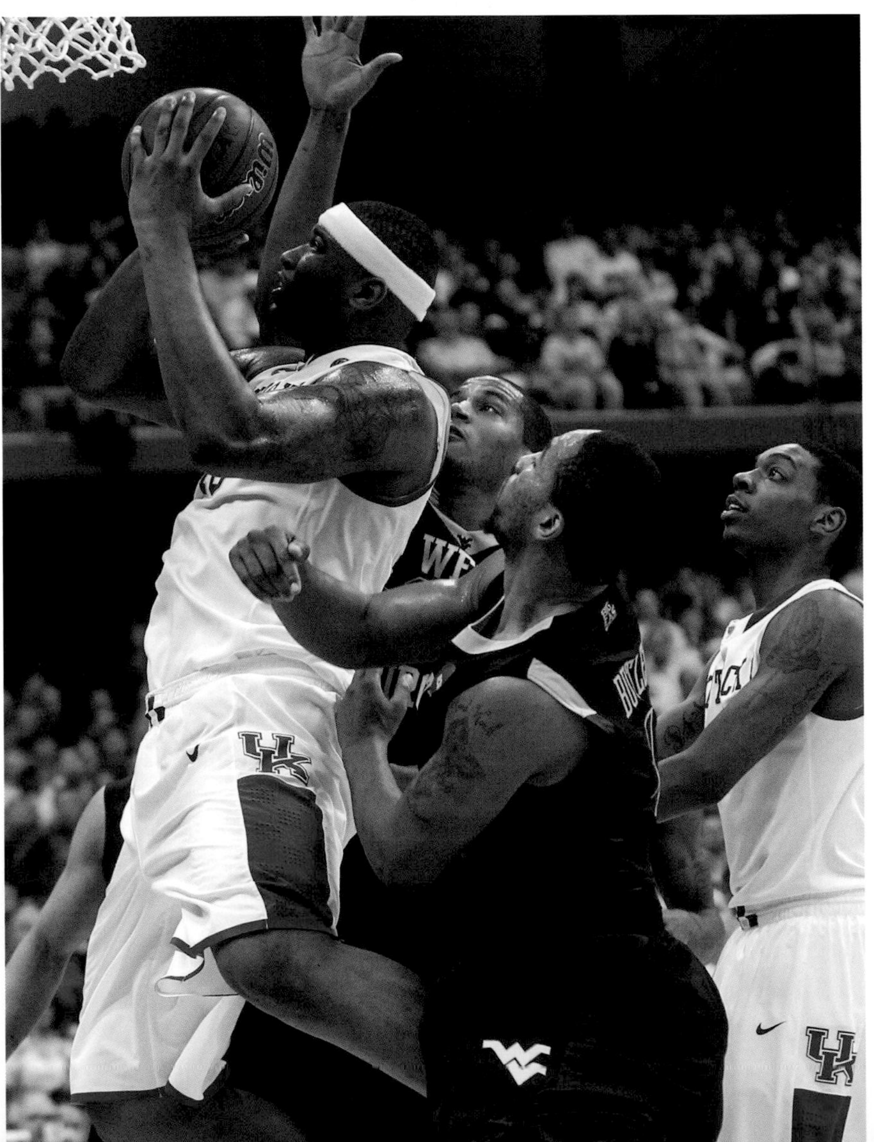

cut off penetration. It forced the Cats to settle for three-pointers. Kentucky settled. And missed. And missed. Kentucky missed its first 20 three-point attempts, before DeAndre Liggins hit a triple with 3:28 left.

You knew West Virginia would play well defensively. Huggins' teams always play well defensively. What you didn't know is that Huggins' team would make shots. While Kentucky was throwing up bricks, WVU was finding nothing but net. The Mountaineers made 10 of 23 three-pointers.

Point guard Joe Mazzulla, pressed into action when starting point guard Darryl Bryant broke his foot earlier in the week, averaged 2.2 points on the season. Saturday, he scored 17.

"He hit some layups that were backbreakers," said Calipari.

There will be those who say this was a back breaking loss. Kentucky basketball has high standards. And this was the program's fourth straight Elite Eight loss. Calipari's team extended the string that started in 1999 with Tubby Smith and continued twice more. Kentucky still hasn't been to a Final Four since 1998, the longest gap in the program's storied history since Adolph Rupp reached his first Final Four in 1942.

If the game was a nearepic failure, however, the season was a near-epic success. In the moment, though, that was of little solace to the team on the losing end at the Carrier Dome.

With 51.3 seconds left,not long before the West Virginia band struck up Country Roads, John Wall fouled out. He walked off the floor rolling up the front of his Kentucky jersey, probably the last time he'll wear that jersey in a college game.

"I didn't want it to stop here," Wall said afterward. "I wanted to make it all the way."

In the end, Kentucky picked a bad day to have its worst day. ■

March 29, 2010

Encore will be a chore for Calipari

First-year Kentucky coach now must re-stock talented roster

JOHN CLAY
HERALD-LEADER SPORTS COLUMNIST

John Calipari proved he's pretty good at square one. Now, looks like he's going to have to prove it all over again. Nearly one year ago, Calipari was Kentucky's new basketball coach, inheriting a proud but battered program that was fresh off a two-year Billy Gillispie bruise, with a fractured fan base and a questionable roster. Calipari more than rallied the base. He schmoozed the boosters. He soothed the sponsors. He wowed the fans. He twittered to over a million followers. Best of all, most of all, he lowered the fish nets and caught some outrageously talented players.

So outrageously talented that, even after Kentucky's 73-66 loss to West Virginia in the NCAA East Region finals, looks like Calipari is going to have to reprise his role.

John Wall is gone. The fab freshman point guard looks like he's the best bet to be the No. 1 pick in the next NBA Draft. Wall said Saturday night he wasn't thinking about his future plans. But there are plenty of others thinking about his future plans, and they can't imagine one in which he'll return to the UK campus. Patrick Patterson is gone. There's a reason the junior forward from Huntington, W.Va., earned his degree in three years. There's a reason Patterson chose to participate in Senior Night activities earlier this month. Given his three years here, no one can begrudge Patterson's inkling that now is the time to move on.

DeMarcus Cousins is gone. Oh, West Virginia proved there can always be surprises. Big Cuz still has some rungs to climb on the maturity ladder. But NBA types no doubt drool over what a man with Cousins' size and athletic ability around the rim could do at the next level. Those types write checks.

Eric Bledsoe is thinking of going, though his sub-par Saturday night performance in Syracuse might give him something to think about in that regard. Even Daniel Orton, who didn't start a game, has said he's considering trading in his college career for a shot at the play-for-pay.

Those are four of Kentucky's five starters, and five of the top six players in Calipari's regular rotation. Only junior-to-be Darius Miller appears to be a sure bet to be wearing whatever uniform Nike has the Cats adorn next season.

Not to fear, of course. Calipari gets players. That's his strength, his calling card. He's a master recruiter/motivator, who has a knack for getting the best players — Derrick Rose to Tyreke Evans to John Wall — to sign on the bottom line.

Yet, given the success produced by his latest collection of talent, even Calipari might have trouble following in his own footsteps.

Brandon Knight, the Florida point guard who many think will end up in Lexington, is a dazzling point guard. But is Knight as good as a Wall?

Terrence Jones is considered a blue-chip big-man prospect, though the Washington native has yet to profess his college choice.It's hard to believe, however, that Jones is as good

BELOW: DeMarcus Cousins greeted fans, waiting at Wildcat Lodge, after returning home from the NCAA East Regional final. JONATHAN PALMER

FOLLOWING: Fans congregated outside the TacAir tarmac at Blue Grass Airport awaiting the UK team plane. JONATHAN PALMER

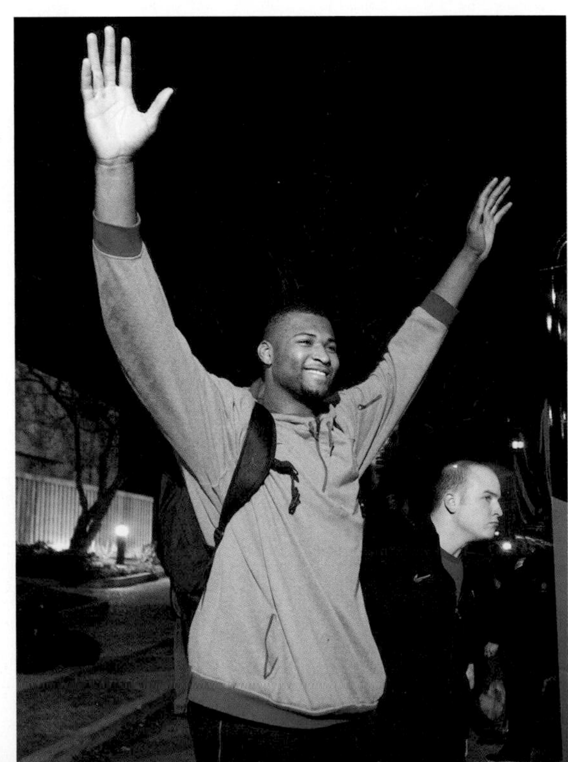

as Cousins, who may be the toughest of all of Calipari's whiz kids to replace.

Consider that Bledsoe was considered by many to be among the best point guard prospects in the land last year, then proved that he could (a) play with another great point guard in Wall, and (b) make a good case that he's a more than credible off-guard.

Plus, there is no potential holdover that will bring to next season what Patrick Patterson brought to the Cats this season.

Great programs don't rebuild, of course. They re-load. Calipari has proven he can provide the ammunition. He'll keep the supply lines open.

But even without a national title, or even a Final Four, the Kentucky head coach has given himself a hard act to follow. ■

Game Log

Date	Opponent	Result	Record
Exhibition			
November 2, 2009	Campbellsville	W 74-38	
November 6, 2009	Clarion	W 117-52	
Regular Season			
November 13, 2009	Morehead State	W 75-59	1-0
November 16, 2009	Miami (Ohio)	W 72-70	2-0
November 19, 2009	Sam Houston State	W 102-92	3-0
November 21, 2009	Rider	W 92-63	4-0
November 24, 2009	vs. Cleveland State	W 73-49	5-0
November 25, 2009	vs. Stanford	W 73-65 (OT)	6-0
November 30, 2009	at UNC-Asheville	W 94-57	7-0
December 5, 2009	North Carolina	W 68-66	8-0
December 9, 2009	vs. Connecticut	W 64-61	9-0
December 12, 2009	at Indiana	W 90-73	10-0
December 19, 2009	Austin Peay	W 90-69	11-0
December 21, 2009	Drexel	W 88-44	12-0
December 23, 2009	Long Beach State	W 86-73	13-0
December 29, 2009	Hartford	W 104-61	14-0
January 2, 2010	Louisville	W 71-62	15-0
January 9, 2010	Georgia	W 76-68	16-0 (1-0 SEC)
January 12, 2010	at Florida	W 89-77	17-0 (2-0)
January 16, 2010	at Auburn	W 72-67	18-0 (3-0)

Date	Opponent	Result	Record
January 23, 2010	Arkansas	W 101-70	19-0 (4-0)
January 26, 2010	at South Carolina	L 68-62	19-1 (4-1)
January 30, 2010	Vanderbilt	W 85-72	20-1 (5-1)
February 2, 2010	Mississippi	W 85-75	21-1 (6-1)
February 6, 2010	at Louisiana State	W 81-55	22-1 (7-1)
February 9, 2010	Alabama	W 66-55	23-1 (8-1)
February 13, 2010	Tennessee	W 73-62	24-1 (9-1)
February 16, 2010	at Mississippi State	W 81-75 (OT)	25-1 (10-1)
February 20, 2010	at Vanderbilt	W 58-56	26-1 (11-1)
February 25, 2010	South Carolina	W 82-61	27-1 (12-1)
February 27, 2010	at Tennessee	L 74-65	27-2 (12-2)
March 3, 2010	at Georgia	W 80-68	28-2 (13-2)
March 7, 2010	Florida	W 74-66	29-2 (14-2)
SEC Tournament			
March 12, 2010	vs. Alabama	W 73-67	30-2
March 13, 2010	vs. Tennessee	W 74-45	31-2
March 14, 2010	vs. Mississippi State	W 74-45	32-2
NCAA Tournament			
March 18, 2010	vs. East Tennessee State	W 100-71	33-2
March 20, 2010	vs. Wake Forest	W 90-60	34-2
March 25, 2010	Cornell	W 62-45	35-2
March 27, 2010	West Virginia	L 73-66	35-3

Team Roster & Stats

No.	Name	Position	Height	Weight	Class	Exp.	Hometown (Last School)
Kentucky Wildcats Roster 2009-2010							
1	Darius Miller	G	6-7	223	Sophomore	1L	Maysville, KY (Mason County)
3	Darnell Dodson	G	6-7	215	Sophomore	TR	Greenbelt, MD (Miami-Dade CC)
4	Jon Hood	G	6-6	195	Freshman	HS	Madisonville, KY (North Hopkins)
5	Ramon Harris	G/F	6-7	218	Senior	3L	Anchorage, AK (West Anchorage)
11	John Wall	G	6-4	195	Freshman	HS	Raleigh, NC (Word of God)
12	Mark Krebs	G	6-5	208	Senior	2L	Newport, KY (Newport Central Catholic)
15	DeMarcus Cousins	F	6-11	270	Freshman	HS	Mobile, AL (LeFlore)
21	Perry Stevenson	F	6-9	207	Senior	3L	Lafayette, LA (Northside)
24	Eric Bledsoe	G	6-1	190	Freshman	HS	Birmingham, AL (Parker)
33	Daniel Orton	F	6-10	255	Freshman	HS	Oklahoma City, OK (Bishop McGuiness)
34	DeAndre Liggins	G	6-6	202	Sophomore	1L	Chicago, IL (Findley Prep)
54	Patrick Patterson	F	6-9	235	Junior	2L	Huntington, WV (Huntington)
55	Josh Harrellson	F	6-10	265	Junior	1L	St. Charles, MO (SW Illinois College)

Name	GP-GS	MIN	FGM	FGA	3PM	3PA	FTM	FTA	OFF	DEF	TOT	PF	AST	TO	BLK	STL	AVG
Kentucky Wildcats Season Stats 2009-2010																	
John Wall	37-37	1288	202	438	37	114	175	232	30	129	159	72	241	149	19	66	16.6
DeMarcus Cousins	38-37	893	206	369	1	6	162	268	156	220	376	122	38	78	67	37	15.1
Patrick Patterson	38-38	1255	215	374	24	69	90	130	116	167	283	61	36	41	51	27	14.3
Eric Bledsoe	37-35	1122	144	312	49	128	82	123	19	95	114	82	107	112	12	52	11.3
Darius Miller	38-32	804	86	215	43	128	31	39	31	62	93	72	58	35	22	22	6.5
Darnell Dodson	35-7	506	70	192	50	144	19	25	16	72	88	40	17	23	9	15	6.0
DeAndre Liggins	29-0	445	36	86	14	44	23	39	18	48	66	42	24	17	8	20	3.8
Daniel Orton	38-0	502	48	91	0	2	33	63	45	81	126	88	15	38	52	21	3.4
Ramon Harris	36-2	395	21	62	5	31	20	33	30	45	75	27	23	26	5	11	1.9
Perry Stevenson	34-1	259	18	27	0	1	8	13	13	35	48	19	7	12	20	4	1.3
Josh Harrellson	22-0	88	12	26	2	4	2	2	9	18	27	8	0	6	7	2	1.3
Jon Hood	17-0	74	6	19	4	11	4	4	7	5	12	6	6	4	0	1	1.2
Mark Krebs	16-1	44	2	17	2	15	0	0	0	2	2	2	1	1	1	1	.4
Team Totals	**38**	**7675**	**1066**	**2228**	**231**	**697**	**649**	**971**	**548**	**1036**	**1584**	**641**	**573**	**547**	**273**	**279**	**79.3**

GP - Games played. GS - Games started. MIN - Minutes. FGM - Field goals made. FGA - Field goals attempted. 3PM - 3-pointers made. 3PA - 3-pointers attempted. FTM - Free throws made. FTA - Free throws attempted. OFF - Offensive rebounds. DEF - Defensive rebounds. TOT - Total rebounds. PF - Personal foul. AST - Assists. TO - Turnovers. BLK - Blocks. STL - Steals. AVG - Average points.